United States History to 1877

HARPERCOLLINS COLLEGE OUTLINE

United States History to 1877

8th Edition

John A. Krout, Ph.D.

Arnold S. Rice, Ph.D.
Keane College of New Jersey

C. M. Harris, Ph.D.

HarperPerennial
A Division of HarperCollinsPublishers

An American BookWorks Corporation Production
Project Manager: Jonathon E. Brodman
Editor: Robert A. Weinstein

Library of Congress Cataloging-in-Publication Data

Krout, John Allen, 1896–
  United States history to 1877 / John A. Krout, Arnold S. Rice,
C. M. Harris. — 8th ed.
       p.   cm.
  Rev. ed. of: United States to 1877 / John A. Krout, 7th ed. 1967.

  Includes bibliographical references and index.
  ISBN 0-06-467111-9 (pbk.)
    1. United States—History—Outlines, syllabi, etc.   I. Rice,
Arnold S.   II. Harris, C. M., 1944–   .   III. Krout, John Allen,
1896–   United States to 1877.   IV. Title
E178.2.K928   1991
974' .02'02—dc20   90-56006

91 92 93 94 95   ABW/RRD 10 9 8 7 6 5 4 3 2 1

Contents

Preface

This eighth edition of *United States History* revises the first volume of John A. Krout's popular and time-tested outlines of American history, first published in the Barnes and Noble College Outline Series in 1933 (7th edition revised in conjunction with Professor Arnold S. Rice, 1971). The original format has now been modernized; the content extensively revised and updated to reflect new scholarship and most recent trends in the teaching and interpretation of American History. Chronologies have been placed at the beginning of each chapter. The appendices have been expanded to include more documents pertinent to the prominent themes of the pre-1877 period.

The revised book is now issued as a reference work and guide to the study of American history, and appropriately, it makes its first appearance as a HarperPerennial title. It provides a concise treatment of American history through the Reconstruction period, designed for students and general readers alike, in the United States and abroad.

Professor Krout's admonition in earlier editions bears repeating here. The book is not a "shortcut" to knowledge of American history. That will be gained only by consulting the many excellent comprehensive and special studies—period and modern works—such as those recommended at the end of each chapter.

C. M. Harris
8th edition

1

Europe and the New World

1682   French explorer La Salle reaches mouth of the Mississippi River

In terms of human history and the history of the North American continent and its peoples, the history of the United States is but a recent episode. The continent itself, the theater of human activity, took its modern form between 54 million and 2 million years ago.

A variety of native cultures had developed in the western hemisphere prior to the first European exploration and settlement in the 15th century. The discovery and conquest of a "new world" was from the European perspective a heroic enterprise. However this process also proved to be destructive of life (natural and human) as it had evolved in North and South America over thousands of years. The European nations had several motives for pursuing colonization in the western hemisphere and they established their colonies in quite different ways.

NATIVE AMERICANS

The first inhabitants of the western hemisphere were themselves immigrants, nomadic hunters who began to migrate from Asia across the Bering Strait at least 15–20,000 years ago. By the time the Europeans discovered the western hemisphere, many different peoples and tribes inhabited what became known as the Americas.

Civilizations of Central and South America

The "new" world was new only from a European perspective. The Mayas in southern Mexico and Central America, the Aztecs in Mexico, and the Incas in Peru had created advanced civilizations and administered extensive empires—although, most noticeably in the case of the Aztecs, whose religion sanctioned human sacrifice, they retained primitive practices. The written language, numbers, and calendar of the Mayas rivaled those of the early Mediterranean cultures. The architecture and civil engineering projects of the Aztecs and Incas continue to exert influence on modern designers.

Early Inhabitants of North America

By the fifteenth century, most of the tribes that inhabited the areas of North America that would become the United States had developed some kind of farming (or fishing), while remaining hunters and retaining nomadic traits. It is estimated that they numbered at least 2 million in 1500. They roamed the high western plains, hunted the mountain valleys, and farmed along the rivers from the Pacific to the Atlantic. These North American peoples did not create great civilizations. Nevertheless there was considerable diversity, and several hundred different languages, among the wide–ranging tribes. The Iroquois, based in upstate New York, were the most successful of these peoples in achieving political unity and extending their influence. Their League of Five (later Six) Nations remained a significant force well into the eighteenth century. Their rivals to the north and south, the larger group of Algonquin tribes, were never as unified, perhaps because they spoke in many different dialects.

The American aborigines or "Indians," as they came to be known after Columbus's voyages, were fiercely proud and independent peoples. They were well adapted to their own environment but vulnerable to the advanced technologies of warfare that the Europeans possessed. Having had no exposure to Europeans, they lacked immunity to their diseases, the most common of which, such as measles, devastated their populations like plagues. The Indians strengthened themselves by taking on some of the European ways—they made effective use of domestic animals and the horse, guns, and metalwork. They derived benefits from their role in the European fur trade, as well as a growing dependency on it.

Without the aid of the Indians, the first Europeans might not have survived in the New World. Many of the Indian vegetables, such as maize and potatoes, became important staples of the Anglo–American diet. The Indian ways however were too strikingly different from those of the European colonists—and superficially too primitive—to gain their respect.

The Europeans' demand for land proved insatiable. In establishing their settlements, whether for purposes of extracting wealth or tilling the soil, they deprived the Indians of their hunting territories and forced them into the interior. The attacks and wars the Indians waged against the inward movement of settlers became excuses for efforts to subjugate or eliminate these indigenous peoples of North America.

Information about the early inhabitants of the Americas continues to accumulate. Since what we know of them derives almost entirely from archaeology and anthropology, and because scientific breakthroughs in diagnostic technologies have been dramatic in recent years, it is likely that knowledge of these peoples and their cultures will grow significantly in the next century, despite the destructive effects that modern life has had on ancient sites.

DISCOVERY

Early Voyagers: The Vikings

Fishermen of the North Atlantic were probably the first Europeans to see the North American continent, but they were not intent on discovery or settlement. In the ninth and tenth centuries the sea–faring Vikings of northern Scandinavia established settlements in Iceland and Greenland. According to the Norse sagas, Leif the Lucky, son of Eric the Red, discovered "Vinland," possibly an area just south of Labrador. His exploits were celebrated in the sagas but had no wider influence.

Medieval Europe

During the medieval period, or Middle Ages (600–1500 A.D.), Europe was fragmented into many small political units, beset with internal rivalries and religious disputes and preoccupied with survival and subsistence. The economic and psychological effects of the Plague of the fourteenth century, in which it is estimated more than one–half of the people of Europe died, were widespread and long–lasting.

Early European Expansion

In the fifteenth century a great movement began that within five hundred years carried Europeans into every part of the world. This was made possible by population growth and the consequent increase of aggregate wealth. Demand for land and products caused prices to rise and trade to expand. This quickening of economic activity created a market for new and exotic things and encouraged traders to extend their enterprises into new and more distant markets. An outward–looking, risk–taking mentality slowly overcame the inward–looking and relatively static outlook of the Middle Ages, with broad effects.

THE LURE OF THE ORIENT

The European imagination had been attracted by the Orient and its trade since the beginning of the fourteenth century. Missionaries, such as the Franciscans who knew Persia, India, China, and Japan, and merchants, like the Venetian Marco Polo, who visited and wrote of the fabulous court of the Great Khan of China in the late thirteenth century, stirred the imaginations of Europeans and revived an east–west trade that had almost disappeared.

By 1400 luxuries of the Orient—silks, precious stones, silver and gold—as well as necessities such as spices and drugs, were carried by sea to the head of the Persian Gulf and then by camel caravan through Baghdad to the Mediterranean, or transported over land routes from China to the Caspian Sea and then by minor roads to the shores of the Black Sea. This growing European trade with the Near East and the Orient was dominated by the Italian city–states—Venice, Genoa, Florence. The merchant princes who enjoyed monopolies as the middlemen in the trade accumulated great wealth.

Economic Motive for Exploration. During the fifteenth century, the costs and uncertain conditions of maintaining the largely overland trade routes with the Near and the Far East, especially after the Turks captured Constantinople (1453), encouraged the emerging nations of western Europe—Portugal, Spain, France, and England—to find a shorter and more reliable (and thus less expensive) route to the East. This in fact was the motive that first led European explorers to sail in the direction of the western hemisphere. The increases in capital wealth that came about as a result of a general expansion of trade in Europe also disposed moneylenders and bankers to be more willing to make credit available for adventurous enterprises.

Powers of the Nation–State. The economic motive for new trade routes to the East was the first stimulus for the European voyages of discovery. But the funds required to support these ventures exceeded the means and the tolerance for risk of private investors and moneylenders. The organizing and outfitting of these overseas expeditions was an enterprise comparable to the launching of a space mission today.

The historical event that was crucial in creating the age of discovery was the consolidation of small principalities into new and ambitious nation-states. The centralization of power in enlarged monarchies and the competition among them provided the means and the will to sustain the great expense of exploring the unknown. Such a commitment, with the economic motive, encouraged the gathering of information about remote geographical areas and the technological innovations in ship construction and navigation that would permit ambitious sea voyages.

CONQUEST AND COLONIZATION

Portugal and Spain were the first European nations to launch voyages of discovery and to exploit the new lands and peoples they encountered. By the seventeenth century most of the European nation–states were engaged in claiming and establishing colonial empires.

The Age of Exploration

The discovery and exploration of the Americas had far–reaching effects on the ideas and aspirations as well as the economies of western Europe during the sixteenth and seventeenth centuries.

PORTUGUESE AMBITIONS

Portugal was the first European nation to establish direct contact with the Far East. Its mariners, trained in the school established by Prince Henry the Navigator (1418), pushed down the western coast of Africa, where the Prince hoped to establish a new Christian nation and to find precious metals. In the years after his death, Portuguese explorers went beyond Africa. Bartholomeu Diaz rounded the Cape of Good Hope in 1486; twelve years later Vasco da Gama reached India. The expansion of trade became Portugal's prime objective. By the early decades of the sixteenth century its merchants had established lucrative posts in Africa, India, China, Japan, and the East Indies, from which Lisbon reaped rich rewards. Brazil, accidentally discovered by Pedro Cabral in 1500, was brought under the control of the Portuguese monarchs(1515–70).

SPAIN'S AMERICAN EMPIRE

By contrast, and as a result of accidental discovery, Spain turned to the west and quickly surpassed the Portuguese in the extent of its voyages and discoveries.

Early Explorers for Spain. In 1492 Cristoforo Colombo, or Christopher Columbus, a seaman and geographer from the Italian port of Genoa, gained financial support from King Ferdinand and Queen Isabella of Spain to make a westward voyage in search of a new route to Asia. In this and three later voyages he discovered parts of the Americas, eventually recognized as a New World. (Although Columbus's name would be used as a secondary name for the United States and for the independent nation of Colombia in South America, the two continents were soon known as the Americas, after Amerigo Vespucci, who in 1500 published an inflated account of a later voyage.)

Soon other explorers were seeking either new lands or new routes to old lands. Spanish expeditions produced a series of rapid achievements and vast claims for the Spanish crown: Vasco de Balboa crossed the Isthmus of Panama to the Pacific Ocean in 1513; in the same year Ponce de Leon landed in Florida. Ferdinand Magellan reached the Philippines in 1513, and one of his ships completed the first trip around the globe, 1519–22. By the Papal Line of Demarcation (1493), modified a year later by the Treaty of Tordesillas between Spain and Portugal, Spain was given control over all "heathen lands" lying west of a line drawn from North to South poles, 370 leagues to the west of the Cape Verde Islands.

Conquistadores and Colonists. Spanish noblemen and gentlemen adventurers, known as *conquistadores*, quickly plundered and subjugated the newly–discovered lands. Hernando Cortes, with an army of only 600, vanquished the empire of the Aztec ruler Montezuma in Mexico (1520). Francisco Pizzaro in Peru (1531), Hernando de Soto along the Mississippi

THE AGE OF DISCOVERY

Spanish   Portuguese   English

(1539–42), and Francisco Vasquez de Coronado beyond the Rio Grande (1540) expanded the reaches of Spanish territory. The *conquistadores* were in search of gold and silver—and they found an abundance of these precious metals, although, as De Soto and Coronado learned, not everywhere in the New World. The Spanish crown, which licensed the private expeditions of numerous *conquistadores*, received one–fifth of their loot and booty. It also gained an empire that by the end of the century extended from the southern regions of what is today the United States to Chile, at the southern tip of South America.

By 1575 approximately 175,000 Spaniards, organized politically into the viceroyalties of New Spain and Peru, were exploiting the resources of the Americas. The rule of the *conquistadores* was replaced by an elaborate bureaucratic system directed from Spain and by the ecclesiastical organization of the Roman Catholic Church. Inspired by the goals of the Counter–Reformation, Spanish priests established missions among the native Indians and set about the work of converting the vanquished to Roman Catholicism.

The Challenge to Spain and Portugal

By the time Spain had conquered Mexico, France had become a force in European power politics. Francois I (1515–47) served notice that he would not permit Spain and Portugal to divide the New World between them.

THE BEGINNINGS OF NEW FRANCE

France based its claims on the activities of French fishermen in American waters and the explorations of both Giovanni da Verrazano, who sailed along the coast of North America (1524), and Jacques Cartier, who tried unsuccessfully to establish settlements along the St. Lawrence (1534–35). It was not until 1608 that Samuel de Champlain, under orders from a monopoly granted by King Henry IV, founded the trading post of Quebec, which was to become the capital of New France.

French Canada existed primarily as a center for the fur trade. French interest in the interior of the continent, demonstrated in the expeditions of Father Jacques Marquette (1673) and of Robert Cavelier, Sieur de La Salle (1682), eventually led to the establishment of a few settlements along the Mississippi River (notably New Orleans). Despite the great extent of its territory, however, New France remained a group of small settlements, the most important of which were along the St. Lawrence River.

THE DUTCH COMMERCIAL EMPIRE

The Dutch provinces of the Netherlands, which broke away from Spanish control (1581), preyed upon Spanish commerce with America and despoiled the Portuguese in their Asian and African trading posts. As Dutch commerce grew in the early seventeenth century, the New Netherland Company and the Dutch West India Company sponsored settlements in South America (Guiana), the West Indies, and the valley of the Hudson River, which Henry

Hudson had discovered in 1609. The first short–lived trading post in the Hudson Valley was established in 1614, and a decade later Dutch settlers began to arrive on Manhattan Island, forming the port of New Amsterdam (later New York).

SWEDES AND DANES IN THE NEW WORLD

Swedish commercial power in the Baltic countries grew rapidly in the seventeenth century. Sweden's merchants established a trading post on the Delaware River (1638), but it was not well supported. Its struggle against great odds ended in 1655, when it was conquered by the Dutch. Greenland and the Virgin Islands, on the periphery of the North American contintent, were colonized by Denmark.

ENGLISH SETTLEMENTS

Although much smaller on maps of Europe than its rivals, England nevertheless surpassed them in developing foreign trade. It possessed a great advantage in the economic strength of its rising commercial middle classes. After 1588, the English navy had no equal on the seas, and England's ambitions became expansive. The English, much more than other European powers, came to the New World with the goal of making successful "transplantations" of their own society.

English Colonization

The English government did not participate in colonial ventures directly as did the governments of Spain and France. Still, English monarchs, from Elizabeth I to Charles II, gave encouragement to subjects willing to undertake overseas adventures that held out promise for the nation.

EXPLORERS AND ELIZABETHAN "SEADOGS"

From the year 1497, when the Genoese captain Giovanni Caboto, or John Cabot, explored the coast of North America for King Henry VII, English mariners searched for the "northwest passage," a route through America to the Orient. Their achievements contributed to geographical knowledge and inspired writers such as Thomas More to imagine utopias in the New World. The English nation, however, remained preoccupied with political, economic, and religious matters until the late sixteenth century. When war with Spain appeared inevitable at that time, Queen Elizabeth gave encouragement to the daring deeds of Captain John Hawkins, who disrupted the Spanish slave trade, and to Sir Francis Drake's raids on Spain's colonies and ships carrying precious metals to Europe. The English navy's complete victory over the Spanish Armada in 1588 eliminated the threat of a Spanish invasion of Britain and made England preeminent on the high seas.

Raleigh and Gilbert. Queen Elizabeth also encouraged several colonization efforts of Sir Humphrey Gilbert and Sir Walter Raleigh, both of whom had been instrumental in the effort to subjugate and secure English settlements in Ireland in the 1560s and 1570s. Gilbert urged the queen to establish colonial bases from which the English could strike at Spanish possessions in the Americas. He claimed Newfoundland for the queen in 1583, but failed in his attempt to establish the first English settlement in the New World. Raleigh sent out several expeditions with a similar goal, the most successful of which landed on Roanoke Island, off the coast of North Carolina, in 1587. The "Lost Colony," of some 120 persons, had disappeared by 1590, when English ships returned with supplies after the conclusion of the struggle with Spain.

Economic and Religious Motives for Expansion

During the reign of James I, the English court became more supportive of projects to plant English colonies in the New World. The desire to weaken Spain and France continued to be a factor, but by this time colonization had also begun to appear useful in resolving England's domestic problems, which derived from economic upheaval and growing religious strife. The seventeenth century proved to be a time of great turbulence in England, an era of civil strife, war, and unrest.

MIGRATION OF THE DISCONTENTED

Government gradually recognized that colonies would provide useful outlets for large numbers of displaced farmers and laborers and for the growing numbers of religious dissenters who objected to the rites of the established Church of England and the authority of Anglican bishops and priests.

Most of the English settlers who migrated to the New World had strong motives for risking the known perils of sea voyages and the unknown perils of life in a remote wilderness. Some, like the Puritans and English Roman Catholics, wished to live free of dictated religious conformity and the threat of (or actual) persecution for their differing religious beliefs. Others were victims of economic changes in England—such as the farmers and workers who were displaced by the "enclosure" process, by which farm land was increasingly given over to sheep–raising for the production of wool. Some were "down and out" debtors seeking a new chance for prosperity; others, some outlaws, had much to gain by escaping their predicaments in England. Whatever their backgrounds and circumstances, those who emigrated to the English colonies were universally attracted to America by the opportunities to own their own land and to start anew.

INVESTMENT CAPITAL AND MERCANTILISM

The growth of overseas trade (largely from exports of wool) increased the capital wealth of English merchants and encouraged many of them to become merchant–adventurers, to take greater risks to secure higher profits on their investments. They became increasingly interested in new enterprises after the collapse of the European cloth trade in the 1550s. The fact that private capital was available to fund colonial ventures in the New World helped convince English monarchs to make the land grants that were needed to begin settlements—the royal purse was not placed at risk.

In permitting new settlements to be established in America, the Crown was also influenced by the prevailing economic ideas that would later be defined as mercantilism, which preached the desirablility of economic self–sufficiency within the borders of the nation. The wealth of a nation, so the mercantilists argued, was measured by its trade surpluses, the balance of gold and silver not required for everyday transactions and expenditures. According to this theory, it was highly desirable for England, an island nation, to gain its own sources of raw materials, without having to import them on the world market. By this pragmatic standard, the colonies became useful sources of commodities, to be organized and governed primarily for the purpose of serving the needs of the mother country.

THE PROMISE OF AMERICA

Richard Hakluyt (the younger), a friend of Sir Humphrey Gilbert, and other writers and promoters developed and sustained popular interest in the colonization of America, despite such setbacks as the death of Gilbert (lost at sea) and the "Lost Colony." Hakluyt broadened the mercantilist appeal, promising that the colonists would get rich by supplying the natural products needed in the mother country. As for England, he wrote in 1584, the establishment of colonies would be a worthwhile enterprise if only for "the hope of the sale of our wool."

The discovery and penetration of the Americas by the European powers marks the beginning of the early modern era. Intense competition among the new European nation-states caused them to see the New World as a source of wealth and strategic advantages in their struggles for power and domination in Western Europe. By exploiting the native populations and extracting treasure from the Americas, Spain set one pattern of colonization and became an international power. After restraining Spain's drive for domination, England began to colonize for a different purpose, establishing settlements in North America primarily for the purposes of transplanting English society and of expanding the English economy.

Selected Readings

Axtell, James. *The Invasion Within: The Conquest of Culture in Colonial North America* (1985)

Bailyn, Bernard. *The Peopling of British North America: An Introduction* (1986)

Bridenbaugh, Carol. *Vexed and Troubled Englishmen, 1590–1642* (1968)

Cronon, William. *Changes in the Land: Indians, Colonists, and the Ecology of New England* (1983)

Davis, Ralph. *The Rise of the Atlantic Economies* (1973)

Eccles, W.J. *The Canadian Frontier, 1534–1760* (1969)

Gibson, Charles. *Spain in America* (1966)

Morison, Samuel Eliot. *The European Voyages of Discovery: The Northern Voyages* (1971)

———. *The European Voyages of Discovery: The Southern Voyages* (1974)

Lang, James. *Conquest and Commerce: Spain and England in America* (1975)

Nash, Garry B. *Red, White, and Black: The Peoples of Early America* (1982 ed.)

Parry, J. H. *The Age of Reconnaissance* (1963)

Washburn, Wilcomb E. *The Indian in America* (1975)

2

English Colonization in North America

1607	English settlement made at Jamestown, Virginia
1619	House of Burgesses formed, and first Africans sold to planters, in Virginia
1620	Pilgrims (Puritan Separatists) settle at Plymouth, Massachusetts
1624	Dutch settle New Amsterdam (New York City); Virginia Company's charter revoked, Virginia made a royal colony
1630	Puritans settle Massachusetts Bay
1634	Maryland settled
1642–1648	Civil war in England
1649	King Charles I executed; monarchy abolished and the commonwealth proclaimed in England
1660	Restoration of the monarchy and King Charles II; Navigation Act of 1660 (reenacting much of the act of 1651) passed
1662	Connecticut organized by royal charter
1663	Staple Act passed; royal charters issued to Carolina proprietors and to Rhode Island
1673	Duty Act passed
1675	King Philip (Metacomet)'s War brings destruction to the New England frontier
1676	Bacon's Rebellion challenges Governor Berkeley's authority in Virginia
1681	Charter granted to William Penn for Pennsylvania
1684	Crown revokes the Massachusetts Bay Company's charter
1685	Accession of James II (formerly duke of York)
1686	Dominion of New England absorbs New England colonies, and briefly New York and New Jersey

1688	The Glorious Revolution; James II deposed, succeeded by William of Orange and Mary
1691	Massachusetts receives new royal charter
1702	New Jersey united by royal charter
1702–1714	Queen Anne's reign
1714	George I of Hanover succeeds to British throne
1727–1760	Reign of George II
1729	North Carolina and South Carolina formed by new royal charters
1732	Georgia trustees receive charter from King George II

Between 1607 and 1732 permanent English settlements were established along the eastern coast of North America from New Hampshire to Georgia. The new colonies provided outlets for tensions and unrest in the mother country—lack of employment and available land, crowded cities and prisons, and religious and political dissent. The peopling of wilderness environments in North America, the process by which the new settlements took hold and grew, significantly altered the development of the colonies and has had an enduring influence on the course of American history.

METHODS OF ESTABLISHING THE COLONIES

The English government authorized the use of two agencies to promote the establishment of settlements overseas—the chartered trading company and the proprietorship. Both were well known to the merchants and landholders of England and proved to be well adapted to the purposes of colonization.

The Chartered Trading Company

The commercial joint–stock companies, operating under royal charters, were composed of "adventurers" (stockholders) who shared pro rata the profits and losses of the colonial venture. Political control of the colony was at first vested in the directors of the company, who were usually more interested in profits than in the settlers. Most charters provided that colonists should have all the rights and privileges of Englishmen and that their governing bodies should pass no law contrary to the laws of England. Two of the colonies were established by English chartered trading companies: the settlement at Jamestown, Virginia, by the London Company (1607), soon known as the Virginia Company; and the Puritan colony of the Massachusetts Bay Company (1630).

The chief characteristic that distinguished the corporate colony from others in English America was the large measure of self–government which it enjoyed. The stockholders of the Massachusetts Bay Company migrated to America with their charter, thus making the colony corporate or self–governing. The qualified voters in the colony chose the governor, the governor's council, and the legislative assembly. Massachusetts was a corporate colony until it lost its charter in 1684. Connecticut and Rhode Island, originally settled by dissident groups from Massachusetts, gained royal charters that conferred upon the colonists control of their own governments.

FOREIGN COMPANIES

Two of the thirteen original colonies were initiated by non–English joint–stock companies: New Netherland, later New York, by the Dutch West India Company in 1623; and Delaware by a Swedish company in 1638. New York was captured by the English in 1664 and became a royal province when its proprietor, James, duke of York, became king in 1685. Delaware fell under the proprietary control of the duke, who then sold it to William Penn, the proprietor of Pennsylvania.

Proprietary Grants

Of the thirteen English colonies, seven were founded as proprietorships: Maryland by Lord Baltimore (1632); New Hampshire by Captain John Mason (1635); New Jersey by Sir William Berkeley and Sir George Carteret in 1663; the Carolinas by friends of Charles II (1663); Pennsylvania by William Penn in 1682; and Georgia by a board of trustees headed by James Oglethorpe in 1732. All except Pennsylvania and Maryland had become royal provinces before the outbreak of the Revolution.

The proprietary charters normally granted huge tracts of land to an individual or a group of persons on terms reminiscent of feudal tenure. In the proprietorships, political control was put in the hands of those who received the royal grant, but in most cases it was delegated in part to representatives chosen by the colonists. The owners usually invested their personal fortunes in developing their lands and thus were placed in the position of having to attract new settlers to purchase or rent small holdings from them in order to reap profits.

Table of English Colonies

Name (thirteen original states in italic)	Founded By	Date	Charter	Assembly	Made Royal	Status in 1775	Remarks
Virginia	London Company	1607	1606–1609–1612	1619	1624	Royal	
Plymouth	Separatists	1620		1639	1691		Merged with Massachusetts in 1691
Massachusetts	Puritans of the Mass. Bay Co.	1628	1629	1634	1684	Royal	Only royal colony to have its charter restored (1691)
Maryland	Lord Baltimore	1634	1632	1634		Proprietary	A royal province, 1690–1715
Rhode Island	Roger Williams	1636	1663	1647		Self-governing	Frustrated Andros's attempt to take away charters, 1686–1687
Connecticut	Emigrants from Massachusetts	1636	1662	1637		Self-governing	Frustrated Andros's attempt to take away charters, 1686–1687
New Haven	Emigrants from Massachusetts	1638		1643			Merged with Connecticut, 1662
Maine	F. Gorges	1641	1639		1691		Bought by Massachusetts, 1677
North Carolina *South Carolina*	Eight Nobles	1663	1663	1669	N. 1729 S. 1729	Royal Royal	Informally separated, 1691; formally separated with different governors, 1729
New York	(Duke of York)	1664	1664	1683–1685	1685	Royal	Dutch colony of New Netherland, 1622–1664
New Hampshire	John Mason	1664	1639	1680	1679	Royal	Towns absorbed by Massachusetts, 1641–1679
New Jersey	Berkeley and Carteret	1664		1664	1702	Royal	Under the governor of New York until 1738
Pennsylvania	William Penn	1681	1680	1681		Proprietary	A royal province, 1692–1694
Delaware	Swedes	1638		1702		Proprietary	Conquered by Dutch, 1655; by English, 1664 Merged with Pennsylvania, 1682, Separate governor (1691) and assembly (1702)
Georgia	Jas. Oglethorpe	1732	1732	1733	1752	Royal	

THE CHESAPEAKE

The colonies that were established on the Chesapeake Bay, Virginia and Maryland, though quite different in organization and motives, developed along similar lines, shaped to a considerable extent by the Bay itself and the many navigable rivers and streams that flowed into it.

Virginia

Jamestown, site of the first settlement (of about 100 men) in 1607, proved to be an unhealthy and dangerous place for human habitation. It would not have survived were it not for the able leadership of Captain John Smith and the strict order and communal discipline maintained by the first governors.

The Virginia Company made little progress, beyond survival and the development of tobacco as an export crop (by John Rolfe), during the first ten years at Jamestown. New incentives for prospective settlers were therefore announced. To increase the population and supply of laborers, the company enacted in 1618 a new system of land grants. Settlers were to receive a "headright" parcel for themselves and another fifty acres for each additional person whose passage they paid. (Private land ownership had been offered as an incentive a few years earlier.) Fulfilling a guarantee in its charter, the company sanctioned the formation in 1619 of the House of Burgesses, the first legislative assembly in the new world. Still, the company failed, in large part because 347 settlers had been killed in an Indian attack in 1622. James I revoked its charter and made Virginia a crown colony in 1624. Of the 8,500 settlers who went out to Virginia during the company's existence, only 1,300 (or 20 percent) had survived.

ROYAL COLONY

Under royal authority, Virginia expanded and grew. By 1650 there were 16,000 settlers; by 1660, 40,000. A distinct pattern unfolded in this expansion: the best land (initially in the tidewater region) was accumulated in large holdings by a small group of planters. This brought pressure from newcomers and have–nots for additional land in the backcountry and frequently led to the forced removal of Indian occupants and hostilities on the frontier.

Under Governor Sir William Berkeley, who dominated the politics of the colony for thirty years, the House of Burgesses (which received royal sanction in 1639) became an exclusive club of large landholders. The electorate was increasingly restricted and representation thereby heavily weighted in favor of the easternmost counties. Landholders in the interior and backcountry perceived the great inequity in this and became increasingly restive. When Governor Berkeley failed to respond forcefully to Indian uprisings on the frontier in 1676, they took matters into their own hands. Led by Nathaniel Bacon, they gained control of the colony for a brief time and even burned Jamestown. Although "Bacon's Rebellion" quickly collapsed after Bacon died of natural causes, it proved to be the most serious challenge to royal authority in the colonies until the outbreak of the American Revolution.

Maryland

Maryland was established by the Calvert family, the earls of Baltimore, who in 1632 gained a charter from King Charles I making them and their heirs "true and absolute lords and proprietaries" of the settlement. They intended it to be a refuge for English Catholics as well as a productive financial venture. The first settlers landed at St. Mary's, on the Potomac River, in 1634; they encountered friendly Indians who sold them land and provisions.

Although they possessed total authority over the colony and provided large grants of land to their relations and friends, the Calverts needed to attract settlers and laborers to make Maryland a successful venture and avoid financial ruin. They recognized that the colony had little hope of growth if it excluded non–Catholics and thus pursued a policy of religious toleration almost from the beginning. This policy notwithstanding, differences between English Catholics and Puritans troubled the colony in its first years. With the Glorious Revolution, Protestants gained a sympathetic royal governor from King William. They proceeded to pass laws in 1691 establishing the Church of England in the colony and denying Catholics the right to hold office. In 1715 the Calverts reassumed the proprietorship, and the charter of 1632 was restored under the fourth earl of Baltimore, who had been raised in the Anglican faith.

Although its charter and religious purpose were unique, Maryland grew much like Virginia. The land was soon organized into large farms or plantations, on which tobacco was the principal crop. In 1635 the proprietor permitted formation of a representative assembly, the House of Delegates, modeled on the House of Commons. A few years later, faced with an acute need for laborers, they initiated a headright system of land grants, similar to that of Virginia, to encourage immigration.

NEW ENGLAND

New England, named by Captain John Smith, who had explored the area for the Plymouth Company, was first settled by Puritans and other Calvinists. Heavily influenced by the Massachusetts Bay experiment, the colonies east of the Hudson River shared a common religious heritage and adopted a social organization based upon the importance of the town.

Calvinism and Puritans

Calvinism, that strain of Protestantism derived from the teachings of John Calvin, a Genevan (Swiss) theologian, became a powerful, revolutionary force in seventeenth-century England. Calvinists believed in an all–powerful God and in the principle of predestination: that God had determined the individual's fate in advance of birth. This belief was only apparently fatalistic, for in practice Calvinism created an inner tension and uncertainty that encouraged industriousness, good works, and piety.

Puritans sought to purify, or to reform, the established Church of England—to eliminate religious practices that had grown from the traditions of the Church without sanction from the Bible. They feared and detested the influence of the pope in Rome and attributed the corruption in England to Roman Catholic influences. Separatist Puritans thought the solution was to withdraw from the Church of England and to remove themselves from England to live a godly existence. The majority of Puritans, however, wished to purify the church and state from within. During the reign of Charles I, their cause merged with that of the Parliamentary faction and eventually brought down the monarchy. For a brief period (1648–60), Britain was a commonwealth or republic; King Charles's son was "restored" to the throne in 1660.

PLYMOUTH PLANTATION

The second English settlement in North America, and first in New England, was made by a group of Puritan Separatists, originally from the small town of Scrooby, in East Anglia, who had suffered persecution and gone into exile in Holland for their refusal to observe the practices of the established church. Led by William Bradford, this group of thirty-five believing "saints," with sixty-seven others, left England for America in September 1620 on board the ship *Mayflower*. They had been permitted to settle on lands claimed by the London (Virginia) Company but came ashore just outside its territory, on Cape Cod.

To govern their settlement, they subscribed to a covenant or agreement that set down a code of civil laws, known as the Mayflower Compact. They disembarked at Plymouth Rock to begin their settlement on December 21, 1620. Plymouth Plantation remained small and poor, but its example led other Puritans to attempt similar settlements that would prosper. The colony was self–governing under the Mayflower Compact until 1691, when King William III placed the Plymouth settlement under the governorship of the new royal colony of Massachusetts.

Massachusetts Bay

Led by John Winthrop, another group of Puritans, better organized and financed than those led by Bradford, left England in 1630. They had formed themselves into the Massachusetts Bay Company and secured a royal charter the previous year. By emigrating together, they were able to use the joint-stock company organization to achieve greater independence from royal interference. They cleverly extended that organization to structure their religious and political community. In a little more than ten years, in what is known as the Great Migration, the population of the settlement reached 20,000.

The Puritans who settled Massachusetts Bay were not Separatists, wishing to secede from the authority of the Church of England. Rather, they believed they had a special covenant with God to establish a true Christian community that would be an example to the world. As Winthrop put it, "we shall be as a city upon a hill, the eyes of all people are upon us." After a difficult first few years, their numbers grew dramatically, largely because of a steady migration of intact families. The Bay was settled as several communities or congregations, largely self–governing.

The civil government of Massachusetts Bay reflected the importance of its churches—only full members of a Puritan congregation, those who had proved they were God's elect (known as saints), had the vote and held civil offices (as freemen). Significantly, the meetinghouse of each community was located in the center of the town and was used for both religious and civil gatherings. Still, even with the religious requirement, a significant proportion of the adult male population of the community was politically enfranchised (40 percent—a higher percentage than in England). The General Court, at first a meeting of the original stockholders, soon became a legislature, composed of a House of Deputies and a council appointed by the governor. In 1648 it issued the Laws and Liberties in the form of an alphabetized code, the first such code in English.

While Massachusetts Bay was largely self-governed, the Puritans enacted laws no more tolerant of diversity than those that had been used to imprison and persecute their fellow Puritans in England. They in effect established their own churches in place of the Church of England, taxing all residents for their support and requiring universal church attendance. Unorthodox Puritan beliefs—such as those of Anne Hutchinson, who challenged the Calvinist doctrine of predestination by insisting that Christians might gain salvation and grace directly from God; and those of non–Puritan groups like the Quakers—were not tolerated and in fact severely punished.

CONNECTICUT

The desire for better lands and a dissatisfaction with the rigidity of life in Massachusetts Bay led two groups to form new settlements in the rich Connecticut River Valley in the late 1630s. Under the leadership of Thomas Hooker, Hartford and two other local towns drafted the Fundamental Orders of Connecticut in 1639; this frame of government drew on the example of Massachusetts Bay but expanded political rights. The Hartford area colony gained a royal charter in 1662, with authority over another, more orthodox settlement on the lower Connecticut, at New Haven, which had framed its own Fundamental Articles.

RHODE ISLAND

Rhode Island was established by Roger Williams, a separatist Puritan, who made a famous escape from Massachusetts Bay after he was ordered to be deported to England. He survived the winter of 1635–36 by living with the Narragansett Indians. He then bought land from them to establish the town of Providence. Williams's settlement was the first to separate church and state—"liberty in religious concernments" was recognized in the royal charter he received for his colony in 1663 (a charter had been granted by Parliament during the interregnum in 1644). In Rhode Island, taxes were not applied to the support of churches, and no requirement of church membership was placed on the right to vote.

NEW HAMPSHIRE

New Hampshire was organized as a proprietary colony but grew in population only after it was settled by supporters of Anne Hutchinson and other Puritans looking for refuge or new lands. Although Massachusetts pressed its claims to the territory, New Hampshire gained its own charter in 1679.

The Dominion of New England. In an effort to assert royal authority over Massachusetts, and to prevent violations of the Navigation Acts, advisors to James II secured the revocation of the Massachusetts Bay charter in 1684. Two years later the king consolidated the colony and its neighbors into one government, the Dominion of New England. The territory of the Dominion was soon extended to include New York and the Jerseys and placed under the authority of a single royal governor, Sir Edmund Andros. The elected assemblies of the settlements were abolished.

The Dominion collapsed when King James II, an advocate of divine right rule of kings and a Roman Catholic, was driven from the throne in 1688. Governor Andros was pursued by a mob and imprisoned. In England the Glorious Revolution ended with Parliament elevating James's daughter Mary and son–in–law Prince William of Orange to the monarchy. Under their rule, Massachusetts Bay and Plymouth were made into a single royal colony. The colony's new charter (1691) restored the General Court and abolished religious restrictions on political rights.

NEW YORK AND THE MIDDLE COLONIES

New York

New York, originally the Dutch colony of New Netherland, was captured by the English in 1664 and given by Charles II to his brother James, duke of York (later James II). The Dutch resisted the English claim but lost the colony for good, after momentarily regaining it, ten years later. Under the duke's direction, the colony was ruled by his governor—without a representative assembly, but with a recognition of the colony's multinational population and a new code of laws. The Dutch were allowed to retain their property, and the Dutch language and culture continued to flourish. Religious toleration was guaranteed by the "Duke's Laws."

The extensive Dutch manorial estates known as patroonships were acknowledged and James himself reinforced this pattern by making large grants of land to friends and relations. This served to thwart productive use of the land and remained a source of political discontent throughout New York's early history. New York City, strongly influenced by its Dutch origins and diverse European population, steadily grew as a port. The fur trade, especially with the Iroquois tribes around Albany, on the Hudson River, was an important part of the colony's economy during the seventeenth century, but it declined rapidly in New York after 1715.

For a brief period New York (with the Jerseys) was merged into the Dominion of New England. When news of the Glorious Revolution arrived, the local militia seized power and Andros's lieutenant escaped to England. A New York City merchant, Jacob Leisler, took control of the colonial government; he was executed in 1691 after refusing to give way to the new royal governor.

NEW JERSEY

The area between the Delaware and Hudson rivers was part of the grant made by Charles II to the duke of York. He in turn had given it to two of his political friends, Sir George Carteret and Sir John Berkeley (also proprietors of Carolina). When the latter sold his holdings to Quakers in 1674 the colony was divided into West and East Jersey. It was reunited in 1702 under a single royal charter.

New Jersey was sparsely populated and loosely administered throughout its early history. Contests over land and related claims of the early proprietors, which pitted the colony against New York, persisted, restricting development. Many settlers came from New York and reflected a similar pattern of diversity in origins; however, few brought or accumulated substantial wealth.

Pennsylvania and Delaware

Pennsylvania (or "Penn's woods") was named by Charles II, who, to repay a debt, made a large grant of land on the Delaware River to William Penn in 1681. Penn enlarged his proprietary holdings when he purchased the "Three Lower Counties" of Delaware in 1682. His objective was to establish a settlement that would serve as a "holy experiment," to be organized in harmony with the beliefs of the religious Society of Friends, or Quakers (dissenters from the Church of England who had taken a different path than the Puritans). The city Penn planned as the center of the colony was named Philadelphia (from the Latin for "brotherly love") to further proclaim the experiment's goals. Born to privilege, Penn had come to accept the Quaker belief that all possessed the "inner light," a divine spark by which one should be guided. This belief led the Society of Friends to be democratic in their worship and plain in their manners and dress. These practices and their pacifism had subjected them to persecution in England and in the New England colonies.

Like other idealistic proprietors, Penn needed to attract settlers in large enough numbers to offset the large sums he had invested to establish the colony. He encouraged Germans, Scandinavians, and other continental Europeans to emigrate to his province, creating a diversity that, with Pennsylvania's rich and well-irrigated lands, caused it to develop quickly. Penn's good faith in dealing with the Indians allowed the new colony to enjoy good relations with the local tribes during its infancy. He even agreed to restrictions on his own powers in accepting the Charter of Liberties in 1701, which also authorized Pennsylvania and Delaware to elect their own representative assemblies. Despite the colony's success, Penn and his family were unable to collect the quitrents from settlers (feudal levies) that had been provided for in the king's grant. He was later imprisoned for debt in England.

THE CAROLINAS AND GEORGIA

North and South Carolina

The Carolinas were Restoration colonies, settled soon after the restoration of Charles II to the English throne in 1660. They were originally granted by the king to eight of his friends, ambitious land speculators, who sought to make large profits by enticing new settlers from other American colonies to their proprietary lands. Interestingly, they attempted to do this by granting religious freedom and promising that laws would be made by an elected assembly. When few responded to these enticements, one of the proprietors, Sir Anthony Ashley Cooper (shortly the first earl of Shaftesbury) convinced the others to sponsor emigration from England. In 1670, an expedition succeeded (despite the loss of more than half its members) in forming a settlement at Port Royal, in the sea islands off the Carolina coast. Ten years later the city of Charles Town (later Charleston) was founded at the confluence of the colony's two principal rivers, named the Ashley and the Cooper.

Shaftesbury and the philosopher John Locke, who never visited America, drew up the Fundamental Constitution for Carolina in 1669. This document responded to England's social problems rather than to the realities of life in the New World. The well–ordered and highly structured aristocratic society they envisioned never took form. The northern portion of Carolina, which became North Carolina, was settled by small farmers. Those who settled about the harbor at Charles Town, in the coastal lowlands, raised provisions for export, notably to the sugar planters of the West Indian island of Barbados. At the turn of the century they began exporting rice, soon a valuable staple crop. Land grants in the form of headrights helped to attract a steady flow of new settlers (often with slaves) to the lowlands.

The Carolinas were ill–fitted as a single political and geographical unit and proved impossible to govern. The proprietors lost control of the settlers after Shaftesbury's death in 1719. In 1729 King George I abolished the proprietorship and divided the original grant into two royal colonies, North Carolina and South Carolina.

Georgia

The last colony to be established by Britain in America, Georgia, was placed under the direction of General James Oglethorpe and a group of trustees in 1732 for a period of twenty–one years. The following year Oglethorpe led the expedition that made the first settlement on the Savannah River. The colony was established primarily for military reasons, to serve as a buffer between the British colonies and Spanish Florida, from which the Spanish had launched attacks against English settlements in 1686. Anticipating future attacks from Florida, the trustees sought to people the colony with only the most reliable settlers and to concentrate the population rather than allowing it to spread out over large areas. They prohibited Roman Catholics and black slaves from the colony, restricted the size of land holdings, and forbade the import of rum, fearing its possible effects on local Indians. The colony also had a social purpose—to serve as an outlet for unfortunate debtors (one could be imprisoned for owing a very small sum) and for the poor of Britain.

Events in Georgia failed to fulfill this idealized mission. Despite the trustees' active efforts to recruit settlers, only a small number of British debtors and paupers migrated to the colony. Land restrictions were soon eased, rum tolerated and permitted; the prohibition on slavery was eliminated in 1751. Recognizing the failure of their experiment, the trustees returned their colony to the crown the following year. Thereafter Georgia grew in the manner of the southern plantation provinces, as settlers from other colonies, especially South Carolina, came to raise rice and other staple crops.

The most successful of the English settlements in North America possessed strong communal purpose and organization in the first years of "transplantation." Once the settlements took hold, they faced an array of social problems and continuing threats to their survival, made worse by lulls in migration or declines in population. Massachusetts Bay benefitted from a steady influx of new Puritan settlers from England until the English Civil War. But most of the colonies, especially the proprietorships, had to abandon or ease their first, idealized plans for new communities to attract and keep settlers. They provided incentives in the form of land grants, political rights, and, gradually, laws to insure religious toleration. As the colonies grew and new settlers pushed into the interior in search of unclaimed lands, conflicts with displaced Indians increased and new tensions emerged between the western or interior regions and the first coastal settlements.

Selected Readings

Andrews, Charles M. *The Colonial Period in American History* (4 vols., 1934–38)

Craven, Wesley Frank. *The Southern Colonies in the Seventeenth Century, 1607–1689* (1949)

Cressy, David. *Coming Over: Migration and Communication Between England and New England in the Seventeenth Century* (1987)

Jones, M.J.A. *Congregational Commonwealth: Connecticut, 1636–1662* (1968)

Kammen, Michael. *Colonial New York* (1975)

Lovejoy, David S. *The Glorious Revolution in America* (1972)

Main, Gloria L. *Tobacco Colony: Life in Early Maryland, 1650–1720* (1982)

Morgan, Edmund S. *American Slavery, American Freedom: The Ordeal of Colonial Virgina* (1975)

———. *Roger Williams: The Church and the State* (1967)

———. *The Puritan Dilemma: The Story of John Winthrop* (1958)

Tate, Thad W. and Ammerman, David eds. *The Chesapeake in the Seventeenth Century* (1979)

Tolles, Frederick B. *Quakers and the Atlantic Culture* (1960)

Weir, Robert. *Colonial South Carolina* (1983)

3

Provincial America

1611 Publication of "authorized" or King James version of the Bible in English

1619 First African slaves sold in Virginia

1636 Founding of Harvard College in Cambridge, Massachusetts

1647 Massachusetts School Act passed

1649 Maryland Toleration Act passed; repealed 1654

1654 First group of Jews to settle in American colonies arrives in New Amsterdam; first American synagogue founded in New York in 1695

1662 "Halfway Covenant" introduced in Massachusetts Bay

1665 Freedom of conscience included in New Jersey proprietors' Concessions and Agreements

1678 Publication of John Bunyan's *The Pilgrim's Progress*, a Christian allegory

1687 Publication of Sir Isaac Newton's *Principia Mathematica*, containing his laws of motion and theory of gravitation

1688 The Glorious Revolution; James II deposed, succeeded by William and Mary

1692 Witchcraft trials begin in Salem, Massachusetts

1693 The College of William and Mary founded

1697 Abolition of the slave trade monopoly of the Royal African Company

1708 First regularly issued colonial newspaper published in Boston, the *News–Letter*

1730s–1740s The Great Awakening begins and spreads

1731 Organization of the Library Company of Philadelphia

1734–1735 Trial of John Peter Zenger for libel

1739 Stono uprising of slaves in South Carolina

1741 Reverend Jonathan Edwards gives sermon "Sinners in the Hands of an Angry God"

1743 Founding of the American Philosophical Society for the Promotion of Useful Knowledge, held in Philadelphia

1747–1752 Franklin's experiments with electricity and lightning

1750 Iron Act passed by Parliament

1766 First Wesleyan or Methodist Church in America established in New York City

Immigrants from the Old World brought English and European habits, customs, and outlooks to new and often harsh environments in the New World. To survive they had no choice but to adjust to the new conditions of life in the American colonies, enforced by nature and by British governments. To prosper they had to overcome great odds: the sheer distance between the settlers, a constant scarcity of labor, and the lack of liquid capital and a circulating currency. In the middle and northern colonies these conditions encouraged diversity and innovation; in the South the prospects of great wealth from large–scale staple crop agriculture led white planters first to use and then to rely on the labor of black slaves. In cultural matters the American colonists continued to look to metropolitan London for direction and examples, much as did the people who inhabited areas in England that were distant from the great imperial capital.

COLONIAL ECONOMIES

Colonial America was largely a land of farmers and planters. Home or plantation "manufactures" or manufactured goods flourished on a small scale. Large–scale manufacturing was restricted by imperial legislation and a lack of capital for investment. More fundamentally, the colonial economies were shaped by the magnet of British demand and handicapped by labor shortages. These hindered the development of local and regional markets, although there was an active intercolonial coastal trade.

New England   Severe winters and poor soil largely determined the economy of the New England colonies. With the exception of the rich Connecticut River Valley, which fit the pattern of the middle colonies, the region proved to be unfit for large scale agriculture and was thus shaped in its development by trading and the sea.

HARVESTING THE LAND AND SEA

Characteristic of the region northeast of the Hudson Valley was the diversified farming of small freeholds. Despite the handicaps of a short growing season and rocky soil, many crops were grown successfully for consumption or local trade. Among the chief products were corn, oats, rye, barley, and fruit.

Fishing as a commercial enterprise was virtually confined to New England. By 1765, 10,000 persons were employed in catching, cleaning, and preserving cod, mackerel, bass, halibut, and other deep–sea fish, which had become an important factor in Anglo–American trade with Europe and the West Indies. By the eighteenth century, New Englanders were hunting whales in the Atlantic, from the Arctic to the coast of Brazil. Some 360 vessels were engaged in the whaling industry at the outbreak of the American Revolution.

MANUFACTURING AND COMMERCE

Domestic production in New England, as elsewhere, was supplemented by the output of small handicraft industries. Woolen textiles, leather goods, household utensils, and iron implements were important, but in the eighteenth century the distillation of rum from West Indian molasses became New England's chief industrial activity. It was part of the profitable trade in molasses, rum, and slaves that brought gold and silver into the maritime provinces. Along the New England coasts, industries related to seafaring and shipbuilding developed in response to the demands of domestic and foreign trade.

New York and the Middle Colonies

The middle region of English America possessed good soil and a moderate climate. Two of the continent's major river systems, the Delaware and especially the Hudson, permitted navigation into the interior. Like their southern neighbors, these colonies developed staple crop agriculture; however, the region was characterized by the diversity of economic activity rather than uniformity.

Diversified farming, not unlike that of New England, was more rewarding in the fertile valleys of the Middle Colonies. They were the principal supplier of wheat to New England and the southern colonies. Corn and other grains, animal products, vegetables, and fruits also contributed to the region's export trade.

EARLY INDUSTRIALIZATION

The wheat-growing areas of these "provision provinces" were dotted with flour mills. Pennsylvania and New Jersey attracted significant numbers of immigrant craftsmen and artisans, especially from Germany. "Iron plantations" and small furnaces spread in Pennsylvania and elsewhere in the region throughout the eighteenth century. The most ambitious enterprise, the

American Iron Company of Peter Hasenclever, operated several furnaces and forges in New York and New Jersey and employed over five hundred men in the 1760s before failing when its English backers went bankrupt. The skilled workmen in this region also produced textiles, paper, glass, and iron.

Southern Colonies

The economy of the Chesapeake region of the upper South was soon dominated by large–scale agriculture. Land was organized into plantations and given over to the production of a single staple or cash crop (at first tobacco) and the generation of profits. This pattern also took hold in the colonies of the lower South.

PLANTATION AGRICULTURE

Although fruits and grains were raised in the southern colonies, agriculture was dominated by commercial cash crops. Tobacco was raised in Maryland, Virginia, and North Carolina. It did not grow in South Carolina and Georgia, but planters there found that rice and indigo (a blue dye) could be produced instead. Before the Revolution, Maryland and Virginia were raising 50 million pounds of tobacco annually, and South Carolina was exporting 500,000 pounds of rice each year.

In good growing years, when market prices were favorable, such large-scale agriculture could be immensely profitable. However, the promise of large profits encouraged overproduction. Consequently there were periodic collapses in prices due to excess supplies; the risks of crop destruction from bad weather and various pests were high. Further, the uninterrupted cultivation of cash crops, especially tobacco, exhausted the soil.

Servitude and Slavery. Plantation agriculture required large pools of labor. Indentured servants, fulfilling fixed terms of work, performed field labor, but there were not enough of them nor predictable supplies of new "redemptioners" to meet the demand. Further, field work was hard and difficult, none more so than that required to cultivate rice paddies. Such work, and the diseases that accompanied it (especially malaria), brought high death rates.

Driven by the desire to accumulate wealth, and often in debt, the first planters were limited in their ability to gain profits by the scarcity of labor. The more land they put under cultivation, the greater their profits; but they could profit only from what they could harvest. Their need and desire for labor, and the nature of field work, led to solutions that dehumanized laborers and made them receptive to slavery. Nevertheless, the labor force of the southern colonies throughout the seventeenth century was chiefly recruited from the poor whites, both free and indentured. By 1700 there were perhaps 25,000 slaves in all of the American colonies, with the great majority in the southern states.

SOUTHERN COMMERCE

Since the cash crops of the South were grown for British markets, and most plantations were located near navigable rivers and streams, southern planters tended to deal directly with British merchants. The shipments of products they sent to British ports were credited to their accounts; they purchased finished goods and supplies against the balances (which usually favored the merchant). This practice limited the growth of local and regional commerce.

SOUTHERN MANUFACTURERS

The southern colonies had fewer manufacturing establishments than the other regions of the country. A small–scale iron industry emerged in Maryland and Virginia, but the work of blacksmiths, tanners, cobblers, and weavers was largely confined to the plantations and their immediate needs. The forests of the Carolina uplands furnished lumber for shipbuilding and naval stores—pitch, tar, and turpentine—for the British navy. In the eighteenth century, Carolina and Georgia traders did a thriving business in furs.

COLONIAL SOCIETIES

American settlers brought European traditions and patterns of living with them to their new homes, but they faced quite different environments in the New World. Life in colonial America was shaped to a great extent by the immensity of nature and the struggle to survive in demanding conditions.

Population Patterns

The real dangers of the transatlantic crossing and survival in an alien and often hostile environment discouraged those without strong motivation from migrating to English America. Most of the early immigrants from England were from the commercial and laboring classes, those from the upper classes usually younger sons without means. More often than not these immigrants were willing to risk a new life to avoid persecution, prison and punishment, business failures or dim prospects for trade and work. The motivation must have been particularly strong among those who came as indentured servants, who signed on usually for terms of five years of hard work in exchange for their transportation and living necessities. This method of gaining transportation to the New World was widely used by those who immigrated to the southern colonies in the seventeenth century; thereafter, as slaveholding increased, it was more common among immigrants to the middle colonies.

By 1700 the population of English America had dramatically increased, due to new immigration throughout the century but also to increases in life expectancy. In New England those who survived childhood lived to an old age comparable to modern life expectancy—probably a testament to the healthfulness of the environment. The region's population reached 150,000 in 1700, having quadrupled since 1650, largely as a result of natural reproduction. In the southern colonies, however, conditions were quite different. The average life expectancy was roughly forty years, reflecting high mortality rates among children, the persistence of malaria and similar diseases, and a significant disparity in the number of males to females.

Social Conditions

The peopling of the English colonies began with a small migration from a few provincial areas of England and, after the first settlements took hold, increased dramatically. By both voluntary and involuntary means, Europeans and Africans, as well as British and Irish, came to North America in significant numbers. The great distances that separated the settlers and a general scarcity of labor had significant effects on the development of colonial societies.

FAMILY AND THE ROLE OF WOMEN

The family was the basic unit of colonial society, sanctioned by religion and tradition. Marriages took place at an early age and families were large, particularly on the frontier, where each new pair of hands counted. The family bond was strengthened in New England by the longevity of the population and by the cluster effect of the town pattern of settlement in New England and other northern communities. Families were less stable on the frontier and the plantation as a consequence of higher death rates, disease, and isolation.

The position of women, who had an almost completely dependent status under English common law, improved rapidly in English America, where their numbers were few. Although they possessed few legal rights and protections, women were often accepted by men as equal partners in the social and business affairs of the family. They played crucial roles on the farm, raising and producing salable items to augment the income from crops.

Social status. Though the primitive conditions of life along the frontier tended to make all men equal in their wilderness environment, class distinctions were obvious in the seaport cities and the older village settlements. A relatively small upper class, having close connections with England, consisted of colonial governors, clergymen, wealthy merchants and planters, and professional men.

In Puritan New England the highest social rank was at first reserved for those leaders (among the "visible saints") considered most pious and worthy of emulation. This later gave way to measures of personal wealth and influence. In the South, and to an extent in New York, wealth, social position, and political power were measured by the extent of lands (and servants or slaves) one held. The English ideal of a permanent landed class was aspired to (though in reality only approximated) and consequently aristocratic manners and trappings were emulated.

Much larger was a growing middle class of prosperous tradesmen, farmers, mechanics, and laborers. The gap between upper and middle classes was much smaller than in England and Europe, where such distinctions endured from generation to generation; in the New World setting they proved far less fixed. In the Chesapeake and other southern colonies, however, social mobility diminished toward the end of the seventeenth century as ruling planter groups began to perpetuate themselves and slaveholding became more firmly identified with wealth and power. Of the two groups of bond servants, those under bond or indenture were decreasing in number late in the eighteenth century, while the number of slaves was increasing.

INDENTURED SERVANTS

Following English precedent, these bondsmen were indentured, or agreed to contracts of service, for fixed terms (usually five years). Many were voluntarily indentured in England in exchange for their transportation to the colonies; these "redemptioners" were frequently skilled artisans and occasionally persons with professional training. Unskilled laborers were often recruited by kidnappers operating in European ports; many others were transported by English courts for political and religious offenses, as well as for misdemeanors and crimes.

THE SLAVE TRADE

After the termination of the slave trade monopoly of the Royal African Company in 1697, white indentured servants were rapidly replaced by enslaved Africans in Virginia and the Carolinas. The first shipload of these slaves arrived in Virginia in 1619.

Africans were first transported to the New World in the sixteenth century by the Portuguese, who captured or purchased men and women on the west coast of Africa for sale as laborers. The slave trade increased rapidly in the eighteenth century. The English colonies were always a small part of the world market for the slave traders—perhaps less than 5 percent of the total number transported (compared to more than 35 percent who were sent to Brazil).

While there is evidence that there was some fluidity in the condition and prospects of black laborers in the seventeenth century, the idea gradually took hold among whites (as the slave population grew) that blacks were fitted only for perpetual enslavement. The fact that they arrived in servitude, and appeared so alien to the ways of the English, contributed to this view. The judgment that they were an inferior race seems also to have grown out of deeply rooted feelings about their color, associated with evil by peoples of British and northern European stock. Before the slave trade was abolished in the nineteenth century, between 8 and 11 million black captives had been brought to the New World to live and work against their wills.

African Slavery. In 1700 there were roughly 25,000 slaves, perhaps one–half of whom were in Virginia. By 1760 it is estimated that there were perhaps 300,000 Africans in English America, of whom more than three-quarters were in the South. In some areas of South Carolina and Georgia they exceeded the white population in number. In the healthier climate of the upper South, the black population increased as a result of natural reproduction.

As the number of black slaves grew, southern states passed various slave codes that gave white owners almost complete control over the lives and persons of their slaves. Slaves, in fact, were defined for legal purposes as chattel or animal property—this invited abuse and affected all aspects of the master–slave relationship. It also had an important effect on human relationships within the slave community. Despite these measures, there were outbreaks of resistance—such as the Stono uprising of 1739 in South Carolina which, while few in number, served to keep all aware of the possibility of armed insurrections.

Immigration

Non–English settlers came to American shores in substantial numbers, bringing ideas and traditions that steadily modified the predominantly English manners and mores. By the early eighteenth century, immigration from England had slowed and was actually being discouraged by the government. The forcible immigration of slaves, from Africa as well as the West Indies, increased throughout most of the eighteenth century.

THE GERMANS

The principal source of immigration from continental Europe to the English colonies after 1700 was the German states. Many German settlers were hard–working peasants, dispossessed by wars or other reverses and often victims of religious persecution. Others had been trained as skilled artisans or professional men. Pennsylvania became the center of German settlement, but Germans also penetrated the Shenandoah Valley and the Piedmont region of Virginia and North Carolina. Probably 200,000 Germans were in the colonies in 1775.

THE SCOTCH–IRISH, SCOTS, AND IRISH

The largest group of new immigrants to the colonies were the descendants of Presbyterians from the Scottish Lowlands who had colonized northern Ireland (or Ulster) early in the seventeenth century. Shortly after 1700, these Scotch–Irish, driven by religious and economic grievances, left Ulster in large numbers for Pennsylvania and the colonies to the south. Drawn westward along the fertile river valleys in search of cheap land, often resorting to violence to remove Indians and others in their way, they exhibited hard qualities that allowed them to adapt to the unstructured life of the colonial frontier. Perhaps 300,000 Scotch–Irish came to America before the Revolution.

Immigration from Scotland and Ireland continued throughout the seventeenth and eighteenth centuries. Scotch and Irish merchants and shippers were active in a number of American ports. Some Scots Highlanders (largely Roman Catholics), defeated in the uprisings of 1715 and 1745, came to settle in the colonies, especially North Carolina. Scots Lowlanders immigrated in increasing numbers at the end of the century to escape poor economic conditions.

OTHER IMMIGRANT GROUPS

Other groups fled Europe to escape religious or political persecution or economic hardship, but in significantly fewer numbers: Huguenots and other Protestants fleeing religious and political persecution in France after the Edict of Nantes was revoked in 1685; the Swiss in North Carolina; the Welsh Quakers in Pennsylvania and New England; and small groups of Jews from Spain and Portugal, who settled in several port cities. Along the Hudson River, the Dutch influence in speech, dress, and building construction persisted into the nineteenth century.

Social Patterns

The greater part of the more than one million inhabitants of America in the mideighteenth century lived in rural settings, reflecting the importance of agriculture to the colonial economies. In New England the town emerged as the defining social unit, in the South the plantation community.

CITIES

The major colonial cities and large towns—Boston, Newport, New York, Philadelphia, and Charleston—were all ports. The largest, and most developed as a cultural center, was Philadelphia, which had a population of over 18,000 in 1750 (almost twice that number by 1775). Beginning as tiny settlements, these cities rapidly developed into commercial centers in which physicians, lawyers, merchants, artisans, and mechanics lived in much the same way they would have in England or Europe. As the increase and concentration of population continued, colonial cities adopted governments and regulations for public health and safety and developed cultural institutions for the most part modeled after those of London. Communication between the colonial cities was at first mainly by sea because roads were poor—for a time the seaports were more closely in touch with England, six weeks away by sea, than they were with one another.

PLANTATIONS

In Maryland and the colonies to the south, and also to an extent in upstate New York, along the Hudson River, society was organized by the large plantations and estates that were formed in the late seventeenth and early eighteenth centuries. The choicest locations were on rivers and navigable streams that permitted vessels to receive produce directly from the dock. The largest plantations were usually well-run and somewhat diversified enterprises, to a large extent economically self–sufficient; slaves were trained to perform skilled work and crafts as well as the support functions of the plantation community. While most holdings were modest in size, the plantation pattern prevailed and had the effect of retarding village and town development.

THE NEW ENGLAND TOWN

The social pattern of New England reflected the agreements or covenants that the Pilgrims and Puritans subscribed to as congregations prior to or during the process of settlement. The civil life of the congregation took place within the town, a hybrid social and political unit Puritans adapted from the English parish, village, and borough. Members of the community lived in a cluster of houses, built about a "common" pasture, that formed the town. They went out from this center to farm and work their portions of the community's fields and wooded lands. In the town center was the meetinghouse, the locus of the community's spiritual and political life. The community was governed by its yearly town meeting, in which all men participated. As populations and pressures for land use rose in the second and third generations of the first town settlements, the town unit model was replicated in inland areas.

Although the town structure was efficient and well suited for new settlements, Puritanism proved incapable of resolving other challenges presented by economic and social changes. The practice of dividing land holdings among the next generation of sons, rather than passing a single estate on to the eldest son, had the effect of fragmenting holdings and dividing family members. The Puritan "saints" were unable to adjust to New England's rapid maritime and mercantile development and the region's increasing wealth. Tensions relating to such changes may have contributed to the fears and accusations of witchcraft that appeared in the 1680's and 1690s.

THE FRONTIER

Compared to the relative comfort of the cities and towns, life on the frontier was rough and dangerous. The danger of Indian attacks was constant—families frequently moved westward in groups and, when beginning a new settlement, erected a stockade for protection before clearing the land. By the eighteenth century the log cabin was the standard dwelling; clothing was often made from the skins of animals; food at first was obtained chiefly by hunting and fishing. Recreation usually took the form of useful community enterprises, such as logrolling, house raisings, and husking bees.

COLONIAL INSTITUTIONS

The role and presence of institutions in the American colonies was slight compared to that of king, church, Parliament, the military, and universities in Great Britain. Those British institutions, with few exceptions, exerted more influence in colonial America than the fledgling colonial institutions that were established in the colonies to serve similar social functions. The tradition of religious dissent, the great distances that separated most Americans from population centers, and a pattern of political differences with the mother country gave a distinctly anti–institutional quality to the emerging Anglo–American culture of the eighteenth century.

Religion

The lives of most American communities were shaped by the churches or religious sects that dominated their colonies, whether their citizens subscribed to religious teachings or not. Although many settlers had left England to gain more religious freedom, a complete separation of church and state was achieved only in Rhode Island.

THE ESTABLISHED CHURCHES

By the middle of the eighteenth century nine of the original thirteen colonies had established churches, supported by colonial laws and general taxation.

The Anglicans. Virginia was the first of the English colonies to give legislative sanction to the Church of England. Prior to the Revolution, Maryland, New York, the Carolinas, and Georgia had also recognized the Anglican Church by voting to support its parishes with taxes. There was no resident bishop of the Church of England in colonial America, and the Anglican clergy, handicapped by difficulties of travel and communication among scattered settlements, never gained a dominant position. The parish structure and the vestry, the lay council or committee of the parish, nevertheless had an effect on the government and politics of Virginia and Maryland.

Puritanism. Calvinism dominated all aspects of the Puritan experiment of seventeenth-century New England. It continued to exert a strong influence in the eighteenth century, although church membership weakened and the individual congregations broke into two groups on the question of church government: Presbyterians recognized a central governing authority of Presbyters; Congregationalists did not.

The Puritan settlers believed that their members had been divinely "elected" for salvation. During the first two generations of their control in Massachusetts, only church members could vote—to become a church member one had to have his spiritual worth approved by the minister and the congregation. Conformity to such strict standards was not easy, and church membership requirements were relaxed by means of measures such as the Halfway Covenant of 1662 (extending provisional church membership to children of church members). The Massachusetts charter of 1691 removed the church membership requirement for voting. In the following century the colony permitted the establishment of some Anglican chapels, adopted a policy of cooperation with Presbyterian Calvinists, and authorized such dissenting sects as Baptists and Methodists to use funds derived from taxes for the support of their own ministers. The New England Congregationalist and Presbyterian clergy nevertheless continued to exercise considerable influence in political matters.

THE MULTIPLICATION OF RELIGIOUS SECTS

In the eighteenth century, thousands of European Protestants who were neither Congregationalists nor Anglicans came to America. Along the frontier particularly, Baptists, Presbyterians, Methodists, and Quakers flourished. Lutherans, Dutch Reformed, Moravians, and Huguenots found a haven in the Middle Colonies, especially in Pennsylvania and New Jersey.

PROGRESS TOWARDS RELIGIOUS FREEDOM

Although the desire for freedom of worship had inspired many nonconformist religious groups to move from England and the European continent to the New World, the English colonies only gradually adopted policies of religious tolerance. Still, the need to survive and to populate settlements exercised a sway in the direction of religious freedom that was unknown in the Old World. Pressed by the demands of the growing non–English population, Massachusetts Puritans for example made notable concessions to dissenters.

The example of Rhode Island, which Roger Williams had founded on the principle of separation of church and state, was nevertheless unique. Despite such measures as the Maryland Toleration Act (1649), the freedom of conscience provision in the New Jersey charter (1665), and the broad invitation to all religious sects sent out by the Quaker William Penn in settling Pennsylvania, Roman Catholic and Jewish minorities were restricted in the practice of their religion and denied the right to vote and hold office (as had been the case in England).

THE GREAT AWAKENING

During the 1730s and 1740s, a revival of religious fervor swept the American colonies, ignited by wandering evangelists who perceived a decline of piety in their congregations. The most prominent preachers in this movement were George Whitefield, an evangelical Anglican from England who attracted large crowds and often spoke out of doors, and Jonathan Edwards, a New England Congregational minister and theologian. Edwards entitled his best known sermon "Sinners in the Hands of an Angry God," which he believed was the predicament of mankind, who could be saved from eternal damnation only by God's grace. In different ways evangelists attempted to win converts with such emotional appeals, which had a powerful effect on their audiences.

The revival stirred both towns and countryside but had its most lasting impact on those who populated the isolated backcountry of the South and west. It produced a split among Presybterian leaders—into "Old Lights," who condemned emotionalism and took a more rationalistic approach to theology; and "New Lights," who put evangelical fervor above church organization. Methodism, the movement founded by John Wesley that sought to reform the Church of England, and Baptist sects that derived from Calvinism also gained converts to the evangelical cause. By giving such emphasis to individual conversion and grace, the Great Awakening contributed to a democratizing trend—and to a questioning of traditional authority and institutions.

Education in the Colonies

Education was judged important by the English colonists, and it began in the home. However poor and isolated, most Americans learned to read and compute numbers, wherever they lived. The King James translation of the Bible was often the only book they had—the unsurpassed English made it an excellent language primer. Many families owned one or more of the works of Shakespeare, a copy of John Bunyan's classic *A Pilgrim's Progress*, and sometimes collections of English literary essays or great speeches.

ELEMENTARY SCHOOLING

In 1647, the Massachusetts School Law required every town of fifty householders to maintain a grammar school. Although not universally enforced, the law was the first to mandate public education in America. In the middle colonies, schools were dependent on religious societies, notably the Quakers, and on other private organizations. In the South the families of the tidewater employed private tutors or relied on the clergy to conduct secondary schools. Most elementary schools were for boys exclusively, but schools for girls were established in the eighteenth century in most cities and large towns. Despite the informal quality of most American schooling, by the mideighteenth century the literacy rate in the colonies was probably equal to if not higher than that in most European countries.

In the crafts and "arts," such as building and carpentry, training was provided under terms of apprenticeship. For slave children there was little opportunity to learn to read or write. By depriving their slaves of the ability to read and write, slave owners sought to prevent insurrections and resistance. Some masters wanted (or permitted) their slaves to improve themselves, but the slaves and even the master risked punishment if caught.

COLLEGES AND MEDICAL SCHOOLS

Before the American Revolution, nine colleges had been founded. Harvard (1636), William and Mary (1693), Yale (1701), the College of New Jersey, now Princeton (1746), Brown (1764), Rutgers (1766), and Dartmouth (1769) were established primarily for the training of ministers, although subjects other than theology and the classics were taught. Two had no religious affiliation or purpose: the Academy and College of Philadelphia (1755), which became the University of Pennsylvania, and King's College (1754), later Columbia University.

By 1720 the natural sciences were being taught and modern languages were considered worthy of study. The College of Philadelphia also offered courses in practical subjects such as mechanics and agriculture. At the end of the eighteenth century, medical schools were established there and at King's College.

Anglo–American Culture

Cultural institutions founded on English models emerged in the colonies in the eighteenth century. The books, manners, and fashions of colonial America reflected those of the mother country and its great metropolitan center, London.

LANGUAGE AND LITERATURE

On the eve of the Revolution, Americans were more predominantly English in thought and aspiration than the large numbers of continental Europeans in the population seemed to indicate. Except among the German groups in Pennsylvania, English was the language of the overwhelming majority in every community. American usage reflected regional differences and, to be sure, the quite new conditions that settlers encountered—but the literary standards of America were still set by the works of English writers in England. The only writer in the American colonies to gain notice in England was Benjamin Franklin, author of many practical–minded essays, notably *Poor Richard's Almanac*, which appeared annually from 1732 to 1757.

EFFECTS OF THE ENLIGHTENMENT

The European Enlightenment had a significant impact on eighteenth–century culture and thereby exerted influence on the American colonies. This broad movement of learning and ideas was in large part the cultural expression of the great scientific advances of the seventeenth century, particularly the discoveries of Sir Isaac Newton in astronomy. The mechanical laws that governed the motion of the planets seemed to prove the existence of a rational God, a benevolent mechanic or clock–maker deity, whose handiwork could be discovered and understood by means of experimental science. Many Christians, especially those close to the world of learning, incorporated such views into their religious beliefs. These "deists" disputed the literal or fundamentalist interpretation of the Bible and looked on the world as God's creation rather than man's temptation.

The great scientific advances of the eighteenth century encouraged experimental inquiries into all aspects of the physical world. In colonial America, where nature so dwarfed the human presence, scientific interests were almost exclusively devoted to practical subjects with technological promise. Benjamin Franklin's celebrated experiments with electricity and the lightning rod demonstrated the validity of such an approach and made him world famous. The many new discoveries helped to foster a confident outlook that age–old social, economic, and political problems might also be solved.

Libraries and Learned Societies. During the eighteenth century there was a large increase in the number of books imported to America and gradually in the number printed in the colonies. The first printing press had been put into operation in Massachusetts in 1639. Private libraries grew in size, and public subscription libraries were founded on the model of the Library Company of Philadelphia, begun by Franklin and others in 1731. As was the case in England and Europe, an interest in science, albeit of a more practical bent, united merchants, lawyers, farmers, and especially physicians. Organizations such as the American Philosophical Society (1743), also formed under Franklin's leadership and modeled after the Royal Society of London, provided a formal structure for such investigations.

Expanded Role of Newspapers. In the great expanse of colonial America, newspapers quickly took on an essential role in communication and information. They printed laws of the colonial legislatures, official communications, news from London and Europe, advertisements and notices, and selections from books of all kinds. The colonial printer (Franklin began his career as one) became an important figure in the shaping as well as the dissemination of early American culture. By 1730, seven newspapers were being published in four different colonies. At the turn of the century there were more than 180 in the United States. Proportionally, there was a larger readership of newspapers in the colonies than in the mother country.

LAW AND POLITICS

English law and governmental institutions gradually took hold, but the great distance that separated the colonies from the mother country, as well as the American setting itself, introduced important modifications to English traditions. The common law and English judicial procedures were adopted, but they were applied in ways that fit American circumstances. General legal ideas and language blended readily into colonial politics and speech, reflecting, it would seem, the frequency with which the colonists felt it necessary to define their liberties and standing within the empire. In general, however, knowledge of English law in the colonies was rarely precise or deep. The idea grew that law represented abstract justice or natural order, rather than the will of the king in Parliament. The decision in the libel trial of the New York printer John Peter Zenger in 1734–35 pointed to an American perspective: Despite the court's refusal to admit Zenger's evidence proving the truth of the alleged libel, he was acquitted of the charge. The case, as historian Daniel Boorstin has pointed out, was significant for having "affirmed the power of juries in libel cases to decide the law as well as the fact."

By the mid–eighteenth century, life in the American colonies had been shaped by both cultural heritage and environment. Since the ethnic character of populations was not uniform, and the landscape and climate of American geographic regions varied, the provincial societies of English America exhibited more diversity than provincial English society. While they did not yet share a distinctly American outlook, there were elements in their work and customs, their language and education, and their laws and politics that made them resemble one another more than their English rulers. Beyond the cities and principal towns of the colonies, British authority and English culture were considerably diluted.

Selected Readings

Ahlstrom, Sydney. *Religious History of the American People* (1972)

Bailyn, Bernard. *Voyages to the West: A Passage in the Peopling of America on the Eve of the Revolution* (1986)

Boorstin, Daniel J. *The Americans: The Colonial Experience* (1958)

Bridenbaugh, Carl. *Myths and Realities: Societies of the Colonial South* (1963)

———. *Cities in the Wilderness* (1938)

———. *Cities in Revolt* (1955)

Bumsted, J.M. and Van de Wetering, John E. *What Must I Do to Be Saved? The Great Awakening in Colonial America* (1976)

Hofstadter, Richard. *America at 1750: A Social Portrait* (1971)

Jordan, Winthrop D. *White over Black: American Attitudes Toward the Negro, 1550–1812* (1968)

May, Henry. *The Enlightenment in America* (1976)

McCusker, John M. and Menard, Russell. *The Economy of British America* (1985)

Morgan, Edmund. *The Puritan Family* (1966)

Tolles, Frederick B. *Meeting House and Counting House: The Quaker Merchants of Colonial Philadelphia, 1682–1763* (1948)

Wood, Peter H. *Black Majority: Negroes in South Carolina from 1670 Through the Stono Rebellion* (1974)

4

American Colonies in the British Empire

1649–1660	Commonwealth governs England
1660	Restoration of the monarchy and King Charles II; Enumerated Commodities (Navigation) Act of 1660 (reenacts much of the act of 1651)
1663	Staple Act passed
1673	Duty Act passed
1685	Accession of James II (formerly duke of York)
1686	Dominion of New England formed
1688	The Glorious Revolution; James II deposed, succeeded by William and Mary
1689–1697	King William's War; concluded by the Treaty of Ryswick
1696	Board of Trade and Plantations established; Parliament passes Enforcement Act
1702	Anne, daughter of James II, becomes queen of England
1702–1713	Queen Anne's War
1707	Union of England and Scotland, forming Great Britain
1714	George I (first Hanoverian) assumes throne
1745–1748	King George's War; concluded by Treaty of Aix–la–Chapelle
1754	The Albany Congress meets, Plan of Union fails; Battle of Fort Duquesne begins conflict with France in British America
1754–1763	The French and Indian War (Seven Years' War in Europe); concluded by the Peace of Paris
1760	Accession of King George III
1763	Proclamation Line of 1763 enacted
1764	Sugar Act and Currency Act passed
1765	Stamp Act and Mutiny Act passed; Stamp Act Congress meets

1766 Stamp Act repealed and Declaratory Act passed

1767 Townsend duties introduced

1768 Nonimportation agreements implemented

1770 The Boston massacre occurs; repeal of Townsend duties

1772 Attack on the Gaspee

1773 Tea Act passed; Boston Tea Party staged

1774 Parliament passes Intolerable Acts (March–May); Continental Congress convenes (September)

During the first 150 years after Jamestown was settled, British governments put in place a mercantilist system of imperial regulation and made repeated efforts to strengthen royal authority over the colonies. However, struggles and conflict between Parliament and crown, wars in Europe, and the great distance that separated the colonies from the mother country prevented officials in London from gaining firm control of the American colonies. The majority of the colonists in the meantime became quite determined about their rights as Englishmen, particularly in matters of taxation. A new attitude and policy toward them emerged in Britain after the victorious conclusion of the Seven Years' War in 1763, prompted by the great increase in the national debt that had been required to wage that worldwide conflict.

EARLY IMPERIAL ADMINISTRATION

Royal Administration Under the Stuarts

James I, who regarded America as an extension of the royal domain, created administrative agencies which he hoped would maintain the crown's authority over the colonies. He appointed a Council of Trade (1622) to see that English laws were enforced in America, and he revoked the charter of the London Company (1624), thus making Virginia a royal province. His successor, Charles I, gave large powers over the colonies to a commission of twelve members of his Privy Council (1634).

THE PURITAN COMMONWEALTH

The activity of the Privy Council in colonial affairs was cut short by the Puritan revolt (1642) against Stuart authority, which resulted in the execution of Charles I and the establishment of a commonwealth. Though the Long Parliament tried to maintain continuity of control by naming a special board of six noblemen and twelve commoners (1643), little was accomplished during the period of parliamentary rule. The colonies were in the main left on their own and allowed to govern themselves in local matters.

THE RESTORATION

Charles II returned from exile to take the throne (1660) and sought the advice of favorites among the nobility and the wealthier merchants in colonial matters. He named two advisory bodies—a Council for Foreign Plantations and a Council for Trade (1660). These were merged in 1674 into a standing committee of the Privy Council for Trade and Foreign Plantations. Preoccupied by domestic strife and foreign wars, the king's advisors finally resorted to a radical scheme to curb the progress toward self–government they had detected in Massachusetts and neighboring provinces. They secured the revocation of the Massachusetts charter and persuaded James II to merge the several settlements of the region into the Dominion of New England. The creation of the Dominion was represented as a measure necessary for military defense, but Americans generally regarded it as a device to impose royal authority on the colonies. The Dominion collapsed when James II was driven from the throne by the Glorious Revolution (1688).

Parliament and Empire

Although Parliament imposed new constitutional limits on the authority of the crown, it continued to believe that colonial affairs could be guided by its commercial regulation.

MERCANTILISM

English parliamentarians generally accepted the prevailing theory of mercantilism—that a nation's prosperity depended upon the amount of precious metals it could accumulate through favorable trade balances. Colonies were judged valuable as suppliers of raw materials and consumers of finished products. The crown had specific reasons for regulating the trade of the colonies—it needed (sometimes desperately) the revenues that flowed from duties and fees. British merchants embraced the regulation of colonial commerce as a means of excluding foreign competitors, principally the very active Dutch merchants.

THE NAVIGATION ACTS

Mercantilist ideas provided the rationale for Parliament to pass a series of trade acts in the second half of the seventeenth century. These were designed to enhance the benefits of the colonial trade for the mother country and to restrict trade by colonials with Dutch and other foreign merchants. This trend in legislation continued after the Restoration.

The Navigation Act of 1651. Parliament decreed that all goods entering England must be carried in ships owned and in major part manned by British subjects, including colonials, or in ships of the country producing the goods.

By this arrangement the Spanish could bring to England their olives and the Portuguese their wines, but Dutch ships carrying such products were barred. The Netherlands retaliated with war (1652–54), the result of which was to further increase the prestige of England's navy and merchant marine.

The Enumerated Commodities Act (1660). In this legislation most of the restrictions of the original Navigation Act were re–enacted. The colonies were forbidden to export certain commodities such as tobacco, sugar, cotton, indigo, and dyes to any country except England or the other English colonies. The list was made to include rice, molasses, and naval stores in 1706. In 1722 it was further extended to copper, ore, and skins. Since the commodities enumerated were much in demand in England, and the colonies had been established to serve the mother country, English political leaders held that the act was justified.

The Staple Act (1663). Designed to protect English merchants against foreign competition in American markets, this act provided that all European imports into the American colonies, with a few exceptions, had to first enter English ports. Such goods could be reshipped only after the payment of a duty.

The Duty Act (1673). To prevent colonials (especially New Englanders) from exploiting flaws in earlier legislation designed to thwart their participation in direct trade with Europe, Parliament levied a plantation duty, to be paid in colonial ports. Provision was also made for the appointment of resident customs collectors in the colonies, who were made directly responsible to the commissioners of customs in England.

The Enforcement Act (1696). The American colonists, who considered the Navigation Acts inconsistent with their rights and destructive of their growing commerce, found many ways to evade them. Customs officials, notably Edward Randolph in Massachusetts (1680), could get little help in carrying out their duties. As a result, the law of 1696 contained stringent clauses to break up smuggling: it required that all English and colonial ships be registered, and it authorized customs officials to search ships, wharves, and warehouses and to seize unlawful goods. Admiralty courts to handle enforcement proceedings were established in all the colonies—such bodies could proceed without the accused having benefit of common law protections, notably a jury trial. In the same year King William III created the Board of Trade and Plantations to oversee colonial commerce.

ENFORCEMENT OF THE NAVIGATION ACTS

After the Glorious Revolution, the victorious Whig faction, which had set constitutional limits on the monarchy, did not repeal the legislation that had extended imperial control over the colonies. Between 1682 and 1752 eight colonial charters were annulled, and the number of royal officials increased in all the colonies. The royal veto was exercised to overturn acts of the colonial legislatures; attempts were made to regulate certain colonial industries (including wool and iron manufacture) so as to reduce competition with those of England; the issuance of colonial currency was closely supervised; and the right of appeal from decisions of the colonial courts to the Privy Council in London was extended. Nevertheless, particularly under the long ascendancy of Sir Robert Walpole as first lord of the treasury and chancellor of the Exchequer (1721–42), the enforcement of these measures was not particularly vigorous and at times purposely lax in order to stimulate trade. Dealing with inconsistent and often inept enforcement of the regulations became as much a part of colonial economic life as the printed provisions of the Navigation Acts.

THE STRUGGLE FOR CONTROL OF NORTH AMERICA

From the Glorious Revolution of 1688 to the Peace of Paris (1763), the development of English America was in large part determined by the contest for power waged by England and France in every part of the world. Early in the eighteenth century royal officials in the colonies, as well as in England, came to believe that French forts and trading posts might "encircle" the English settlements along the Atlantic coast.

French Policy   France's goals in North America were ambitious, if at times subordinate to its worldwide struggle with Britain. From settlements at Quebec and Montreal on the St. Lawrence River, the French pushed toward the Great Lakes and down the Mississippi Valley. The empire they claimed was a huge territory, extending from settlements on the lower St. Lawrence River, to the Great Lakes and beyond, and down the Missisippi River Valley to the Gulf of Mexico. But, in fact, beyond Montreal, it was a series of trading posts, missions, and forts strung along the route of the fur traders—the total population of New France was only 75,000. To maintain their authority over this great extent, the French formed alliances with the Algonquins (particularly the Hurons) and other tribes who were threatened by the English settlers or their Indian allies, the Iroquois.

THE ENCIRCLING FRENCH

EXPLORATION OF THE INTERIOR OF THE CONTINENT

In 1763 Father Jacques Marquette, the adventurous Jesuit missionary, and Louis Joliet, a successful fur trader, explored Lake Michigan and the tributaries of the Mississippi. They then sailed southward on that great river to the mouth of the Arkansas. The count de Frontenac, then governor of New France, realizing the strategic importance of control of the Mississippi, gave strong support to a daring expedition of Robert Cavelier, sieur de La Salle. In 1682 La Salle's small band of French and Indians reached the Mississippi delta and the Gulf of Mexico, claiming the whole valley for France. The French then began to erect a series of forts to bar the English and their Iroquois allies from the region.

Colonial Wars

The military conflict between Britain and France in America was but one aspect of a worldwide struggle between the two nations that was waged from Canada to the West Indies, on the high seas, and through Europe and Asia. Of principle concern for the English and French colonists in America were control of the fur trade, supremacy in the North Atlantic fisheries, and possession of the great Ohio–Mississippi basin.

KING WILLIAM'S WAR (1689–1697)

The outbreak of the War of the League of Augsburg in Europe led to hostilities in North America known as King William's War. The French, aided by their Indian allies, the Hurons, launched a series of raids from Canada. Settlements at Dover, New Hampshire, and Schenectady, New York (1690), were destroyed. The English took Port Royal (today Annapolis Royal), Nova Scotia, in 1690 but failed in a later attempt with their Iroquois allies to capture Quebec. Hostilities formally ended the inconclusive Treaty of Ryswick (1697), but the Huron and Iroquois continued their conlfict.

QUEEN ANNE'S WAR (1702–1713)

The French king Louis XIV's desire to place his own candidate on the throne of Spain precipitated a general war in Europe, known as Queen Anne's War in America. In 1710 France lost the province of Acadia (Nova Scotia), long a source of attacks against New England. On European battlefields the brilliant leadership of the duke of Marlborough was decisive for the British. By the Treaty of Utrecht (1713), Great Britain secured the Hudson Bay region, Newfoundland, and Nova Scotia. Spain yielded to British merchants (in the Assiento) a monopoly on the slave trade to Spanish America.

Troubled Truce. For thirty years after the Treaty of Utrecht the French and British competed for advantage in establishing trading posts, building strategic forts, and arranging agreements with the Indian tribes most active in the fur trade. Spanish raids on British settlements in South Carolina during earlier conficts eventually led to the founding of Georgia, primarily as a buffer colony.

KING GEORGE'S WAR (1745–1748)

The bitter Anglo–French rivalry again erupted, first in Europe in the War of the Austrian Succession (1744). There, as well as in America, the conflict was inconclusive. New Englanders captured the fortified town of Louisbourg on Cape Breton Island, but, to the colonists' dismay, it was returned to France under the terms of the Treaty of Aix–la–Chapelle (1748). After the war, fighting continued on the frontier, particularly in the Ohio Valley, as both nations competed for the control of the region and of the fur trade.

The French and Indian War (1754–1763)

The contest for empire reached its climax in the war that was known in Europe as the Seven Years' War. In Asia and America, as well as on the European continent, Britain finally prevailed over France and her allies. The war in America was bitterly fought.

EARLY DIFFICULTIES

Although the American colonies had almost twenty times the population of New France, the war went badly at first for the British cause. General Braddock's army regulars, supported by Virginia militiamen under Colonel George Washington, were routed while on an expedition against Fort Duquesne (today, Pittsburgh). The French captured Fort Oswego (in upstate New York), while in Europe, Russia, Austria, and Sweden joined France to defeat Britain's ally, King Frederick of Prussia. The demands in other theaters, or locations of the conflict, limited Britain's ability to commit troops to North America. Thus the early fighting against the French in the American theater was largely assigned to the local militia of the individual colonies. The coordination of these groups proved difficult, giving France and its Indian allies a temporary military advantage.

WILLIAM PITT'S LEADERSHIP

At the low point in British fortunes, William Pitt brought a new spirit into the war. As England's prime minister he established effective control of military forces and foreign policy. In 1757, in an attempt to strengthen British forces in America, he initiated impressments (forcible inductions) of colonists into the British army. He also authorized seizures of their produce and possessions and approved the quartering of soldiers in their homes against their wills. These measures were so resisted by the colonists that Pitt issued new directives the following year. The colonial assemblies regained responsibility for raising troops, and compensation was stipulated when goods and other support were requisitioned by the army. Pitt enlarged the force of British regulars stationed in America.

BRITISH VICTORIES

In 1758 a colorful army of English, Scots, and Americans, led by British generals Jeffrey Amherst and James Wolfe, stormed the French fortress of Louisbourg. Later that year General John Forbes's troops cut their way across Pennsylvania and blew up Fort Duquesne, erecting Fort Pitt on its ruins. In 1759 Wolfe lost his life in the spectacular capture of Quebec, the capital of New France. The following year Montreal fell to the British and the war in America came to an end.

The Peace of Paris (1763)

The treaty that concluded the conflict redrew the map of the world. Britain ended the influence of France in India and gained Florida as compensation from Spain for the return of Cuba and the Philippines, seized during the conflict. In America the boundaries of British colonies were extended to include Canada and all of France's territory east of the Mississippi River, except New Orleans. France was compelled to cede to Spain the port of New Orleans and the rest of Louisiana that lay west of the Mississippi. The French empire in America was reduced to the small islands of Martinique and Guadeloupe and half of Hispaniola (Haiti), in the West Indies.

CONSEQUENCES OF BRITAIN'S TRIUMPH

The defeat of France was secured at great expense to the British government—the national debt soared, restricting Britain's financial resources. With this constant reminder of the high cost of victory, the British government, believing the American colonists had not contributed sufficiently to the war effort, quickly concluded that the colonial system needed to be changed and new regulations implemented.

INTERCOLONIAL COOPERATION

The removal of the French presence in Canada was of considerable significance for English America. It made the colonies less dependent on Great Britain for military defense, and it opened the eyes of the colonists to many defects in the imperial system. The wars with the French convinced many colonial leaders of the usefulness of intercolonial cooperation in dealing with military matters, Indian relations, and commercial issues.

THE ALBANY CONGRESS (1754)

Even before the opening clash of the French and Indian War, delegates from seven colonies met in Albany to discuss the possibility of a closer union among the English provinces. The congress accepted Benjamin Franklin's suggestion that a federation be formed, to consist of a federal council chosen by the colonial assemblies (who were to retain their powers) and a president–general appointed by the crown. The council was to provide for common defense, guide Indian negotiations, and levy taxes for general purposes. The

Albany Plan was rejected by the British government and received little support in the colonial assemblies.

STRENGTH OF COLONIAL LEGISLATURES

The Anglo–French conflict dramatized the rise of the colonial legislative assemblies. Their responsibility for raising troops and their power to levy taxes within their borders had been indirectly acknowledged (if not directly approved) by Pitt in 1758. His decision to ask the colonial assemblies to raise taxes to pay for the war in America was interpreted by the colonists as recognition of their authority to tax themselves.

THE REORDERING AND EXTENSION OF IMPERIAL CONTROL

With the Peace of Paris, the British empire virtually doubled in size. The great increase in the extent of British territory resulted in new thinking about the purpose of empire. The administration and control of the new lands had to be dealt with immediately. The pressing problem of the national debt caused royal officials and parliamentarians alike to devise ways to raise additional revenues.

The Grenville Ministry

In 1763, the young and at times unstable King George III designated William Pitt's brother–in–law, George Grenville, chancellor of the Exchequer, to be the prime minister. Faced with the need to significantly raise revenues and to gain control of a vastly enlarged empire, Grenville set out to reinvigorate the mercantilist system. The general goal of his colonial policy was to secure tighter control over the colonies in imperial matters and to gain greater returns from them for the benefit of the mother country.

PRESSURES OF BRITISH PUBLIC OPINION

British merchants complained that the American colonists had long evaded the Navigation Acts with impunity, and that colonial merchants had made handsome profits during the French wars by trading with the enemy. They pressed Parliament to strictly enforce the commercial regulations in the colonies.

Merchants and landlords in Parliament demanded that the burden on British taxpayers be lessened by compelling the colonies to bear a larger share of imperial expenses. Great Britain's debt had doubled between 1756 and 1764, while the cost of maintaining the civil and military establishments

OWNERSHIP OF THE CONTINENT, 1682-1783

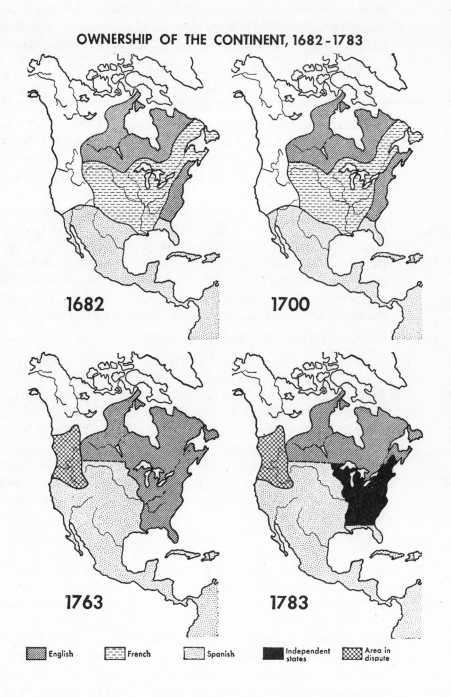

1682

1700

1763

1783

English | French | Spanish | Independent states | Area in dispute in America had increased fivefold since 1748. Although a few of the American colonies had met the requisitions imposed by the British government, most had contributed little to the costs of the French wars.

TROUBLE ON THE AMERICAN FRONTIER

The western frontier of the American colonies exploded in warfare in 1763 when a chief of the Ottawa tribe, Pontiac, formed his followers into a confederacy to drive English settlers out of the Ohio Valley. Though this attack was soon crushed, it had a significant effect in setting the new British policy on western lands in North America. It seems also to have convinced the British government that a permanent standing army in America was necessary.

Proclamation Line of 1763. Initially a temporary measure in response to hostilities in the Ohio Valley, the Proclamation Line reserved the region between the Alleghenies and the Mississippi—from Florida to 50° north latitude—for the use of Indian tribes. The colonists were ordered to remain east of a line drawn along the crest of the Alleghenies. Those who had already settled in the region were forced to withdraw. The new policy was protested by American traders, frontier settlers, and land speculators.

GRENVILLE'S NEW TRADE REGULATIONS

By tighter enforcement of the trade laws, Grenville expected to obtain larger revenues from the American colonies to defray imperial expenses. British ships were stationed along the American coast and customs agents were deployed in American ports to force compliance. Colonial exports of finished goods were restricted so as to prevent competition with manufacturers in the mother country.

Writs of Assistance. These general search warrants, against which James Otis of Boston had made his famous plea in 1761, were used ever more frequently to locate illegal shipments and to collect customs duties formerly lost through smuggling.

The Sugar Act (1764). An enlarged customs service was charged with enforcing the Molasses Act of 1733. It set almost prohibitive duties on rum, spirits, sugar, and molasses imported into the colonies from foreign sources. In 1764 the duty on foreign molasses was slightly reduced, that on refined sugar was increased, and new taxes on wines, silks, and other luxuries were imposed. The act stipulated that charges of smuggling were to be decided in vice–admiralty courts (effectively denying the accused trial by jury).

The Currency Act (1764). At the solicitation of British creditors, Parliament forbade further issuance of paper money in the colonies, thus preventing colonial debtors from settling their accounts in depreciated currency.

The Stamp Act (1765). Grenville hoped to secure considerable revenue by requiring that all official and legal documents, newspapers, almanacs, and pamphlets that were circulated in the colonies bear stamps showing that a tax on them had been paid. Unlike the Sugar Act, which revised previous duties on similar products, the Stamp Act was clearly a new form of tax, not a measure to regulate trade and raise revenue. A Stamp Act Congress of representatives from nine colonies gathered in New York in October 1765. It recognized Parliament's authority but asserted that taxes could only be levied by the colonies' elected representatives.

The Quartering, or Mutiny, Act (1765). An attempt was made to reduce the cost of the military establishment by compelling the colonists to quarter, or furnish lodging and supplies for, British troops if colonial barracks were inadequate.

COLONIAL PROTESTS

Opposition to Grenville's laws was much more widespread and violent than the British government had anticipated. This in itself demonstrated how effectively they were being enforced—revenues collected in the colonies increased tenfold. The new measures were implemented at a time when the American colonial economies were in a postwar downturn. They extracted hard money from every class, region and area—in cities and towns, plantations, large and small farms.

Americans particularly objected to the new pattern of taxation and enforcement. By empowering British officals, troops, and courts to collect revenues, Parliament circumvented the traditional authority of the colonial assemblies. The new measures were thus perceived to be threats to the rights of the colonists as well as to their prosperity.

Boycotts and Mobs. Aroused by the threat to their lucrative West Indian trade implicit in the Sugar Act, colonial merchants organized intercolonial nonimportation and nonconsumption agreements. These grew in effectiveness after the passage of the Stamp Act. In Boston, New York, and other ports, the more radical opponents of the measures, often calling themselves the Sons of Liberty, held public demonstrations, terrorized the stamp collectors, and destroyed the stamps.

Reaction to the new British policy served to unite disparate elements of the American colonies in a common cause. It blunted, for example, the strong differences that set the interior and western regions in opposition to the eastern seaboard. (Such differences had earlier produced Bacon's Rebellion in Virginia; they caused the rising of the Paxton Boys in Pennsylvania in 1763 and would also lead to a revolt known as the Regulator movement in North Carolina in 1771.)

RETREAT FROM GRENVILLE'S POLICY

While colonial resistance was noticed in London, it was the perception of a sharp decline in the colonies' trade with Great Britain that persuaded the new ministry of the marquis of Rockingham to repeal the Stamp Act and to reduce the duties imposed by Grenville in 1764. At the same time, Parliament also passed the Declaratory Act, reasserting its right to tax the colonies as it saw fit. The fruits of concerted action were not lost on the colonists.

The Townshend Program

Under the new ministry of the aging William Pitt, Charles Townshend, chancellor of the exchequer, persuaded Parliament to make a new attempt to increase revenues from America through comprehensive regulation of trade.

TOWNSHEND'S LEGISLATION

In 1767 Parliament passed a Duty Act imposing duties on glass, lead, tea, paper, and paint pigments, to be collected by British commissioners in America. Enforcement of the existing laws was given further emphasis—the New York Assembly was suspended for refusing to comply with the mandatory Quartering Act. In 1768 the Massachusetts legislature was dissolved for issuing a "circular letter" calling for united resistance to Parliamentary taxation, and the Virginia House of Burgesses was dissolved for endorsing the letter.

RENEWED COLONIAL PROTESTS

The imposition of the Townshend duties revived nonimportation and nonexportation agreements in the colonies. British finished and luxury goods were boycotted; American "homespun" products were worn defiantly.

The Boston Massacre (1770). When members of a new board of customs officials for the colonies were threatened, four regiments of British troops were quartered in Boston. Soon thereafter, a slight brawl between the "redcoats" and a group of "liberty boys" developed into mob action. The British troops fired at the shouting civilians, killing five and wounding several others. The incident was purposely distorted and exaggerated by American dissidents, anxious for a dramatic issue to use in building resistance to the new British policy.

EFFORTS AT CONCILIATION

When King George's favorite minister, Lord North, took over the control of governmental policy, he promised to heal the breach that had been developing between the colonies and the mother country. In 1770 Parliament was persuaded to repeal all duties on colonial imports except a small tax on tea. Lord North's conciliatory attitude strengthened the conservatives in the American colonies, who wished to avoid trouble. But the radicals, who distrusted North, prepared to meet any new infringement of their political and economic rights. Incidents such as the attack organized by merchants of

Providence, Rhode Island, on the customs schooner *Gaspee* in June 1772 and the unsuccessful attempt by customs officials to send the accused to England for trial rekindled animosities.

THE TEA ACT

In 1773 Lord North and his colleagues attempted to help the British East India Company sell its surplus tea in America and thereby save itself from financial disaster. Parliament relieved the company of the duty that it had paid to import tea into England and granted it a monopoly on the transport of tea to America, specifying that it could be sold in the colonies only by company agents (thereby undercutting colonial merchants). Prices for tea fell, but colonial consumers boycotted the product, reacting to the principle in the legislation, which they identified as yet another example of Parliament's attempt to levy taxes on them without their consent.

The Boston Tea Party. In Boston in December 1773, some 150 men disguised as Mohawk Indians boarded three of the East India Company's ships and dumped cargoes of tea into the harbor. In other colonies the company was either refused permission to unload its tea or prevented from selling it.

Coercion and Resistance

Parliament passed four Coercive Acts, known in America as the Intolerable Acts, to punish the residents of Boston and the Massachusetts. The Boston Port Bill closed the city's harbor to all commerce until the province of Massachusetts had paid for the destroyed tea. The Massachusetts Government Act suspended the charter of 1691, making all colonial officials appointees of the crown and forbidding town meetings without permission from the royal governor. The Administration of Justice Act permitted British officials charged with capital offenses in enforcing the law to be tried in England. The Quartering Act ordered Massachusetts to provide lodging and food for British soldiers stationed there.

THE QUEBEC ACT OF 1774

The Quebec Act was carried in Parliament at the same time as the Coercive Acts. It placed the area west of the Alleghenies and north of the Ohio River within the province of Quebec, to be governed directly by British officials. The law also recognized the authority of the Roman Catholic Church. It antagonized several colonies that had claimed lands in the region and raised fears of new imperial measures to introduce ecclesiastical control over religion.

The First Continental Congress (1774)

The Intolerable Acts roused the colonies to again take cooperative action to defend what they regarded to be their liberties. In answer to the many calls for a Continental Congress, representatives from all of the colonies but Georgia met in Carpenters' Hall, Philadelphia, in September 1774. They were chosen by Committees of Correspondence, Committees of Safety, provincial mass meetings, and county conventions.

PETITION OF GRIEVANCES AND THE SUFFOLK RESOLVES

The Continental Congress narrowly defeated Joseph Galloway's proposal for a colonial union along the lines of the Albany Plan (with a congress that would accept or reject legislation enacted by the British Parliament). It drafted a Declaration of Rights and Grievances in the form of a petition to "His Most Gracious Sovereign," the king, in which document they demanded the repeal of the parliamentary measures that had produced their grievances since 1763. The representatives moved closer to asserting their continuing authority when they endorsed the resolves of Suffolk County, Massachusetts, which declared the Intolerable Acts unconstitutional, and made arrangements for a second meeting of the congress the next spring.

THE CONTINENTAL ASSOCIATION

The most important action taken by the Continental Congress was to urge the American colonies to join in an agreement, the Association, to boycott both import and export trade with Great Britain. Detailed methods were worked out for the enforcement of such an agreement in all the colonies.

The Navigation Acts imposed duties and penalties on the colonial trade, but they were not (and could not be) enforced consistently, given the great extent of the American coastline. Their effectiveness depended on the compliance of the colonists. This was grudgingly given as long as the commercial system was loosely enforced, which, despite periodic intervals of zeal, proved to be the case until 1763. By that time the colonists had developed sufficient independence of mind that new and more aggressive legislation by Parliament designed to increase tax revenues and punish evaders took on the distinct appearance of purposeful oppression. The persistence of the British in such efforts, which in each case bypassed the colonial governments and assemblies, strengthened this perception. By 1774 the colonists could conclude quite reasonably that the objective of Parliament's colonial laws was to restrict or diminish what they had come to believe were their fundamental rights as Englishmen.

Selected Readings

Bailyn, Bernard. *The Ideological Origins of the American Revolution* (1967)

Christie, Ian R. and Labaree, *Benjamin W. Empire or Independence, 1760–1776* (1976)

Ernst, Joseph. *Money and Politics in America, 1755–1775* (1973)

Gipson, Lawrence Henry. *The British Empire Before the American Revolution* (15 vols., 1936–70)

Kammen, Michael. *Rope of Sand: The Colonial Agents, British Politics, and the American Revolution* (1968)

Labaree, Benjamin W. *The Boston Tea Party* (1964)

Maier, Pauline. *From Resistance to Revolution: Colonial Radicals and the Development of American Opposition to Britain, 1765–1776* (1972)

Morgan. Edmund S. and Helen M. *The Stamp Act Crisis* (1953)

Nash, Gary B. *The Urban Crucible* (1979, 1986)

Pares, Richard. *Yankees and Creoles: The Trade between North America and the West Indies before the American Revolution* (1956)

Parkman, Francis. *France and England in North America* (9 vols., 1865–1892)

Peckham, Howard R. *The Colonial Wars, 1689–1762* (1963)

Sydnor, Charles S. *American Revolutionaries in the Making: Political Practices in Washington's Virginia (1965); also published as Gentlemen Freeholders* (1952)

5

The American Revolution and the Confederation

1774 First Continental Congress assembles in September, adjourns October 26; Continental Association forms (October)

1775 Battles at Lexington and Concord, Massachusetts (April); Second Continental Congress convenes (May); American forces capture Fort Ticonderoga and Crown Point (May); fail to take Montreal, Washington appointed commander–in–chief (June), British win costly Battle of Bunker Hill (June 17)

1776 Thomas Paine's *Common Sense* published (January); British depart Boston (March); occupy New York City (September); Congress votes to declare independence (July); Washington crosses the Delaware to surprise the Hessians at Trenton (December)

1777 Defeat of General Burgoyne at Saratoga in October foils British invasion plans; British occupy Philadelphia (September); Articles of Confederation formally adopted (November); ratified March 1, 1781; Washington's troops go into winter quarters at Valley Forge, Pennsylvania

1778 Treaties of alliance and commerce with France concluded (February); British take Savannah, begin southern campaign (December)

1780 British take Charleston, win Battle of Camden, South Carolina (May, August); Benedict Arnold's treason exposed (September); passage, ratification of state constitution of Massachusetts

1781 Fierce fighting in the Carolinas causes Lord Cornwallis to reposition his troops in Virginia (January–May); decisive Franco–American victory at Yorktown results in Cornwallis's surrender (October)

1782 Impost tax rejected in Congress

1783 Last large contingent of Loyalists (7,000 of some 100,000) evacuated with British forces from New York (April); Treaty of Paris confirms American independence (September); soldiers' march for compensation causes Congress to leave Philadelphia (June)

1785 Land Ordinance of 1785 passed (May)

1786 Annapolis Convention meets (September); Shays's Rebellion rises in western Massachusetts (August–December)

1787 Northwest Ordinance passed (July)

In taking up arms the American colonists believed they were defending fundamental political rights conferred on them by the British constitution. From 1763 they had protested, resisted, and now were defending themselves against a series of measures Parliament wished to impose on their communities without their consent. By 1776 many had come to believe that an anti–American conspiracy existed in the highest circles of the British government. After the Battle of Yorktown a new British ministry would offer to restore imperial relations to conditions pre–1763. By that time, however, the Revolution had produced more ambitious aims.

FROM PROTEST TO RESISTANCE

In 1775 few Americans thought that the mounting quarrel with the British government would lead to independence for the colonies. As reluctant "rebels," they hoped for a modification of imperial regulations that would satisfy their demand for a greater measure of self–government.

The Appeal to Arms

After the adjournment of the First Continental Congress, the radicals among the colonial leaders created Committees of Safety to enforce the nonimport and nonexport features of the Association agreement (see chapter 4). After Massachusetts had been declared to be in a state of rebellion in February 1775, Lord North offered a plan of conciliation on the issue of taxation in the House of Commons: Parliament would "forebear" to tax the colonies (beyond those measures intended for trade regulation) if the colonial assemblies would vote taxes to support royal government within their boundaries. This overture was offset by Parliament's passage of the Restraining Act (March 1775), which required New England to trade only with the mother country and the British West Indies, a measure also applied to middle and southern colonies after they joined the Continental Association.

LEXINGTON AND CONCORD

Before the Second Continental Congress assembled in Philadelphia in the spring of 1775 the Massachusetts Minutemen had fought the British regulars at Lexington and Concord. The clashes occurred when General Gage ordered his troops to destroy military stores in the hands of Americans and to arrest such colonial leaders as John Hancock and Samuel Adams. The British suffered over a thousand casualties. Militia from all the New England provinces, some 16,000 in arms, promptly surrounded Gage's regiments in Boston, while Massachusetts leaders appealed to all other colonies for aid. In May 1775 colonial militia under Benedict Arnold and Ethan Allen took two strategic garrisons in upstate New York, Fort Ticonderoga and Crown Point.

THE SECOND CONTINENTAL CONGRESS

In response to these appeals, the Second Continental Congress, while sending a final "Olive Branch" petition to the king, took steps to raise and equip an army, appointed Washington commander in chief, issued a Declaration of Causes for Taking up Arms, and began seeking alliances with France and other European nations.

In July 1775 Congress rejected the North plan for reconciliation. In November news was received that the king had not considered the "Olive Branch" petition but declared the colonies to be in open rebellion. Parliament was sending an additional 25,000 troops to join the force of 15,000 already in the colonies. In December 1775, the king issued a proclamation and Parliament passed the Prohibitory Act to close all American ports.

From Moderate to Radical Consensus

The movement for political separation grew slowly but steadily among Americans in response to London's punitive actions. The colonists continued to believe that they had taken up arms to defend themselves and asserted that they would lay them down when their grievances were redressed. They did not need to be reminded that Britain possessed the world's finest naval and military forces. The brutal suppression of previous risings against the crown, especially those in Ireland and Scotland in the eighteenth century, also gave American colonists pause—the penalty for rebellion was death.

RELUCTANCE TO DECLARE INDEPENDENCE

Fighting in the colonies had been going on for more than a year before the Continental Congress decided in favor of independence. There were several reasons for this delay: (1) the sentimental attachment of most of the colonists to the mother country as well as strong connections of language and culture; (2) the fear that either anarchy or despotism might take the place of British authority; (3) the hope among colonial leaders that, as had previously occurred, there would be a change in the British ministry and policies; (4) the reluctance of colonial merchants to give up trade privileges which they enjoyed under the British flag; and (5) the inertia of many colonials, their failure to give specific instructions to their delegates in the Continental Congress, and the lack of effective apparatus for building a national or intercolonial consensus for such a dramatic move.

THE LOGIC OF POLITICAL SEPARATION

The colonists were pushed farther down the road to a decision for independence by British actions, which suggested that compromise and accommodation were no longer possible.

Lord North's Provocations. Americans were universally incensed by the North ministry's decision to pay foreign mercenaries, especially the Hessians (soldiers from the German state of Hesse) to fight in America, which they interpreted as evidence of an intention to use brutal means to suppress the resistance. Equally revealing of the ministry's closed–mindedness about reconciliation were reports that British agents were inciting the Indian tribes against settlers of the western regions of the colonies and the extraordinary action of Lord Dunsmore, royal governor of Virginia, who had offered freedom to black slaves if they would join British forces in the fight against their masters.

Common Sense. Although King George III had no sympathy for the colonials' cause, the Continental Congress, who were not fully aware of this, persisted in asserting that they were resisting the "tyranny of irritated ministers" and Parliament rather than taking up arms against the crown. The arguments presented by the English radical Thomas Paine in his pamphlet *Common Sense; Addressed to the Inhabitants of America,* published in Philadelphia in January 1776, exposed the rhetorical nature of such distinctions.

Paine identified the source of the colonists' grievances as the aristocratic society created by the monarchy, an unnatural and arbitrary system. "Of more worth is one honest man to society and in the sight of God," he wrote, "than all the crowned ruffians that ever lived." He argued for independence as a means of establishing a new republican order, free of the absurdities and follies of artificial distinctions. Indicting George III as the "Royal Brute," he suggested that if "earthly honors" were required, America should proclaim that the "Law is King." "Everything that is right or natural pleads for separation," he observed. "[T]here is something very absurd in supposing a continent to be perpetually governed by an island. In no instance hath nature made the satellite larger than its primary planet."

Paine wrote with great power in a plain style, calculated to reach the widest possible audience. That he had succeeded in his intentions was quickly evident. More than 100,000 copies of the pamphlet were bought in less than three months after the first printing. The extent of Paine's influence is best measured by the events that followed. He cut the ground out from under the moderate position, creating a logic for declaring independence (and revolution) that made more sense to the common man than talk of "attachments" and tradition.

The Irrevocable Step

During the spring of 1776 several colonial legislatures instructed their delegations to the Continental Congress to work and vote for independence. South Carolina set up a republican constitution; Rhode Island eliminated the required oath of allegiance to the king. It was also felt that a decisive act on the part of the Continental Congress would help to inspire American troops in the field.

RICHARD HENRY LEE'S RESOLUTION

Throughout the spring, the Continental Congress became more assertive. It sent an agent to Europe to procure military supplies, proclaimed that the ports of the colonies were open for trade (but not with Great Britain), and gave sanction to American privateers preying on British shipping.

On June 7, 1776, delegate Richard Henry Lee, of Virginia, moved that "these united colonies are, and of right ought to be, free and independent states." After debate and delay, Congress on July 2 formally approved Lee's resolution by a unanimous vote, with New York abstaining.

THE DECLARATION OF INDEPENDENCE

A committee appointed on June 11 to draft a declaration—consisting of Thomas Jefferson, Benjamin Franklin, John Adams, Roger Sherman, and Robert R. Livingston—had reported a draft document on June 28. Although amended in committee and on the floor of Congress, the Declaration of Independence was largely the work of Thomas Jefferson, who "turned to neither book nor pamphlet" in composing it, but rather sought to reflect the sense of Congress and the people. The document was signed by most of the delegates on July 4, 1776, and communicated to the colonial capitals. New York's approval enabled the Congress to prepare a "unanimous declaration" for a formal signing ceremony that took place the following month.

The Declaration falls logically into two parts: first, a preamble containing a statement of the natural rights philosophy, developed by John Locke and the English liberal thinkers of the late seventeenth century, with whose writings Jefferson and his colleagues, as well as most educated Americans, were well familiar. Jefferson was thus able to refer to "self–evident" truths, "that all men are created equal, that they are endowed by their Creator with certain unalienable rights; that among these, are life, liberty, and the pursuit of happiness." He then stated the Lockean tenet that governments were formed "to secure these rights" by means of a contract and derived "their just powers from the consent of the governed." When "any form of government becomes destructive of those ends, it is the right of the people to alter or to abolish it."

In the second part of the Declaration, Jefferson listed the "repeated injuries and usurpations" that led the colonies to declare the "political connection between them and the state of Great Britain" to be "totally dissolved." This was the evidence offered to justify the breach of contract. His indictment was levelled at the king, accused of the "direct object" of establishing "an absolute tyranny over these States." Since the king (not Parliament) was sovereign under the British constitution, the breach had to be made with the monarchy, even if the measures listed by Jefferson had been passed and largely advanced by Parliament. Paine's Common Sense had prepared the way for such an indictment.

THE EFFECT OF THE DECLARATION

The Declaration was composed as an announcement and explanation to the world of the colonists' reasons for dissolving the union with Great Britain. It had the additional responsibility for stating a clear purpose and objective, with justifications, for making a revolution, and of convincing the undecided to join the patriot cause. It was not written for abstract or academic purposes. The language of the Declaration was, and is, powerful, at the same time universal and concrete—the French Revolution of 1789 was inspired by it and the course of American history has been continuously affected and at times shaped by it. The Declaration continues to exert influence in the world. When published in 1776, it had the additional effect of sharpening the lines between Whigs and Tories (or patriots and loyalists) and forcing individual Americans to make difficult choices.

THE WAR FOR INDEPENDENCE

With but three million people, the colonies confronted a world military power with a population of nine million. Poor strategy on the part of the British army, and Washington's skillful and economical use of the Continental Army, prevented superior British troops from destroying American forces. In time, French and other European assistance, as well as the size of the continent itself, proved decisive.

THE REVOLUTIONARY WAR ON THE ATLANTIC SEABOARD

Mobilizing the Revolution

The need to obtain the material of war—guns, cannon, horses, ammunition—and to pay for clothing, food, and housing to keep armies in the field posed enormous problems for the revolutionary patriots. Unlike the British government, which had the constitutional authority and well-established procedures to obtain what it needed to wage war, the Continental Congress lacked the power to tax and had no treasury or stream of revenue upon which to rely. It resorted to various devices to raise monies.

FINANCING THE REVOLUTION

In 1776 the economies of the thirteen United States were overwhelmingly agricultural and cash–poor. The few commercial centers were dominated by British merchant houses, the principal sources of credit for colonial Americans. The lack of hard currency resources, purchasing power among consumers, and available credit made it necessary for the Congress and the state governments to issue scrip or paper money, which was backed by no other resource but the government's promise to make it good.

By 1780 almost $192,000,000 had been issued in paper money or "Continentals." More than $60 million in additional bills of credit and certificates was pledged for quartermaster's compensation, loans, and soldiers' pay. The paper money depreciated rapidly, contributing to a rapid inflation; about $120 million was finally redeemed at one-fortieth of its face value. Many American merchants (notably those in Philadelphia during the winter of 1777–78) refused to accept payment for provisions in "Continentals." The Congress directed requests for specific sums to the states in the form of requisitions. Despite the urgency, the states were inclined to ignore them; they contributed only $6,000,000 to the Continental treasury during the war.

Congress assigned financial administration to several committees and treasury boards before selecting Robert Morris as superintendent of finance in February 1781. He persuaded them to charter the Bank of North America as a means of establishing order in the financial system. Morris also instituted a contract system for army purchases, previously managed by means of requisitions on the states.

Foreign Loans. While loan certificates similar to modern bonds were sold through loan offices in the various colonies, the war effort could not have been sustained without foreign loans. These amounted to approximately $8,000,000, and were placed in France, Holland, and Spain.

ORGANIZING MILITARY FORCES

It took all of General George Washington's political as well as military skills as commander in chief to keep American forces intact and in fighting form once the war began in earnest. Early victories, which led to overconfidence, made the task of raising a regular army more difficult.

The Continental Army. The Congress relied upon the state militias until October 1776, when they finally yielded to Washington's pleas that a national army be created. He raised about 10,000 volunteers, initially to serve until the end of 1776, and was given control of some 7,000 more militia troops. This nucleus of Continental troops was augmented by volunteers who joined temporarily, as the locations of battles and skirmishes changed.

Washington's forces, including most of his American officers, were for the most part inexperienced and poorly trained. The local militia were the least reliable in the field, but they did operate effectively in checking Loyalist activities and in denying the British much of the behind–the–lines cooperation that their hard currency would otherwise have purchased. Washington's command of the Continental Army was weakened by political jealousies and disputes over the conduct of military affairs. The war effort was further impeded by negligent and incompetent officials.

American Naval Forces. Although Captain John Paul Jones won several naval engagements and for a time terrorized the North Sea, the rebellious colonists had no sea power worthy of the name until the French navy came to their aid in 1780. Some two thousand privateers (in effect, licensed pirates) and thirty–four commissioned ships of war constituted the naval force in the early years of the war. American privateering significantly disrupted British merchant shipping, sending insurance rates soaring.

Early Encounters

Having evacuated Boston after the skirmishes that began in Lexington and Concord, British forces under General Sir William Howe captured New York City. Some 32,000 regular troops and over 100 ships were deployed about the harbor.

THE BATTLE OF LONG ISLAND

On August 26, 1776, the British defeated a division of Washington's army (of perhaps 19,000 men) on Brooklyn Heights, but failed to prevent the escape of the American forces. Howe leisurely followed Washington northward, content to fight light skirmishes at Harlem Heights and White Plains. Believing that most Americans did not support the rebellion, he failed to press the attack to destroy the Continental Army. Washington retreated across New Jersey into Pennsylvania, while Howe distributed certificates of loyalty to more than 3,000 inhabitants who were willing to swear loyalty to the king.

TRENTON AND PRINCETON

On Christmas night, 1776, Washington crossed the Delaware River and surprised Hessian detachments of the British army at Trenton, taking almost a thousand prisoners. He also surprised the British at Princeton early in the new year before moving into winter quarters at Morristown, New Jersey. These encounters were not in themselves significant, but they clearly demonstrated that the British army, despite its great superiority and advantages, was not invincible.

British Strategy in the Middle Colonies

In 1777 the British tried to execute a plan to capture the state of New York and split the colonies. Three British armies were to meet near Albany: General John Burgoyne to move southward from Canada via Lake Champlain; Colonel Barry St. Leger to advance eastward from Lake Ontario by way of the Mohawk Valley; and General Howe to lead an army north from the port of New York.

CAPTURE OF PHILADELPHIA

Howe failed to carry out his part in this campaign, having decided to pursue Washington's forces instead. He took the rebel capital with little difficulty. After overcoming Washington's stubborn resistance at Germantown, he quartered his army comfortably in the Pennsylvania capital, while the Americans went into winter quarters at Valley Forge (1777–78).

SARATOGA

During the summer of 1777 Burgoyne had quickly retaken Fort Ticonderoga, then begun a slow march south. When St. Leger's advance eastward in the Mohawk Valley was checked, he found himself cut off from aid and reinforcements. Bands of New York and New England farmers harassed and slaughtered his regiments. On October 17, 1777, at Saratoga, New York, he surrendered the five thousand men who remained in his army to General Horatio Gates.

The Turning Point: The French Alliance

The French government, under the influence of the able foreign minister the comte de Vergennes, saw opportunity in an alliance with the Americans against its archenemy Great Britain. However, it withheld formal recognition of the United States until events demanded it.

SECRET FRENCH AID

The American cause, aided immeasurably by the presence of the celebrated Franklin as ambassador, was popular in France from the outset of the Revolution. By several means, including the use of secret agents (notably the versatile playwright Caron de Beaumarchais) and the creation of a phony trading company, the French government secretly aided the American war effort. Most of the gunpowder and other military supplies required at the outset of the war came through these channels. Ammunition, clothing, shoes, and other supplies were shipped from France in a steady stream during 1777.

The Treaty of Alliance of 1778. The news of the great American victory at Saratoga, and the report that the British were readying a new peace initiative, induced the French government to make a decisive diplomatic move. On February 6, 1778, France recognized the independence of the

United States and signed a military alliance and a treaty of commerce with the new nation. Spain and Holland followed France in declaring war on Great Britain.

The Military Conclusion, 1778–1781

British forces pursued and inflicted much damage on Washington's army in Pennsylvania and New Jersey, but failed to take steps to destroy it. Continuing in the belief that loyalist sentiment was strong, the British command, under General Henry Clinton after Saratoga, turned its attention to the South, where the most bitter fighting of the war occurred. Washington skillfully executed a defensive strategy, avoiding a decisive battle and attacking only when he had the advantage.

THE WEST (1777–1779)

American victories in the interior help to relieve the gloom cast by the military stalemate in the mid–Atlantic states and the discovery of General Benedict Arnold's treasonous plot to help the British take West Point. Virginia's outpost, Kentucky, had been ravaged by Indian raids, and the Kentuckians were eager to strike the British posts northwest of the Ohio River. George Rogers Clark led American troops against Kaskaskia and Vincennes (1778–79) and broke British power in that area.

THE WAR IN THE SOUTH

Expecting support from the Loyalists of the Carolinas and Georgia, the British captured Savannah (December 1778), occupied Charleston (May 1780), and soon thereafter won a brilliant victory under Lord Cornwallis at Camden, South Carolina. Although they managed to hold the seaport towns in the Carolinas, they failed to maintain control of the countryside and could not subdue the guerrilla leaders Francis Marion, Thomas Sumter, and Andrew Pickens. After a decisive defeat by Carolina frontiersmen at King's Mountain (N.C.) and a few costly victories, the British commander Lord Cornwallis withdrew north to receive supplies and reinforcements.

Yorktown. When Cornwallis took up a position at Yorktown on the James River, in Virginia, Washington organized a bold attempt to entrap him. Late in the summer of 1781 he and the comte de Rochambeau, commanding newly arrived French troops, marched southward and joined forces under the command of the mrquis de Lafayette in Virginia. Additional troops were deployed by a French fleet under the command of the comte de Grasse, who closed the trap by sealing off the Chesapeake Bay. On October 19, 1781, Cornwallis was compelled to surrender his army (of 7,000). British troops remained in control of the port cities of New York, Savannah, and Charleston, but launched no new offensives.

The Peace of Paris (1783)

Pressed by enemies in Europe, Britain was now eager to make peace with her American colonies, initially on terms of a restoration of imperial relations as they had existed before 1763. An extended period of diplomatic negotiation and intrigue ensued in which the various belligerents explored several solutions. American representatives in Paris (Benjamin Franklin, John Adams, and John Jay) were instructed by the Congress to insist on the recognition of the independence of the United States.

THE TREATY WITH GREAT BRITAIN

In the final version of the treaty, signed September 3, 1783, Great Britain recognized the independence of the United States and its claim to the territory westward to the Mississippi and from the Canadian border to Florida (which was returned to Spain by a separate treaty). The Americans were confirmed in their fishing privileges off Newfoundland and adjacent territories; their efforts to obtain Canada, however, went unrewarded. From the United States the British government secured pledges that (1) no legal impediments would be placed in the way of British crediuors seeking to collect sums owed by American debtors; (2) Congress would urge the states to restore to the loyalists their confiscated property; and (3) navigation of the Mississippi from source to mouth would be open to subjects of Great Britain and the United States.

Social Effects of the Revolution

The Revolution had its origins in political protest but also fed on tensions within the colonial societies. It generated social and economic as well as political changes but worked no great upheaval in the structure of American society as the French Revolution would effect in the 1790s. Class–related grievances against colonial elites did emerge, but the disputes varied from colony to colony and were frequently geographical (east–west, upland–lowland) in nature. Furthermore, the distance from the top of the social ladder to the bottom in America was, by European standards, relatively slight.

THE LOYALISTS

Between one–fifth and one–third of the inhabitants of the American colonies actively worked for or favored the British cause. It is difficult to generalize about their economic and social backgrounds—but their numbers included well–to–do imperial officials and agents, most of the Anglican clergy, and merchants and farmers more directly linked to British interests as well as many Americans of quite modest means. Many of these Tories were city–dwellers, although the isolation of others probably accounted for their loyalty to British rule. Ethnic backgrounds also played a role in determining loyalties: Scots immigrants, for example, were largely Tory, the Scotch–Irish settlers from Ulster or Northern Ireland overwhelmingly rebels (or patriots after Yorktown).

Exodus of the Loyalists. By using state militia and vigilante groups, the rebel or patriot state governments effectively controlled the countryside and towns. They constantly menaced the Loyalists, imprisoning thousands, tarring and feathering or banishing many others. It is estimated that about 100,000 of them left America voluntarily or fled to Canada or England. Their lands and other property were confiscated and only rarely returned after the war.

THE NEW SOCIAL ORDER

The Revolution itself and the Articles of Confederation formulated by the Continental Congress eliminated the monarchy and its authority from the American states. Since the political aims of the Revolution were eventually embraced by most of the wealthy and powerful in the colonies, and a large proportion of the adult male population held property, revolutionary fervor was directed almost exclusively to the institution of the monarchy and the trappings of royalty and aristocracy, not to economic status. Many Americans in fact openly pursued economic opportunities presented by the cutting of imperial ties and the confiscations of Loyalist properties. Those who made fortunes in privateering, speculation, and profiteering in army contracts during the Revolution were seldom condemned.

Other Effects. Although the rhetoric of liberation and freedom had broad social implications, the revolutionary movement in America made use of such language for specific political rather than general purposes. Patriots might speak and write with passion about Britain's plot to "enslave" them, but the only significant emancipations of the Revolution were made by the British army, which freed captured black slaves, notably in Virginia, in the hope of disrupting the colonists' war effort. Most of these blacks were transported to Britain, where they met with neglect and misery.

THIRTEEN STATES

Although the conflict with Great Britain had forced the thirteen colonies into united action, most Americans still regarded themselves as citizens of the particular state in which they lived. Nationalism was to grow slowly.

The State Governments

In May 1776, the Continental Congress recommended that the colonies form new frameworks of government. Their new status as free and independent states, proclaimed by the Declaration, required fundamental adjustments. By the following year, twelve of the states had adopted new constitutions.

A DECADE OF CONSTITUTION–MAKING

Following colonial rather than British precedents, the new compilations of fundamental laws were in each case written documents. All eliminated the monarchy and established republican governments, deriving the authority to govern from the will of the corporate citizenry as expressed through their elected representatives.

The colonists' grievances against the mother country had a strong impact on the first state constitutions. The separation of legislative, judicial, and executive powers was carefully worked out, leaving little to interpretation— the legislatures were given the greater powers, the executive or governor quite purposely weakened; in two states, Pennsylvania and Georgia, the executive was eliminated.

Participation in government continued to be confined to male property holders, although by a series of measures, notably the elimination of primogeniture and entail (traditional methods of preventing the division of estates), property ownership was widened. Still, universal suffrage was not enacted. Andwhile eight states eventually incorporated declarations of the "natural rights" of the governed in their constitutions, establishing a precedent that later contributed to the passage of the Bill of Rights, slavery was abolished only in the New England states and in Pennsylvania.

Despite the fact that women played key roles in the struggle, notably the writer Mercy Otis Warren and the almost mythic "Molly Pitcher," only one state, New Jersey, gave them the right to vote (repealed in 1807). The legal status of married women remained one of complete subordination to their husbands.

THE MASSACHUSETTS CONSTITUTION OF 1780

Massachusetts was the last of the states to enact a new constitution, but the document and the convention process that produced it proved to be the most influential. In general, the first state constitutions, written and passed by state legislatures, proved to be inadequate to the practical needs of governing. During the years before the Federal Convention, many states turned to the Massachusetts model, which provided for a bicameral legislature and a governor (directly elected), who was given the power to veto bills passed by the legislature.

The Articles of Confederation

As soon as the colonies decided on independence, the Continental Congress, which served as an intercolonial steering committee for the war, authorized a committee of thirteen to draft articles of more permanent union. The colonies had made tentative ventures toward federation in the New

England Confederation (1643), the Albany Congress (1754), and the First and Second Continental Congresses.

STRUCTURE OF THE CONFEDERATION GOVERNMENT

The Articles of Confederation provided for a league between sovereign states and reflected deep suspicions of power. Each state had one vote in the federal Congress, and unanimous consent was required to amend the Articles. The Confederation Congress was empowered to borrow money, regulate the currency, establish a postal service, regulate Indian affairs, and settle interstate disputes. It assumed all financial obligations of the Continental Congress.

The weakness of the Confederation became apparent soon after the Articles were ratified. In seeking to prevent concentrations of power, the Continental Congress limited the new national government's capacity to govern. The most serious omissions were the absence of a federal executive and judiciary; and the failure to give Congress power to levy taxes, to regulate foreign and interstate commerce, or to enforce its laws.

Creation of a National Domain. Congress approved the Articles of Confederation in November 1777, but ratification of the instrument was delayed until 1781. Maryland refused to agree to the federal arrangement until the states claiming western lands consented to cede them to the central government. The resolution of this difficult issue removed a significant obstacle to formation of the union.

WESTERN LAND CLAIMS

The colonial charters of six of the states had granted them indefinite westward extension. When the Revolution wiped out the Proclamation Line of 1763 and the Quebec Act of 1774, some of these states expressed ambitions to extend their authority to the Mississippi. However, a growing awareness of the impracticalities of governing territories of such great extent led Virginia and other "landed" states to assign their western claims to Congress in 1781; the other states followed, although the last cession was completed only in 1802.

ORDINANCE OF 1784

As soon as the Treaty of Paris had confirmed the title of the United States to the region between the Alleghenies and the Mississippi, the Confederation Congress adopted an ordinance, drafted by Thomas Jefferson, guaranteeing that the territory would be divided into ten new states, each to be admitted into the union as soon as it had a population equal to that of the least populous state in the Confederation. This measure, which also provided universal suffrage for adult white males, was superceded by the ordinance of 1787.

LAND ORDINANCE OF 1785

Eager to secure revenue from the public domain, Congress authorized surveys to divide the land northwest of the Ohio River into townships—each township was divided into thirty–six sections of 640 acres to be sold at public auction for a minimum price of $1.00 (hard currency) per acre. One section in each township was set aside for the support of public schools. Demand for parcels remained weak until Congress agreed to take wartime government loan certificates at full face value in payment for the land, a measure that favored speculators but also those veterans and other original holders who had retained the depreciated paper.

THE NORTHWEST ORDINANCE (1787)

Responding to requests from the land companies, notably to those of Manasseh Cutler, who had secured a grant of six million acres for his company, Congress extended more control over the government of the Northwest Territory and its inhabitants, revising the previous ordinances. There were to be not less than three nor more than five states carved out of the area northwest of the Ohio River, as soon as 60,000 inhabited the territory. An assembly (to be elected by property holders when 5,000 had settled) was provided for in the interim, but an appointed governor was given a veto over its acts. (The states of Ohio, Indiana, Illinois, Michigan, Wisconsin, and part of Minnesota would be formed from the region, soon referred to as the Old Northwest.) The ordinance banned slavery from the Northwest Territory, made provision for public education, and guaranteed to the settlers civil rights and freedom of religion. The status of the new states to be formed from the territory (as full equals of the original states) was also specified.

The western region below the Ohio River was never organized in such a systematic way. There the process of settlement was uneven and confused by conflicting land claims and endless lawsuits. The populations of Kentucky and Tennessee grew dramatically during and immediately after the Revolution.

Uncertainty in Foreign Affairs

The American government under the Articles of Confederation was ineffective in dealing with foreign nations. The restrictions placed on Congress's powers led foreign diplomats to believe that Britain's former colonies now constituted thirteen states rather than one nation.

HOSTILITY OF GREAT BRITAIN

The British government, citing the failure of Americans to indemnify the Loyalists and to pay the debts owed to British merchants, refused to withdraw British forces and abandon its fur–trading posts along the southern shores of the Great Lakes (which it had pledged to do in the treaty of 1783). Britain refused to open her West Indian ports to American ships and (until 1791) to send a diplomatic representative to the United States.

SPAIN'S WESTERN INTRIGUES

From their colonies in the Floridas, the Spanish made attempts to gain the loyalties of American frontiersmen and settlers of the interior. Since Spain held the mouth of the Mississippi and thus controlled the principal highway and lifeline of American settlers of the interior, its intrigues posed a serious threat to the new nation. John Jay, as secretary of foreign affairs, tried to settle these difficulties in negotiation with the Spanish diplomat Diego de Gardoqui. The agreement they reached in 1786 would have required the United States to relinquish claims to navigation on the Mississippi in return for commercial privileges. Congress rejected these terms, and settlers in Kentucky and Tennessee threatened either to leave the union or to wage war on the Spanish.

Economic Disruption

The artificial prosperity of the war years disappeared within a year of the treaty of peace. The first years of American independence brought severe economic problems caused by a postwar deflation, increasing national debt, and the changes in commerce and business brought about by the loss of economic participation within the British colonial system.

GOVERNMENT FINANCES

Lacking the power of taxation, Congress had to rely upon requisitions, which the state governments frequently failed to meet. The national debt steadily increased, as soldiers and foreign creditors went unpaid. The credit of the American government was so poor that loans required to meet its operating expenses could be obtained only with great difficulty and at exorbitant interest rates. Two attempts (in 1781 and 1785) to keep the government solvent by means of a national impost or tax on imports were defeated. Congress's efforts to gain the help of the states in retiring largely devalued Continental paper money issued during the war were unsuccessful; the individual states further compounded the currency problem by issuing paper money of their own.

IMPEDIMENTS TO ECONOMIC RECOVERY

Lack of a uniform national currency severely hindered economic transactions. Specie or hard currency was scarce and made up of a bewildering variety of coins. Heavy importation of European goods immediately after the war drained hard currency from the country. The means of replenishing it were lacking, because Great Britain barred American ships and many American products from her ports in the West Indies and in Europe. (Spain and France also closed their West Indian islands to American ships.) Paper money was uncertain in value and easily counterfeited. Tariff barriers between the states discouraged trade.

The Debtor's Plight and Shays's Rebellion. With economic depression came a fall in prices and a rise in the value of scarce hard money. Debtors found it increasingly difficult to secure funds with which to pay interest, settle mortgages, or meet tax assessments, and they pressed for the issue of paper money for these purposes.

In 1786 a group of disgruntled Massachusetts debtors, led by former Continental Army officer Daniel Shays, organized to prevent the courts from issuing judgments against debtors, collecting debts, and conducting foreclosure proceedings. Shays's band of farmers and veterans was quickly suppressed, but the incident dramatized the dangers of weak and unstable government and convinced many that drastic changes were required to preserve the republican experiment.

Americans achieved their independence as reluctant revolutionaries. They had resisted and protested a series of taxes and imperial regulations and taken up arms as their last available means to stop what they believed to be London's calculated usurpation of their liberties. In protest and in arms, they invoked their inherited rights as Englishmen rather than a new standard of rights and citizenship.

Victory could be savored only temporarily. Its fruits proved to be bitter by everyday standards as depression set in after the war had ended. The first independent state governments and the national confederacy created by the Articles of Confederation proved incapable of dealing effectively with post-war problems. These governments, largely deprived of executive power and authority, reflected the former colonists' belief that an oppressive and distant central government had been the source of their troubles. After the war, Americans found that by depriving their governments of the powers to govern effectively, they had also restricted their ability to carry out the people's will.

The sacrifices of war and pride in victory contributed to a new sense of nationalism, but the experience had not yet created a nation. However, the frustrations and disappointments that emerged during what has been called the "Critical Period" of American history, 1781–87, did produce a growing recognition of the importance of union to the survival of the republican experiment and a sense of urgency among those who wished to strengthen it.

Selected Readings

Bailyn, Bernard. ed. *Pamphlets of the American Revolution, 1750–1776* (1965)

Calhoon, Robert M. *The Loyalists in Revolutionary America* (1973)

Fiske, John M. *The Critical Period of American History, 1783–1789* (1883)

Foner, Eric. *Tom Paine and Revolutionary America* (1976)

Freeman, Douglas Southall. *George Washington* (7 vols., 1948–1957)

Ferguson, E. James. *The Power of the Purse: A History of American Public Finance, 1776–1790* (1961)

Higginbotham, Don. *The War of American Independence* (1971)

Jensen, Merrill. *The Founding of a Nation: A History of the American Revolution, 1763–1789* (1968)

Main, Jackson Turner. *The Sovereign States, 1775–1783* (1973)

Middlekauff, Robert. *The Glorious Cause: The American Revolution, 1763–1789* (1982)

Morris, Richard B. *The Peacemakers: The Great Powers and American Independence* (1965)

Norton, Mary Beth. *Liberty's Daughters: The Revolutionary Experience of American Women, 1775–1800* (1980)

Quarles, Benjamin. *The Negro and the American Revolution* (1961)

Shy, John. *A People Numerous and Armed: Reflections on the Military Struggle for American Independence* (1976)

6

Framing and Implementing the Constitution

1787 Constitutional Convention gathers in May, document adopted and published in September; first number of *The Federalist* appears in New York newspapers (running to April 1788)

1788 *The Federalist* issued in book form (March–May)

1787–1788 Ten states ratify the Constitution; ratifications by Virginia and New York (June, July 1788) were considered crucial

1789 First election for president under the Constitution (January–February); first federal Congress meets (March 4); outbreak of the French Revolution (July); Bill of Rights passed (September); from which first ten amendments ratified (December 1791); passage of Judiciary Act of 1789 (September); North Carolina is twelfth state to ratify the Constitution (November)

1790 Rhode Island ratifies the Constitution (May); Hamilton's plan for disposing of national and state debts approved (July); national capital fixed at Potomac River site from 1800, at Philadelphia until then (July)

1791 Congress legislates the Bank of the United States, the president signs bill (February); Congress passes wiskey tax (March); Vermont admitted to statehood in the union

1792 President Washington reelected unanimously (December); design competitions for the capitol and president's house held; Kentucky admitted to statehood in the union

1793 President Washington announces the Proclamation of Neutrality (April); Jefferson resigns as Secretary of state (December)

1794 Whiskey Rebellion in western Pennsylvania rises and is suppressed (July–November); Jay treaty signed (November)

1795 Hamilton resigns as secretary of treasury (January); terms of Jay treaty made public in March 1795, resulting in political turmoil; Pinckney's treaty with Spain is signed (October)

1796 Washington's Farewell Address (September); John Adams elected to succeed Washington, defeating Jefferson, the new vice–president (December); Tennessee admitted to statehood in the union

1797 Episode of the "XYZ Affair" in France (October)

1798 News of "XYZ" is made public in April and embroils the nation; establishment of Navy Department (May); Congress repeals treaties with France (July)

1798 Congress passes the Alien and Sedition Acts (June–July); Kentucky and Virginia resolutions passed (November–December; second set of Kentucky Resolutions issued November 1799)

1798–1800 Incidents in the quasiwar with France

1799 Death of George Washington at Mount Vernon (December)

1800 Convention of 1800 (Treaty of Mortefontaine) signed with France (September; ratified December); Presidential election results in large popular victories for Jefferson in a sufficient number of states to win in the electoral college (December)

The struggle to thwart, circumvent, and defeat the colonial policy of the British government in the years 1763–76 had guided the American lawmakers in drafting the Articles of Confederation and the first state constitutions. The objective of these documents had been to keep decisions in the hands of the people and to diffuse power so as to prevent its concentration in a central authority. In practice, most of the new governments were quickly revealed to be poorly designed instruments for the new demands of self–government.

In the first years of independence, government under the Articles of Confederation and the first state consitutions proved incapable of dealing with sizeable postwar problems. A growing sense of crisis contributed to a broad movement led by advocates of reform in the individual states who projected a bold nationalist vision of the future. By means of intelligence, persuasion, and clever maneuver, these nationalists succeeded in gaining popular support for a new constitutional order, which introduced a far stronger central government to the federal system. The emergence of two distinct models for the nation's growth and development sharpened political differences over the proper powers of the national and the state governments. The wars that raged in Europe, though distant, continued to menace the new nation.

"THE GRAND CONVENTION"

The political, economic, and diplomatic difficulties of the first critical years of independence contributed to the strength of a growing movement to place the national government on an entirely new basis. The refusal of the state legislatures to approve amendments designed to give Congress larger powers over national commerce and finance demonstrated the weaknesses of the postwar union and made it clear that the Articles of Confederation would have to be revised if the American people were intent on forming a new nation.

The Campaign for a New Fundamental Law

Even before Shays' Rebellion in 1786, which gave dramatic emphasis to the consequences of weak government, there was clear evidence that the relationship between the thirteen states and the Congress was flawed. The dissenting vote of a single state had prevented the national government from raising adequate revenue to deal with the national debt. The individual states continued to have their own legal tender—several issued paper money knowing it was valueless. Lack of adequate checks on the power of state legislatures encouraged majorities to overlook or ignore minority interests.

The powerlessness of government contributed to a growing sense of crisis. In March 1783, when discontent among officers of the Continental Army encamped at Newburgh, New York, began to take a conspiratorial tone, General Washington had to intervene personally. The following year Spain indicated it would ignore the boundary between the United States and Spanish Florida set down in the Treaty of Paris. With the clear intention of alienating western settlers from the United States, the Spanish government announced that Americans would no longer have access to the lower Mississippi River. The political instablity contributed to the postwar economic depression, which deepened through the end of 1786.

COALITION OF INTERESTS FOR CHANGE

In addition to those who feared the consequences of social disorder, the desire for reform was particularly strong among groups that depended on stable government policy or who required a uniform standard, such as a single national currency, to conduct their businesses or gain their living. These included (1) holders of government securities; (2) army veterans seeking back pay and the funding of their pensions; (3) manufacturers advocating protective tariffs to allow them to dominate the home market; (4) merchants with interstate or international business, who required an intelligible and credible financial order; (5) creditors who wished debts repaid at face value or better; (6) investors and financiers, in fear of the inflationary schemes of state legislatures; and (7) settlers and land speculators, who wanted the government to suppress Indian hostilities on the frontier and open western lands to settlement.

PRELIMINARY CONFERENCES

In March 1785, committees from the Maryland and Virginia legislatures met at George Washington's Mount Vernon estate to discuss navigation of the Potomac River and the Chesapeake Bay. They decided to invite all the states to confer on commercial problems of the Confederation. The Annapolis (Md.) Conference held in September 1786 was attended by delegates from five states, who adopted a report by Alexander Hamilton calling for a convention of all the states to meet in Philadelphia in May 1787, to "render the constitution of the Federal government adequate" to the needs of the union. The Confederation Congress endorsed this call, which, following the example of the Massachusetts Constitution of 1780, was made directly to the people (requesting them to send delegates) rather than to the state legislatures or other established bodies.

The Constitutional Convention

The fifty–five men who attended the meetings at Philadelphia in the summer of 1787, the lawgivers or "framers" of the American Constitution, formed a remarkable assembly. They were mostly practical men of affairs who had been active in the patriot cause—merchants, lawyers, planters, farmers. While many delegates were familiar with the ideas of political philosophers such as John Locke and the baron de Montesquieu, and some had read more deeply in political theory, most shared the view of John Dickinson of Delaware, a lawyer and respected political thinker, who remarked during the deliberations, "Experience must be our only guide. Reason may mislead us."

LEADERSHIP OF THE CONVENTION

The delegates to the "Grand Convention" were all prominent figures in their home states. Benjamin Franklin was preeminent among them in age (eighty-one), fame, and knowledge of the old, European world. Many had held offices in their respective states, but only a few, notably Franklin and John Jay, possessed diplomatic experience. Hamilton brought exceptional ability in financial matters; James Madison extensive study of ancient and modern governments. Others contributed legal knowledge and experience in drafting legislation, notably James Wilson of Pennsylvania and George Mason, of Virginia (who would not sign the final document). George Washington presided over the sessions, which by agreement were conducted in secrecy, without official record. Conspicuiously absent were the "radical" revolutionary leaders Thomas Paine, Patrick Henry, and Samuel Adams, as well as Thomas Jefferson, then minister to France, and John Adams, minister to Britain.

PLANS FOR RECONSTITUTING GOVERNMENT

A consensus quickly emerged in the convention on the need to strengthen the central government, but not on the means by which this should be accomplished. The delegates agreed, however, that a new government had to be given adequate powers to levy taxes, regulate commerce, protect private property, pay the national debt, coin and borrow money, and provide for the national defense.

Two major plans were presented. The first, upon which most of the discussions proceeded, was submitted by Virginia, then the largest of the states in area and population. It called for a new "national government" composed of "a supreme Legislative, Executive, and Judiciary," and proposed that population determine representation. The smaller states countered with the New Jersey Plan, which called for a "federal" government with a single-house legislature—in effect a proposal to strengthen the existing Articles of Confederation.

Resolution by Compromise. Differences on questions of representation were particularly difficult to resolve, owing to the problem of how to count slaves in the slave states. A sense of the urgency as well as of the importance of their work made it possible for the delegates to reach compromises.

The convention eventually accepted a proposal, worked out by a "grand committee," which became known as the "great compromise." The lower house of the national legislature would represent the states according to population; the upper house would be based upon equal representation, with two members for each state. In calculating population, the slaves would be counted as three–fifths persons. Other compromises were made on matters relating to slavery in order to retain the support of the southern states—for example, the new government was prohibited from levying taxes on exports and from making any restrictions on the slave trade for twenty years.

The Constitution

The delegates at Philadelphia concluded their secret deliberations on September 17, 1787, and promptly published the completed document, the first words of which declared a new basis for the fundamental law of the nation. "We the People of the United States do ordain and establish this Constitution for the United States of America." The Preamble, modeled after the opening sentence of the Massachusetts Constitution of 1780, clearly stated that the new fundamental law derived from the authority of the people themselves. The Articles of Confederation had been the creation of the individual states.

THE STRUCTURE OF GOVERNMENT

As James Madison, its principal architect, would observe, the new Constitution established a political system that was a composition of national and federal government. The new federal system accommodated the thirteen state governments, derived from the colonial tradition, while establishing new bodies and powers designed to deal with national questions. The national government created by the union of states stood above the state governments in specified national matters, while it acknowledged the role of the states or shared power with them in others. State officials were required to take an oath to support the Constitution, state courts to recognize the Constitution and the laws and treaties made under it as the supreme law.

The Constitution greatly increased the power of central government but carefully divided its functions into three distinct branches—executive, legislative, and judicial. The principle of separation of powers was applied throughout the document. Carefully measured checks and balances were inserted to prevent usurpation or concentration of power in any one branch and for the purpose of protecting minority rights from the potential tyranny of the majority. In their powers to amend the Constitution and to elect the President and members of the Senate, the states also gained a role in applying checks and balances.

The chief executive, the *president*, to be chosen by a college of electors in such fashion as the legislatures of the states would direct, was designated commander–in–chief of the armed forces and given the veto over legislation and the power of appointment.

The national legislature, the *congress*, was to consist of two houses: the lower house, the House of Representatives, to be elected directly by popular vote; the upper, the Senate, composed of two senators from each state, to be chosen by the state legislatures. Congress was given the powers to tax, to regulate interstate and foreign commerce, to control the army and navy, and to oversee foreign relations.

The *judiciary* was to consist of a Supreme Court and such lower courts as Congress might create, the judges appointed for life or good behavior by the President, with the consent of the Senate. The House was assigned the power to impeach the president and members of the judiciary; the Senate the role of trying and judging such charges.

The Campaign for Ratification

Since most of the delegates had come to the convention with instructions to amend the Articles of Confederation, there was immediate and sharp reaction to the decision to draft a new Constitution (which only thirty-eight of the designated fifty-five delegates had in fact signed). An intense campaign was required in several states to secure its ratification. By calling for special conventions in the states to ratify the document, the framers were able to avoid the amendment process specified in the Articles of Confederation, which required unanimous approval of the thirteen states through their legislatures. They gained important rhetorical advantage in the contest by calling themselves the true Federalists (or supporters of a federal system, of national and state governments) and casting defenders of the status quo system as the Antifederalists. The fact that they avoided representing themselves as nationalists, which in fact they were, suggests that they perceived public opinion to be a formidable obstacle to the changes they proposed.

CRITICISM OF THE CONSTITUTION

Critics and opponents believed that the Constitution concentrated too much power in the central government and suggested it would ease the way to despotism. They identified a retreat from the principles of the Revolution, citing that (1) the document had been drafted in secret, by representatives of a propertied aristocracy; (2) the delegates had gone beyond their powers in writing a new framework of government; (3) the states would be reduced to dependent provinces; (4) the document contained no "bill of rights" to protect the citizen against tyranny; and (5) the rights of property and not the rights of man were emphasized in the Constitution.

STRENGTHS OF THE FEDERALISTS

The Federalists were able to mobilize powerful forces in the struggle for ratification. They enlisted most of the business and financial interests, the professional classes, and the influential newspaper editors. They had money, they were well organized, and they counted among their numbers the most prominent men in the country, most notably Washington and Franklin.

The Federalist Papers. Under the penname "Publius," Alexander Hamilton, James Madison, and John Jay wrote eighty-five essays that appeared in New York City newspapers during the debate over ratification in that crucial state.

These essays were written with an immediate purpose, to persuade contemporaries to support the new Constitution and to allay fears raised by the Antifederalists—but were soon acknowledged to be classic works in western political thought.

Of particular importance was *The Federalist Number Ten*, written by Madison, which dealt with the argument that republican (or representative) government could only survive in small geographical areas. It was generally believed that the ancient Roman republic had declined as the Roman Empire expanded; the more sophisticated reading public knew the works of the influential French writer the baron de Montesquieu (1689–1755), who had demonstrated the tendency of central power to become more despotic as the distance between the rulers and the people grew. Madison effectively countered the conventional view. "The smaller the society, the fewer probably will be distinct parties and interests composing it, and the smaller the compass within which they are placed, the more easily will they concert and execute their plans of oppression. Extend the sphere," he argued, "and you take in a greater variety of parties and interests; you make it less probable that a majority of the whole will have a common motive to invade the rights of other citizens; or if such a common motive exists, it will be more difficult for all who feel it to discover their own strength, and to act in unison with each other."

RATIFICATION

The contest over ratification in the thirteen states was prolonged and often bitter. The lines of debate, however, were not clearly drawn, and local and regional factors were significant. Support for the new Constitution came from those whose work and interests were tied to the commercial life of the country; those more in control of their circumstances, such as farmers who had few commercial contacts, tended to oppose a change in the status quo. Residents of the small states, feeling their interests could only gain by the strenghthening of the national government, were overwhelmingly in favor.

Delaware, New Jersey, Georgia (by unanimous votes), and Connecticut promptly ratified the Constitution by January 1788, and victories for the Federalists in Maryland (April) and South Carolina (May) were also decisive. But in Pennsylvania, Massachusetts, Virginia, and New York the margins were narrower and the contests tough and often bitter. Although nine states (sufficient to implement the Constitution) had ratified by June 1788, it was not certain that there would be a new government until the next month, when both Virginia and New York had ratified. North Carolina and Rhode Island had not decided when Washington took the oath of office on April 30, 1789 (they ratified, respectively, in November 1789 and May 1790).

ESTABLISHING AUTHORITY AND PRECEDENTS: THE WASHINGTON ADMINISTRATION

The Constitution provided a framework and outline for the executive, legislative, and judicial branches but no specific instructions for setting up the new government. It was left to the first officeholders to interpret the terse language of the Constitution and to set precedents.

The First Federal Congress

The first Congress to serve under the Constitution was elected in early 1789 and convened in September of that year. The members of the new Senate and the House of Representatives completed the work of the Constitutional Convention—filling in the framework of the federal government and setting it in motion. Members quickly passed legislation to establish departments within the executive branch, to create federal courts, and to raise revenues.

Having decided to secure most of its revenues through customs duties, Congress passed the Tariff Act of 1789, which placed a 5 percent duty on all imports. It then created the executive departments of state, treasury, and war and other administrative offices. In passing the Judiciary Act, it established the Supreme Court (with six justices) and federal circuit and district courts. The act also assigned the Supreme Court the authority to determine questions concerning the constitutionality of state laws. John Jay was appointed first chief justice of the Supreme Court.

THE "BILL OF RIGHTS"

From the more than one hundred proposed amendments to the Constitution urged by the state conventions, the first Congress, following Madison's recommendations, approved and referred twelve to the states for ratification in September 1789. Ten of these amendments, which became known as the "Bill of Rights," had been ratified by 1792. The first nine protect the citizen against the possibility of tyranny or infringement of civil rights by the federal government. By declaring that powers "not delegated to the United States by the Constitution, nor prohibited by it to the States" were reserved to the states or the people, the Tenth Amendment further emphasized the "federal" nature of the document.

The President

George Washington, the hero of the American Revolution, was elected the first president of the United States by a unanimous vote of the electoral college. His role was the most controversial in the new government and by his actions and demeanor he had much to do with establishing the tradition of a strong and independent executive branch in America. Some proposed titles such as "His Elective Majesty" for the president and compared him to a king. Washington discouraged such talk while carefully establishing the authority of the presidency. He succeeded in this by merging his personal dignity with his public role as chief magistrate and by making effective use of formal ceremony.

THE PRESIDENT'S "CABINET"

President Washington named Thomas Jefferson secretary of state, Alexander Hamilton secretary of the treasury, and Henry Knox secretary of war. For his legal adviser, he chose Edmund Randolph, making him attorney general. These four executive officers supervised departmental offices that, with the General Post Office, were run by only 130 employees in 1801.

During the course of his first term in the presidency Washington gradually came to rely on private meetings with the four executive officers "in cabinet," or behind doors, to gain advice on policy and legislation. In August

1789 he visited the Senate to ask its advice and consent on matters pertaining to a treaty that was being negotiated with the southern Indians. But after the Senate responded with hesitation and offered its own suggestions, in his opinion going beyond the legislative to infringe on executive power, he made a practice of communicating with that body only in a more formal way, after obtaining advice from within the executive.

Hamilton's Financial Plan

The financial chaos that confronted the new government posed a serious challenge to the credibility, and even the survival, of the republic. The reports and legislation that Alexander Hamilton prepared for Congress sought to bring order to the nation's finances but were also intended to establish the supremacy of the new national government over the states.

The brilliant Hamilton, who had served as General Washington's personal aide and secretary during the Revolutionary War, was a political realist who viewed the world from a commercial perspective. Born on the sugar island of Nevis, in the British Windward Islands, he'd grown up under difficult circumstances on St. Croix, in the Danish Virgin Islands. As a boy and young man he had worked as a clerk in the store of a St. Croix merchant (providing for himself from the age of twelve); with the help of friends he had been sent to study at King's College (Columbia University) in New York at the age of seventeen.

Hamilton believed the republic could survive and prosper in its infancy only by enlisting the support of the wealthy—the merchants, capitalists, and investors—and harnessing their interests to those of the national government. Similarly he thought it folly for the young republic to challenge British economic and military supremacy, whatever the provocation. Like most Federalists (and many Republicans), he believed that pure democracy would lead to "mob rule." He looked to the "mixed government" of the British constitution, at least in theory a perfect balance of democratic (House of Commons), aristocratic (House of Lords), and monarchical (king or queen) elements, for useful models.

THE NATIONAL DEBT

In his first report to Congress, Secretary Hamilton estimated that the national debt was $54 million, that of the states some $25 million. He proposed to fund the national debt, incurred during the Revolution and the Confederation period, by paying the full face value of all federal obligations, those held by foreigners as well as by citizens of the United States. This was judged unfair by many, especially Revolutionary War veterans, who had been forced to sell paper money or certificates the Congress had issued (often their pay) at large discounts. Hamilton argued that it was more important for the new government to gain financial credibility abroad and to signal its good faith to investors, so that they would be encouraged to keep or put their money in the United States.

Hamilton also persuaded Congress to assume payment of the debts of the several states, on the ground that such indebtedness had been incurred chiefly during the Revolution by colonies fighting in a common cause. While those states that had paid back most of their debt (notably Virginia) objected, Hamilton stressed that this measure would establish the supremacy of the national government in finance and further strengthen the new nation's credibility.

Congressional opposition to Hamilton's proposals was led by the influential Madison. The assumption and funding measures passed the House of Representatives (in July and August 1790) only after extensive debate and much legislative maneuvering. Hamilton's willingness to support a Potomac River site for the new national capital seems to have caused several southern members, as well as Secretary Jefferson, to reluctantly accept the assumption legislation.

ESTABLISHING THE BANK AND THE CURRENCY

In his second report to Congress, Hamilton proposed the creation of a national bank empowered to issue a uniform national currency. After a long and sometimes bitter debate, Congress passed the bill chartering the Bank of the United States in February 1791. It authorized the formation of the institution by issue of $10,000,000 in capital stock, a fifth of which was to be purchased by the government, the remainder by the public. The Bank was authorized to issue notes—that is, paper money—backed in part by gold and silver but chiefly by government bonds. Hamilton modeled it on the Bank of England.

Washington hesitated to sign the bill, which Madison and Jefferson strongly opposed. They protested that the Bank would nurture a dangerous monied interest and argued that the Constitution contained no provision to authorize the act and it was therefore unconstitutional. However, Hamilton's opinion, which relied on a "loose" rather than a "strict" construction, or interpretation, of the Constitution, convinced the president to sign the bill. Hamilton argued that by empowering Congress "To make all Laws which shall be necessary and proper for carrying into execution" (article I, section 8 of the document, which included the responsibility for coining money), the Constitution had implied the authority to establish the Bank. Thus was born the constitutional theory of "implied powers."

THE PROTECTIVE TARIFF

Hamilton's Report on Manufactures boldly urged the adoption of a high or protective tariff, well above the level required to raise revenues. Such a measure, he believed, would aid fledgling American industries (by hindering foreign competitors) and thereby stimulate the development of new domestic industries. His goal was the creation of a balanced economy that would strengthen the nation and in time free it from dependency on foreign suppliers for finished goods. The House, again led by Madison, who feared a concentration of power in the national government, rejected this third and most controversial of Hamilton's reports. The Revenue Act of 1792 but slightly raised the tariff rates.

Through systematic refunding and payment of the national debt, Hamilton managed to reduce interest charges, thus effecting savings for the government. To secure the income needed to meet expenses, he outlined in detail proposals for (1) customs duties on imports; (2) excise taxes on domestic goods, especially distilled liquor; and (3) procedures for the rapid sale of lands in the national domain.

THE NEW NATION IN FOREIGN AFFAIRS

The first government under the Constitution faced formidable challenges, from Indians of the interior and from the British and Spanish, in asserting its authority over the great extent of its boundaries. Great Britain's hostility to its former colonies further emphasized the fragile condition of American independence. The French Revolution and the ensuing wars in Europe complicated the Washington administration's efforts to establish good relations with the European powers while maintaining American neutrality.

Securing the Nation's Boundaries

On the periphery of the original thirteen states, where settlers confronted Indian attacks and the difficulties of getting their produce to market, loyalty to the union wavered. In Vermont, Kentucky, and Tennessee, there was open talk of separation. To anchor these areas to the union, Congress quickly admitted all three to statehood—Vermont (formed from parts of New York and New Hampshire) in 1791; Kentucky (from Virginia), in 1792; Tennessee (from North Carolina), in 1796.

MILITARY ACTION ON THE FRONTIERS

One of the most pressing problems for the Washington administration was to prevent attacks on settlers by Indian tribes. Although some tribes proved conciliatory, others continued to raid border settlements in their attempt to halt the westward advance of land–hungry white settlers. The president did not hesitate to deploy the U.S. army to frontier areas to make clear the government's intention to secure its boundaries.

The Northwest Territory. From their forts and fur–trading posts along the Great Lakes, the British occasionally incited the tribes that still roamed the Northwest Territory against the American settlers. U.S. army regulars and militia under General Arthur St. Clair attempted to establish control of the region south of Lake Erie in 1791 but suffered a humiliating defeat at the hands of Indians. Three years later General Anthony Wayne, with some 4,000 troops, won a decisive victory in the Battle of Fallen Timbers. In 1795 Wayne persuaded the leading chiefs to sign the Treaty of Greenville, whereby the Indians surrendered their claims to most of the area that is now Ohio.

The Southwest Territories. Spanish agents in Florida and Louisiana subsidized attacks on border settlements by Creeks, Cherokees, Chickasaws, and Seminoles. By offering the Creeks favorable terms in the Treaty of New York (1790), President Washington had quieted their Chief Alexander Mc-Gillivray (son of a Scots trader), but the agreement had only a limited effect. The militia of Tennessee managed to check Indian resistance in 1794, but the probability of new outbreaks of hostilities, encouraged by the Spanish, kept the region unstable.

The Whiskey Rebellion. Fearing the effects of a new Shays's Rebellion, the president led some 15,000 troops to western Pennsylvania to suppress a farmers' revolt against the excise tax on whiskey. The show of force was criticized when the perpetrators hid and dispersed; it nevertheless signaled the government's intention to assert its authority on the frontier.

American Neutrality

The terms of the treaty of alliance (1778) with France provided that the United States would defend the French West Indies in the event of a British attack. However, the Washington administration ignored the provision when a general European war broke out in 1793, after King Louis XVI was executed by French revolutionaries.

AMERICAN NEUTRALITY AND CITIZEN GENET

On the advice of Secretaries Hamilton and Jefferson, the president issued a proclamation that extended official recognition to the new French government but stated that the United States would remain at peace. Ignoring the proclamation, Edmond Genet, newly appointed minister of the French republic, who had landed in Charleston early in April 1793, rashly and openly recruited support for his country. Calling upon the United States to fulfill the terms of its alliance with France, he began to fit out privateers, enlist seamen, and organize military plans before he had presented his credentials to the president. Though President Washington received Genet, the administration demanded his recall. Hamilton defended the Administration's policy on the grounds that the alliance of 1778 had been made with the government of Louis XVI, not with the French republic, and that the treaty had not pledged the United States to support France in a war against European monarchies.

The Neutrality Act (1794). The president's proclamation had warned United States citizens not to "take part in any hostilities on land or sea with any of the belligerent powers." The Neutrality Act made illegal the activities Genet had engaged in and prohibited Americans from joining the forces of foreign countries.

Jay's Diplomatic Mission

In an attempt to gain a settlement of American grievances against Great Britain, and to avoid war, Washington sent Chief Justice John Jay to London. His special mission produced a treaty that achieved a modest degree of success. However, the agreement caused a tumult in American domestic politics and disruption in the new nation's foreign affairs.

BRITISH PROVOCATIONS

Although Great Britain had recognized American independence in the Peace of Paris, its posture toward the United States remained hostile. The British government committed, or allowed to be directed, against Americans several provocative acts, including (1) a refusal to evacuate British trading posts in the Northwest Territory, specified in the treaty of 1783; (2) the encouragement and support for Indian tribes that regularly warred on American settlers; (3) a failure to open up British ports in the West Indies to American commerce; (4) beginning in early 1794, seizures of United States ships trading with the French West Indies; and (5) the boarding of American ships and impressment of American seamen into British naval service. Jay was instructed to obtain British withdrawal from the trading posts and forts, compensation for ship confiscations, a trade agreement, and British acceptance of the United States's neutral rights.

OUTCOME OF THE NEGOTIATIONS

Jay's discussions resulted in a treaty in which the British (1) agreed to surrender the fur posts by June 1796; (2) opened their East Indian ports to the United States; and (3) made some minor concessions in the West Indian trade. No mention was made of the seizure of American ships or the impressment of seamen. The question of debts owed to British creditors by Americans and of American claims for damages to shipping were referred to arbitration commissions.

Reaction to the treaty was violent. Opponents calling themselves "true republicans" denounced it as a capitulation to the British. In the fight to defeat ratification in the Senate and the necessary appropriation measures (to implement the treaty) in the House of Representatives, their coalition was transformed into a political party (see "The Republican Opposition," below). The administration barely succeeded in getting the Federalist Senate to ratify the agreement and had to go to extraordinary lengths to secure appropriations.

The episode dramatically underscored the new nation's inexperience and uncertainty in foreign affairs. During Jay's negotiations, Secretary Hamilton provided confidential information about the American objectives to British officials; Secretary of State Edmund Randolph (who succeeded Jefferson) and James Monroe, U.S. minister to France, had similar exchanges with French officials in efforts to defeat the treaty.

PINCKNEY'S TREATY

Jay's negotiations in London had a more positive effect on American relations with Spain. Convinced that the United States and Great Britain were drawing closer together, the Spanish government determined to settle differences. In October 1795, Thomas Pinckney negotiated the Treaty of San Lorenzo, whereby Spain (1) recognized the 31st parallel as the boundary of Florida (the U.S. claim); (2) promised that Spanish officials would restrain the Indians from making raids across the borders of the United States; and (3) granted the United States free navigation of the Mississippi, with the right to deposit goods at New Orleans free of duty.

Hostilities with France

The news of the Jay treaty aroused intense indignation in Paris, where the American representative, James Monroe, had been trying to establish more friendly relations. In seeming retaliation for American overtures to Britain and Spain, French ships began seizing American vessels and sailors.

THE XYZ AFFAIR

When the ruling French Directory refused to acknowledge Charles C. Pinckney, Monroe's successor as U.S. minister to France, President John Adams, Washington's successor, sent John Marshall and Elbridge Gerry to join Pinckney as negotiators in Paris. This commission was waited upon by three agents of the French foreign minister, Prince Talleyrand, who demanded a bribe and a loan as preconditions for the commencement of negotiations. "Messieurs X, Y, and Z," as they were referred to in official documents, also made threats to organize revolutionary activities in America. News of the affront to the American commissioners caused popular sentiment, increasingly expressed in outbreaks of violence, to shift dramatically from an anti–British to an anti–French bias.

THE UNDECLARED OR QUASI WAR (1798–1799)

The country was soon gripped by war fever. President Adams convinced Congress to suspend trade and the treaties with France and to establish a Navy Department. Harbors were fortified, frigates built, and cooperative measures undertaken with the British navy. During 1798 more than eighty French armed vessels were seized by United States warships and privateers. Although he recalled George Washington to assume the chief command of

U.S. forces, Adams successfully resisted pressures to activate the provisional army that was being championed by Hamilton and the "High Federalists," the more extreme elements in the Federalist party.

THE CONVENTION OF 1800

Neither the French Directory nor President Adams wanted an outright war. Adams dispatched a new commission (William Vans Murray, Oliver Ellsworth, and William R. Davies), which reached France in 1800. Napoleon Bonaparte, now in power as first consul, signed a convention permitting the United States to abrogate the treaty of alliance of 1778 and providing a new basis for commerce and maritime relations between the two nations.

THE LEGITIMACY OF POLITICAL OPPOSITION: THE DEVELOPMENT OF POLITICAL PARTIES

During the 1790s the first American political parties took form. The development of party politics was not anticipated by the framers of the Constitution, who believed partisan activity invariably led to corruption of representative government. Rather, political parties grew almost by necessity to accommodate strong differences over domestic and foreign issues. At issue were fundamental disagreements about the future of the United States.

The Federalists in Power

The Federalists in office expected the consensus they had reached in 1787–89 to continue in the new government. Roughly half of the first Federal Congress had attended the Constitutional Convention. As appointments were made, legislation was introduced, and policies took hold, however, members of Congress representing interests that were hurt or hindered by new measures began to voice their opposition. They quite naturally began to join together to pursue common aims. Most Federalists, however, notably President Washington, considered factions to be dangerous to the republic and believed the administration's opponents, by forming a party, wished to undermine the legitimate government.

EMERGING POLITICAL FACTIONS

In the congressional battles over the assumption of state debts, the Bank of the United States, the excise taxes (on domestic goods, especially distilled liquor) of 1791, and the protective tariff, factions were formed to advance or oppose Secretary Hamilton's proposals. His program for economic development, and the strong and active central government that was necessary to bring it about, roused those agricultural, landed, and state–oriented interests that stood to lose from the creation of a new and distant pole of power. At first these groups were loosely organized and not always composed of the same members.

THE ELECTION OF 1796

President Washington had been inclined to retire from office in 1792 but had been persuaded by Hamilton, Jefferson, and Madison to stand for reelection, which he won without opposition. In the summer of 1796, however, he prepared his Farewell Address, in which he would warn of dangers to the union, the principal of which he identified as "entangling alliances" with foreign powers.

Vice–president Adams defeated Jefferson for the presidency by three electoral votes in 1796, but his victory was diminished by serious dissension among the Federalists. The followers of Hamilton, notably such key members of Adams's cabinet as Timothy Pickering (war), Oliver Wolcott (treasury), and James McHenry (navy), were hostile to the president and sought to minimize his influence. Jefferson was elected vice–president and became president of the Senate, while Madison retired from the House of Representatives and began to coordinate political strategy for the opposition.

The Republican Opposition

Following the leadership of Madison and Jefferson, elements of the original Federalists, joined by former Antifederalists, coalesced in opposition during the administrations of Washington and Adams. After Jefferson's resignation from Washington's cabinet in 1793 he became the principal spokesman for this coalition, which identified itself as Republican or Democratic–Republican.

The Republicans shared a common distrust of the growing centralized power and identified in Hamilton's measures a pattern reminiscent of British imperial regulation before the Revolution. Many were alarmed by his Report on Manufactures, concluding that he wished to model America after Europe, where the Industrial Revolution had begun to destroy the agrarian landscape and lifestyle in several countries. Jefferson and his party agreed that America should remain predominantly agricultural and that the seemingly limitless supply of land available for settlement promised a unique destiny. In economic matters, he would note in 1801, the proper role of government was the "encouragement of agriculture and of commerce its handmaid."

Protest and Resentment

Republicans believed that they kept alive the "Spirit of '76" and that the Federalists in office, like the British before them, had been corrupted by power and had formed a political party to promote the interests of financiers and manufacturers. Hamilton and some of the more prominent Federalists in fact openly stated that government should be in the hands of substantial property holders. But there were many more modest Federalists who supported the politics of stablility and law and order out of real fears of godlessness, social disorder, and the threat of foreign invasion. Many Americans believed Jefferson an atheist, the head of a "French party" and a dangerous demagogue.

Republicans objected strongly to the manner in which the Washington administration had suppressed the the Whiskey Rebellion, the farmers' revolt in western Pennsylvania against Hamilton's excise tax on distilled liquors. They argued that (1) the excise was an unnecessarily burdensome tax imposed on the farmers for the benefit of the capitalists; and (2) that the government had put in doubt the western settlers' loyalty to the union.

The Republicans were also quick to denounce the Jay treaty, which they argued benefited Great Britain to the detriment of the United States. Most wished to fulfill the obligations of the Franco–American alliance. They had rejoiced in the establishment of the French republic and, despite the excesses of the guillotine, continued to believe that it confirmed a favorable, worldwide trend toward republicanism. At the least, they could agree with Jefferson that it was necessary to expand commercial relations with France if only to reduce Britain's domination of America's overseas trade, which had actually increased since the Revolution.

The Political Revolution of 1800

Issues raised by the undeclared war (also known as the Quasi War) with France further intensified differences between Federalists and Republicans. The Federalists regained control of the Congress as a result of popular reaction to the news of the XYZ Affair, although differences between Hamilton's "high" Federalists and the Adams Federalists continued to divide their councils.

Republicans directed their energies to the states and prepared for the election of 1800. Their hostility to the war effort and friendly posture toward France led the Federalist Congress to take actions to put the country on a war footing. Republicans feared, with some reason, that the Federalist pressures for an expansion of the army were made for the purposes of suppressing opposition rather than repelling an invasion.

THE ALIEN AND SEDITION LAWS (1798)

During the height of the war fever of 1798, the Federalists in Congress, not without some legitimate fears of French threats, passed a series of harsh measures directed against foreign nationals (principally the large number of

French in the country) and the Administration's domestic critics. The legislation included (1) the Alien Acts, consisting of the Alien Enemies Law, which authorized the President to detain or deport foreigners when the nation was at war, and the Alien Law, which gave the President power to expel any alien deemed dangerous to the country (both were never used); (2) the Naturalization Act, which required all aliens to live fourteen years in the country before they could become citizens; and (3) the Sedition Act, which introduced fines or imprisonment for persons convicted of conspiring to oppose the execution of the laws or of publishing false and malicious writings concerning the president or the government. This last piece of legislation, which was used against several Republican newspaper editors (resulting in the conviction of ten persons), represented the first serious test of the scope of the First Amendment.

THE KENTUCKY AND VIRGINIA RESOLUTIONS, 1798–1799

To counter what they regarded to be oppressive acts, Jefferson and Madison turned to the states for authority to declare the Alien and Sedition laws unconstitutional. They drafted the Virginia Resolutions (Madison) and the Kentucky Resolutions (Jefferson), which were endorsed and published by the legislatures of those states. Defining the Constitution as a "compact" entered into by the states, they argued that the states had the right to declare acts of the central government "void" when they went beyond the powers that had been specifically delegated. Jefferson's argument that "a nullification" by the states was "the rightful remedy" in such instances was not pursued by Kentucky. While other states did not endorse the Virginia and Kentucky rn the campaign of 1800.

THE ELECTION OF 1800

The presidential campaign was bitterly contested. Mudslinging and rumormongering were commonplace, political passions extreme and often violent. Electioneering brought unprecedented numbers to the polls; Jefferson's supporters in particular went to extraordinary lengths to get out the vote. President Adams carried New England, New Jersey, Delaware, and parts of Maryland and North Carolina but lost the electoral vote (by 73–65) as well as the popular vote to Jefferson.

The Burr Intrigue. Since all the Republican electors had voted for both Jefferson and Aaron Burr, a New York party leader, there was a tie vote in the electoral college. The election was thus thrown into the House of Representatives, where the Federalists held a majority. Some of their leaders connived with Burr in an attempt to prevent the election of Jefferson, but after thirty-six ballots, Jefferson was elected president, Burr vice–president. The Federalists who voted for Jefferson did so thinking him the lesser of the two evils. The Twelfth Amendment, ratified in 1804, changed the method of electing the president and thus prevented a recurrence of the tie vote of 1800.

SIGNIFICANCE OF JEFFERSON'S ELECTION

The election of Jefferson represented more than the substitution of a Republican administration for a Federalist one. Although there is some evidence that civil war might have broken out if Jefferson had been denied the presidency, there is no way to know if such threats would have been acted upon. The most significant fact in the outcome of the election of 1800 was that the party in control of the central government had been defeated and removed by means of the ballot box, rather than bullets. The first contested transfer of power had been accomplished peacefully.

The creation of the United States Constitution, the world's oldest and most influential written organic law, was an extraordinary achievement, drawn from, and shaped by, the frustrations of the American experience in self-government. With the ratification of the document, accomplished by skillful and in some ways deceptive political means, the thirteen states gained a new central government that was far more "national" (a seldom-spoken word) in emphasis than the prevailing political consensus could sustain.

The efforts of Federalists in power to create a strong national interest by governing vigorously achieved some territorial and security objectives, but they overreached the new republic's tolerance for direction from a new source of central power, alienating popular sentiment. Secretary Hamilton's efforts to extend the financial powers of government effectively empowered a national commercial interest. At the same time, however, his program roused a new political coalition of local, state, and regional forces, formed of anti-Federalist democrats and disaffected agrarian interests. This coalition gradually took the form of a new Republican party and reasserted the majority consensus by reenacting the revolution of '76.

Fragments of the national program advocated by the Federalists would reemerge in the political life of the nation but never again in the same way. The peaceful transfer of power to the Republican opposition in 1800 removed the fear that party activity would be destructive to the republic and effectively established the legitimacy of organized political opposition.

Selected Readings

Adair, Douglas. *Fame and the Founding Fathers* (1974)

Buel, Richard Jr. *Securing the Revolution: Ideology in American Politics, 1789–1815* (1972)

Combs, Jerald A. *The Jay Treaty* (1970)

Cooke, Jacob E., ed. *The Federalist* (1961)

DeConde, Alexander. *The Quasi-War: Politics and Diplomacy of the Undeclared War with France, 1797–1801* (1966)

Hofstadter, Richard. *The Idea of a Party System: The Rise of Legitimate Opposition in the United States, 1740–1840* (1969)

Kohn, Richard H. *Eagle and Sword: The Federalists and the Creation of the Military Establishment in America, 1783–1802* (1975)

Levy. Leonard W. *Legacy of Suppression: Freedom of Speech and Press in Early American History* (1960)

Main, Jackson Turner. *Political Parties Before the Constitution* (1974)

Rutland, Robert A., et. al., eds. *The Papers of James Madison , vols. 8–14* (1973–1983)

Stourzh, Gerald A. *Alexander Hamilton and the Idea of Republican Government* (1970)

Wood, Gordon. *The Creation of the American Republic, 1776–1787* (1969)

7

Jeffersonian Republicanism

1801 Jefferson–Burr ticket wins but ties in the electoral college; Jefferson chosen president by the House of Representatives (January 20); passage of Judiciary Act of 1801 (February 27); Adams makes "midnight appointments" until March 3 at 9 p.m.; Jefferson inaugurated president March 4. Tripoli declares war on the U.S. (May 14); Jefferson determined to respond with force

1802 Repeal of the Judiciary Act of 1801 (March); passage of Judiciary Act of 1802 (April).

1803 Decision in *Marbury v. Madison* handed down by Chief Justice Marshall (February); Louisiana Purchase transacted; U.S. takes occupation (December)

1804 Death of Hamilton in duel with Burr (July); Lewis and Clark expeditionary party sets out (August); Jefferson reelected with Vice–President George Clinton (N.Y.)

1805 Judge John Pickering impeached by the House and convicted by the Senate (March); Supreme Court Justice Samuel Chase impeached but acquitted; Zebulon Pike begins first of two expeditions

1806 Return of Lewis and Clark expedition

1807 *H.M.S. Leopard* stops and attacks *U.S.S. Chesapeake* off Norfolk, Virginia (June); The Embargo Act becomes law (December 22)

1808 Presidential election won by the ticket of James Madison–George Clinton over Federalists C.C. Pinckney–Rufus King (December)

1809 Repeal of embargo; passage of Non–intercourse Act (March 1); Madison inaugurated (March 4)

1810 Passage of Macon's Bill No. 2, reopening trade and revising terms of nonintercourse (May)

1811 Madison administration loses effort to recharter Bank of the United States General Harrison surprises Tecumseh's forces at Battle of Tippecanoe (November)

1812 War declared against Britain (June 19); British suspend orders in council (June 23); Madison narrowly reelected over anti–war Republican DeWitt Clinton, supported by Federalists (128–89 electoral votes), who made large gains in Congress (December)

1813 Britain blockades U.S. coastline; Commodore Perry's victory in Battle of Lake Erie (September); American offensive against Canada repelled

1814 Andrew Jackson slaughters Creeks at Horseshoe Bend, Alabama, removing them from war (March); British burn Washington but fail to take Baltimore; their northern invasion stopped at Plattsburgh, New York (August–September); Hartford Convention convenes (December); Treaty of Ghent concluded (December)

1815 Jackson's victory at New Orleans (January); news of treaty reaches New York (February 11)

After the extreme partisanship of the campaign of 1800, it was expected, by supporters and foes alike, that the presidential administration of Thomas Jefferson would introduce substantial and even radical changes. The federal government was now firmly in the control of a man and a party that proposed to diminish its size and influence. But although he reversed the principal Federalist domestic and foreign policies, Jefferson generally pursued a moderate course as chief executive, observing in his inaugural address that "we are all Federalists, we are all Republicans." With "true" republicans occupying most of the seats of power, except in the Judiciary, he saw the apparatus of government less as a potential instrument of oppression than the means to achieve republican aims.

PEACE, ECONOMY, AND LIMITED GOVERNMENT

Jefferson assumed the presidency believing that his election represented the triumph of the true republican principles of the American Revolution, the defeat of those who had reverted in varying degrees to policies derived from monarchism. His first acts were to reduce the size of government and to cut spending. The strongest government, he believed, was that which placed the lightest burden on its citizens.

The "Philosopher–President"

Jefferson is a large and now almost mythical figure in American history. In the flesh he was a man of great intellect and learning, of subtlety, and of contradictions. The hand that had drafted the Declaration of Independence continued to keep accounts for more than a hundred slaves until his death. Although he admired their courage, he had little sympathy for the plight of the American Indians, largely because they stood in the way of the American farmer, whose prosperity he deemed essential to the survival of the republic. This conformed to his belief in the progress of civilization and his ambition to put in place "a government founded not on the fears and follies of man, but on his reason."

Although an intellectual and scholar, Jefferson was the first president who was also, unquestionably, the leader of a political party. He skillfully made use of party politics in making appointments to office and in pursuing his legislative aims, entertained members of Congress at the president's house as a means of keeping himself in touch and them in line, and occasionally used less than honorable means in the service of a worthy political end. The exponent of limited government and the initiator of the concept of nullification, Jefferson more than either Washington or John Adams used the powers of the presidential office to achieve his goals.

CABINET MEMBERS

James Madison, Jefferson's close friend and political colleague, the principal framer of the Constitution and first parliamentary leader of the Republicans in Congress, was named secretary of state. Albert Gallatin, a Swiss by birth who had rallied western Pennsylvania for Jefferson and was skilled in accounts, became secretary of the treasury. The four other cabinet posts went to loyal Republicans from Massachusetts, Connecticut, and Maryland.

Political Patronage. Jefferson appointed no Federalists to high office and none of Burr's supporters. He removed some who had been appointed by Washington and John Adams, complaining that few died and none resigned, and when there was a vacancy to fill he invariably named a dependable Republican. However, he resisted the demands of the more radical members of his party for wholesale removals and rarely discarded the competent moderate Federalist, a type he largely succeeded in converting to the Republican cause. In four years he was able to replace about half of the Federalist holdovers with Republican appointees.

FINANCIAL RETRENCHMENT

Soon after taking office Jefferson took steps to repeal Hamilton's financial program and to reduce and eliminate the national debt (by this time, some $83 million). He gained congressional repeal of internal or domestic taxes, including the detested excise tax. The federal government was to be funded solely from duties on imported goods and from the sale of western lands. To reduce government expeditures, Secretary Gallatin imposed sharp cuts in spending by means of (1) reductions in military and diplomatic expenditures; (2) strict accounting in the expenditure of all appropriations; (3) and a rapid reduction of the principal of the national debt.

The number of diplomatic missions overseas was reduced from seven to three (London, Paris, and Madrid). The U.S. army, deprived of a general staff, was cut by about a third, to an authorized force of 3,312. Jefferson justified the reductions by citing the dangers posed by standing armies and touting the civilian militia in the states. The navy was also drastically reduced, to a mere six active ships; after cutting nineteen captains, only nine remained in active service. A large navy, the president reckoned, would give undue weight to the demands of commerce and, by posing a threat to the European powers, increase the chances for war. In 1802 naval expenditures dropped by more than a half to a total outlay of $915,000. However, in response to international events, the budget for the navy increased thereafter.

RESTRAINING THE JUDICIARY

After Republicans won majorities in both the House and the Senate, and the Federalist ticket was defeated for the presidency in 1800, the Federalists in Congress passed the Judiciary Act of 1801. Because appointments to the federal bench were for life, they expected to extend their control of that branch of government. The Judiciary Act of 1801 created ten new positions on the federal district courts and a new category of appellate court, the circuit courts of appeals, between the Supreme Court and the district courts. The act also reduced the size of the high court by one justice. Prior to leaving office, President Adams had appointed as many Federalists to these new positions (derisively called the "midnight appointments") as he could.

Faced with a decidedly hostile judicial branch, the Republicans quickly took steps to counter Federalist moves. In March 1802 Congress repealed the 1801 act, eliminating the new judgeships and designating one Supreme Court justice and one district court judge to sit on the traveling circuit courts. Republicans in Congress, with the encouragement of the president, then moved to impeach two federal justices who had openly attacked the administration from the bench. The first, John Pickering of New Hampshire, was mentally deranged, presenting a constitutional dilemma—his incompetence fell short of the requirement for removal (high crimes and misdemeanors). He was nevertheless convicted by the Senate and removed in

1804. The following year House Republicans impeached Supreme Court Justice Samuel Chase, citing only his partisan excesses; this time the Senate failed to vote conviction. The Chase trial was a pivotal event, for if the Senate had voted to convict on merely partisan political charges, it is likely that impeachments of judges and justices would have continued and perhaps significantly influenced the development of the judiciary. Many Republicans were in fact pressing at this time for constitutional changes to make federal judges more accountable, notably by means of election.

Chief Justice Marshall and the Marbury case (1803). One of Adams's "midnight appointees," William Marbury, sued the new secretary of state to gain a commission as justice of the peace for the District of Columbia, which had not been delivered before the Republicans took office. Citing a provision of the Judiciary Act of 1789, he asked the Supreme Court to order Madison to deliver the commission. Chief Justice John Marshall, speaking for the Court, found the appointment valid but no authority to order delivery of the commission, ruling that the enforcement provision of the 1789 law was unconstitutional. By finding that the Supreme Court was powerless to act for Marbury, Marshall avoided a direct confrontation with the administration while asserting the Court's right to review acts of Congress and rule upon their constitutionality.

In Marshall, a distant cousin whom he despised, Jefferson had gained his most formidable political adversary. Like Lincoln and many other presidents, it should be noted, Jefferson did not consider himself obligated to enforce all rulings of the Supreme Court, interpreting the enforcement power of the executive branch to be a constitutional check on the judiciary.

BARBARY WARS

An advocate of military retaliation against the Barbary pirates of northern Africa since his service as secretary of state, President Jefferson chose in 1801 to respond with force to affronts against the American flag and consulate in Tripoli (today the capital of Libya) and the seizure of American hostages. To prevent attacks on American merchant shipping in the Mediterranean, the United States, like the European nations, had been paying tribute and ransom money to the Barbary states of North Africa—Morocco, Algiers, Tunis, and Tripoli. Having decided that Tripoli's declaration of war allowed him to proceed without a similar declaration from Congress, Jefferson ordered a squadron of four ships to sail for North Africa in 1802.

The continuing difficulties with the Barbary states and growing concern for defense of the American coast led the president to request funds from Congress for the construction of, ultimately, several hundred gunboats. These light vessels (derisively referred to as the "mosquito fleet") gradually replaced the frigates then in service. Nine gunboats had reached the Mediterranean by 1805, when the first of the Barbary wars ended in a standoff. In order to free American prisoners who were threatened with execution, Commodore James Barron signed an agreement that purported to end the requirement of tribute while exacting ransom for the freedom of the hostages.

The Louisiana Purchase

Soon after taking office, Jefferson learned that Spain had ceded the vast province of Louisiana back to France. This raised troubling questions about French intentions, particularly regarding navigation on the Mississippi River. Access to that highway to the American interior was considered vital by some 50,000 Americans who lived and traded in the valleys of the Ohio and the Tennessee rivers (which flow into the Mississippi).

NAPOLEON'S COLONIAL AMBITIONS

France's reacquisition of Louisiana (with the port of New Orleans) in the secret Treaty of San Ildefonso (1800) was part of Napoleon's ambition to re–create the French colonial empire in America. The scheme was defeated in part by Toussaint L'Ouverture, revolutionary leader of the blacks of Santo Domingo (on Hispaniola in the West Indies) who had gained control of their island and established a republic; their new government had been officially recognized by the Adams administration. Aided by an outbreak of yellow fever among the French troops and delays in reinforcing them from Europe, L'Ouverture's forces successfully resisted Napoleon's efforts to retake his island.

On hearing that Louisiana had been ceded, Jefferson, who had gone so far as to suggest to the French that the United States might be willing to join them in overturning Toussaint, shifted course. New Orleans, he observed, was so connected to American interests that if the French gained control of that port, "we must marry ourselves to the British fleet and nation."

THE TREATY OF CESSION (1803)

When news that the Spanish had suspended the right of Americans to deposit goods in New Orleans reached Washington, the president asked Congress to appropriate funds ($2 million) to purchase the port—he also requested funds to increase the army and to build riverboats suitable for a war in the west. The president's determination was given emphasis when he instructed the American negotiators in Paris, Minister Robert R. Livingston and special envoy James Monroe, to open discussions with the British government in the event the French refused to sell New Orleans.

Events were, characteristically, determined by Emperor Napoleon himself. Before the American negotiators could make their proposals, he had determined to be rid of Louisiana. His friend (and Jefferson's), the French traveler C. F. Volney, had given him a firsthand report on the degradation of French settlements in the territory. Calculating his losses in the West Indies, the possibility of renewal of war with Great Britain, and no doubt the geographical advantages enjoyed by the Americans, Napoleon was ready to

THE
UNITED STATES
AFTER THE
LOUISIANA PURCHASE

sell the entire province for the right sum. While Livingston had suggested that the French might wish to part with the northern part of Lousiana, he and Monroe were surprised when offered the whole province. They were not authorized to bid for it, but, aware of the urgency of proceeding and of the enormity of the prize, they agreed to a purchase price of $15 million. A treaty was signed in May, the Senate ratified the document in October, and the territory was transferred to the United States in December 1803.

Although Jefferson doubted the constitutionality of the purchase and at first believed an amendment to the Constitution was required to legally acquire Louisiana, he put aside his scruples and accepted a loose construction of the executive's constitutional power to make treaties. The acquisition was immensely popular, except for the moment with New England Federalists, who reacted to the promise that several new states would be formed from the new territory, further diluting the political power of the northeast.

The Lewis and Clark Expedition (1804–1806). Responding to a secret request from the president, Congress appropriated $2,500 to fund an expedition of the territory beyond the Mississippi to chart and gain information about the region. Jefferson designated Meriwether Lewis, his private secretary, to lead a carefully selected group up the Missouri, across the Great Divide, and into the valley of the Columbia River. An experienced backwoodsman, Lewis and his associate William Clark (brother of George Rogers Clark) set out from St. Louis in May 1804 with a party of fifty, guided by the Shoshoni princess Sacajawea. They reached the Pacific a year and a half later. The work of Lewis and Clark strengthened American claims to the Oregon country (derived from the Louisiana Purchase), which was also claimed by Britain and Spain.

Zebulon Pike's Expeditions (1805, 1806). A second expedition into the new territory set out in late 1805 under Lieutenant Zebulon Pike to explore the upper Mississippi Valley and search for the source of the great river. The following year Pike led another group up the Arkansas River to the easternmost Rocky Mountains of modern–day Colorado and New Mexico, a region he later described as a desert.

PARTISAN BATTLES

By the end of his first term, President Jefferson had doubled the size of the national domain, eliminated the foreign threat to the southwest, and checked the Barbary menace to American commerce in the Mediterranean, while eliminating internal taxes and reducing substantially the national debt. Not surprisingly, he trounced his Federalist opponent for reelection in 1804, Charles Cotesworth Pinckney of South Carolina, by 126–14 electoral votes (losing only Connecticut and Delaware). His second term, however, was dominated by factional strife and political intrigue.

Republican Factions

Although the Federalist party made some inroads by fashioning popular appeals to the electorate, their gains were confined to a few states and posed no national threat to Jefferson's leadership. Without the discipline that the Federalist opposition had forced upon them in 1800, the Republican party became diverted by local quarrels between rival factions (especially in New York and Pennsylvania), while ideological differences among Republicans gave the administration serious trouble in Congress. The rise of factions exposed the weakness of the Republican consensus and enhanced Congress's powers at the expense of the executive.

THE "QUIDS"

In his first term Jefferson had wielded the powers of his office with an authority that Presidents Washington and Adams would not have been permitted. His political moderation and willingness to compromise had won over many of the moderate or Adams Federalists. At the same time those Republicans who had rallied behind him in expectation of a radical departure from previous administrations grew increasingly frustrated. Led by the colorful and eccentric John Randolph of Roanoke, a group of Republicans in the House, who called themselves the "Quids" (or "something or others"), objected to what they identified as "federalism" in the administration's policies. Relying on the Virginia and Kentucky resolutions, they advocated a strict construction of the Constitution and states rights and became the most troublesome of the president's opponents.

THE YAZOO CONTROVERSY

Randolph achieved his most notable success in opposing Jefferson's plan to resolve the Yazoo land claims. When Georgia ceded her western claims to the federal government, the United States had inherited numerous law suits lodged by those who had made purchases from the Yazoo land companies. The original land grants to these companies had been annulled by the Georgia legislature in 1796 on the grounds that they had been made fraudulently.

After several years of dispute, a special commission appointed by President Jefferson proposed a compromise solution that was acceptable to the state of Georgia and to the Yazoo claimants—an appropriation of five million acres of public land was to be made to compensate bona fide purchasers. This compromise solution gained the president's support, but Randolph and his supporters blocked the settlement for ten years, charging that the claims (many of which were held by members of Congress) were undeserving of compensation.

The matter was ultimately resolved by the Supreme Court in the case of *Fletcher v. Peck* (1810). Chief Justice Marshall, for the Court, ruled that the original sale contracts were not invalidated because of fraud and took the opportunity to affirm the Supreme Court's authority to review state laws to determine their constitutionality.

Federalist Intrigues

The extreme elements of the New England Federalists, aware that the center of political power had shifted to the South and west and that New England's role in the union would be diminished, eventually came to believe that secession was better than accepting such a fate.

THE ESSEX JUNTO

A small group of these "high" Federalists of New England, known as the Essex Junto, even deliberated upon the possibility of a union with Canada in order to escape from policies framed by southern planters and western farmers. They determined to work for a "Northern" or "Eastern Confederacy," defending their position with state–rights arguments that echoed those of the Virginia and Kentucky resolutions. Their plans were effectively thwarted, however, when Hamilton stated his opposition to "a dismemberment of our empire."

THE COALITION WITH BURR

In the hope of joining New England with New York and New Jersey in a confederacy, the "high" Federalist faction supported Vice–President Aaron Burr in the election for governor of New York in 1804. Hamilton accused Burr of treasonous activity and impugned his character in such an open way that his comments were reported in the newspapers. After his defeat, Burr, blaming Hamilton, challenged his nemesis to a duel and killed him.

Burr's Conspiracy. Burr avoided possible prosecution in New York by leaving the state, but, because dueling was considered a private (if not entirely just) affair among gentlemen at that time, he was not universally condemned as a murderer, particularly in the southern states, where the practice of dueling was less frowned upon. He presided over the Senate as vice–president until his term ended in March 1805, then made a curious trek that took him and a small group of armed men to the southwest, probably with the ultimate goal of "liberating" Mexico from the Spanish. Burr's ambitions were thwarted when he was indicted on a charge of treason in late 1806.

The principal evidence against Burr was supplied by an admitted collaborator in the scheme, General James Wilkinson, governor of the Louisiana Territory, who had warned of Burr's intention to attack New Orleans. In a dramatic episode worthy of the ancient Roman writer Cicero's accounts of conspiracies, President Jefferson, convinced that Burr was an enemy of the republic, directed the government's prosecution of the trial, which was presided over by Chief Justice Marshall in Richmond. Marshall, strictly interpreting the language of the Constitution (which required two witnesses to the "overt act" of treason for conviction), refused to admit crucial evidence against Burr and thus all but determined his acquittal.

The Burr conspiracy was the most noteworthy incident of its kind in the early history of the United States. Although government presence in the United States and its territories was slight, the strong ambitions and conflicting interests that flourished in the politics of the young republic never combined to threaten the Constitution. By contrast, the ancient Roman republic had been continuously threatened by plots and conspiracies, the first French republic quickly destroyed by them.

THE DIPLOMACY OF "PEACEABLE COERCION"

Europe's brief respite from war ended in 1803. Napoleon's drive to control and reshape Europe roused Great Britain and her allies to renew their struggle to destroy him. The American merchant fleet at first derived great benefits in its role as a neutral carrier, but as losses in the conflict mounted, the belligerent powers ignored the maritime rights of neutral nations in attempts to gain advantages and punish their enemies. Once again, "the exterminating havoc" in Europe disrupted the republican experiment and threatened American independence.

British Maritime Policies

After Admiral Lord Nelson smashed the French fleet at the Battle of Trafalgar in 1805, Britain ruled the seas. Pressed by British merchants, who had become alarmed at the rapid growth of American shipping, the British government invoked imperial regulations to control the exchange of goods with the continent.

ORDERS IN COUNCIL

Taking full advantage of her superior sea power, Great Britain issued several orders in council (the first in April 1806) to restrict the trade of neutral shippers. By November 1807 these measures, at least on paper, had put in place a blockade of European ports and forced neutrals to trade with the continent through Great Britain.

Impressment and the *Chesapeake* Incident. Conditions in the British navy and merchant marine were hard and often subhuman, leading British sailors, most of whom had been impressed into service by physical force, to jump ship when they could. Many joined the U.S. navy or took assignments on American merchant ships. The British considered these men deserters and maintained their right to apprehend them by stopping and searching American ships and removing suspects. Under this claim, they seized thousands of men—many in fact deserters, but also many naturalized Americans who had been born within the dominions of the British empire as well as native–born Americans.

The attack and seizure of the U.S. frigate *Chesapeake* just outside of Norfolk by the British warship *Leopard* in June 1807 gave dramatic emphasis to the issue of British impressments. Although the British government agreed to return the sailors abducted from the *Chesapeake* and to pay damages, it persisted in claiming the!right to board and search foreign vessels to apprehend deserters.

The Emperor Retaliates. In an effort to cripple Britain and in response to the orders in council, Napoleon put in place his Continental System. The Berlin Decree (November 1806) forbade all commerce with the British Isles and ordered the seizure of ships coming from Britain or her colonies to ports under French control. The Milan Decree (December 1807) declared that all ships that paid a tax to the British or obeyed the orders in council were "good prize." By subsequent decrees (1808–1810), Napoleon sequestered American vessels in French ports and confiscated their cargoes. His measures, combined with those of the British, severely hindered the neutral carrying trade and violated the traditional rights of neutral or nonbelligerent nations.

Jefferson's Alternative to War

Although the president recognized that the *Chesapeake* incident had roused Americans to "a state of exasperation" not seen since the Battle of Lexington, he knew that the success of his domestic program—limiting the size of government, reducing the national debt, and eliminating internal taxes—depended on the maintenance of peace. Having long believed that economic measures could be fashioned to serve as an effective alternative to war, he now determined to make the experiment.

THE EMBARGO (1807)

Jefferson and Secretary of State Madison believed that the British and the French were dependent on American foodstuffs, the principal products carried by American ships. Believing that the nation was willing to make sacrifices to gain redress, they designed an economic boycott to force the belligerents to recognize American neutrality and to observe the neutral rights of American shippers. In late December 1807, Congress enacted the administration's embargo, which prohibited all foreign commerce.

The embargo resulted in a serious economic contraction, which severely disrupted the businesses of the merchants and shipowners of New England and other northern states. Those whose livelihood and work depended upon foreign commerce not surprisingly perceived in this policy, with some justice, an overt bias against the interests of merchants and for those of farmers. Opposition steadily grew. Owing to the nation's long coastline and extended border with Canada, the embargo proved difficult to enforce and relatively easy to evade. Congress passed several force acts, some reminiscent of onerous British imperial regulations, to empower customs officials to seize ships and cargoes on suspicion of intent to sail for Europe. The administration found itself closely monitoring the coastal trade and the president even sent troops to upstate New York to prevent violations.

NONINTERCOURSE WITH GREAT BRITAIN AND FRANCE (1809)

With no evidence to suggest that the boycott was having the desired effect in Britain or France, but clear indications that the Federalists were reaping political gains from it, the Republican Congress repealed the embargo legislation at the end of Jefferson's second term. Commerce with the world was again permitted, if only in theory. The Nonintercourse Act of 1809, which replaced the embargo, prohibited all trade with the nation's principal trading partners, Great Britain and France, until they recognized the maritime rights of neutrals.

Madison's Diplomacy

James Madison, who succeeded Jefferson in the presidency in 1809, continued to guide American relations with Europe by the policy of "peaceable coercion." During his administration, the challenges posed by the Napoleonic Wars became more frequent and menacing.

THE ERSKINE FIASCO

David Erskine, British minister in Washington, persuaded Madison that Great Britain would rescind her orders in council if the United States would reopen trade. Accordingly, the president proclaimed resumption of commercial relations with Great Britain only to discover that Erskine had not stated all of the conditions demanded by his government, which refused to confirm the agreement. Many American ships that had set sail under the assumption that the dangers to commerce had been removed were in fact taken by the British navy.

MACON'S BILL NO. 2

In May 1810, Congress, with Madison's approval, passed a bill submitted by Congressman Nathaniel Macon of North Carolina that revised the Nonintercourse Act. The new measure reopened trade with all nations, including France and Great Britain, but it empowered the president to take action against those belligerents under certain conditions. If either of them ceased "to violate the neutral commerce of the United States," and the other refused to do the same, the president could then declare an embargo or resume nonintercourse with the other power.

Napoleon, seeking an advantage against Britain, responded to Macon's bill by proclaiming, in the Cadore letter, his intention to observe the rights of neutral traders (the insincerity of which was revealed only in time). Relying on the French statement, Madison announced that nonintercourse with Great Britain would resume early in 1811 unless the British orders in council were revoked.

REPUBLICAN INDIAN POLICY

Jefferson believed that the American farmer was the backbone of the republic, his prosperity crucial to its health and survival. "Those who labor in the earth are the chosen people of God, if He had a chosen people, whose breasts He has made His peculiar deposit for substantial and genuine virtue," he wrote in his *Notes on the State of Virginia* (1785, 1787). The Republican Indian policy he fashioned and implemented, which was continued under Madison, derived from this conviction about the use of the land. In practice it provided a basis for removing the Indians west of the Mississippi. Tribal claims to hunting grounds in the Northwest Territory were considered illegal and were not recognized. The Indians were offered the opportunity to either assimilate themselves into the "civilized" white agricultural communities or to resettle west of the Mississippi.

Settlement of the Northwest Territory by American farmers had dramatically increased during Jefferson's two terms, aided by the Harrison Land Bill of 1800, which had made it easier to acquire land in the region. To enforce this policy and encourage settlement, Jefferson appointed William Henry Harrison, author of the 1800 law, as governor of the Indiana Territory, a position he held until 1812.

Tecumseh's Confederacy. In reaction to the encroachments of the white man and Republican policy, the Shawnee chief Tecumseh and his brother Tenskwatawa (a shaman, called the Prophet) organized a confederacy of tribes in the Mississippi Valley and attempted to revive their native cultures. The chief told Governor Harrison that the settlers had "driven us from the sea to the lakes—we can go no farther." Along the frontier, from the Great Lakes to the Gulf of Mexico, the Indians rose up in opposition to white settlers, who largely blamed the British for their troubles. When Harrison's troops, after destroying the central Shawnee village at the Battle of Tippecanoe (November 1811), reported that the Indians had been armed with English guns and ammunition, the western regions and states pressed for war.

Anti–British Sentiment. Since 1783, the British presence in Canada and in the Great Lakes region claimed by the United States had been an irritant to American settlers, who detected British influence in the hostilities directed at them by Indian tribes. The British needed friendly relations with the Indian tribes to maintain the fur trade and their control over the vast and thinly populated extent of Canada, but in fact they did not organize them for military purposes, as had the French. They provided supplies and on occasion directly aided their Indian allies in resisting the relentless sweep of American settlers. After the *Chesapeake* incident of 1807, however, the British in Canada took measures to strengthen these alliances in anticipation of an American invasion.

THE WAR HAWKS

The failure of Jefferson's and Madison's economic and diplomatic alternatives to war, with the repeated insults of the European powers and the increasing hostilities on the western frontier, eventually eliminated the administration's options. Demand for war came not from New England shipping interests but from a rising generation of Republicans sent to Washington to represent the western and southern states. They feared the consequences of war less than those of national humiliation. This group of War Hawks dominated the new Congress that convened in December 1811. Prominent among them were Henry Clay of Kentucky, elected speaker of the House, and John C. Calhoun of South Carolina, whom Clay appointed to the House Foreign Affairs Committee, Felix Grundy of Tennessee, and Peter B. Porter of western New York.

The War Hawks and their followers were not merely frustrated nationalists; they were also united by expansionist ambitions and eager to acquire new territory to resolve the nation's problems. Their principal objective, clearly identified by Calhoun, was to gain Canada and thereby remove the British influence from North America. In the South and southwest, their objective was the eastern portion of Florida, still a possession of Spain, now an ally of Great Britain. It had been a base for Indian attacks against white settlements and a refuge for runaway slaves. In 1810 American settlers in western Florida (then consisting of portions of Louisiana, Mississippi, and Alabama) had gained control of that portion of Spanish Florida, which was annexed to the United States in 1812. With Madison's sanction, a similar but unsuccessful effort had been made to take eastern Florida in 1811.

Declaration of War. Recognizing that pressures in Congress could no longer be resisted, Madison abandoned the policy of "peaceable coercion" and recommended war against Britain on June 1, 1812 (approved by Congress two weeks later). In his war message the president cited Britain's refusal to observe the maritime rights of neutral nations, its impressment of

American sailors and merchantmen, and its agitation of the western Indians against American settlers. Assuming that Canada could easily be taken, the administration now entertained the idea that an invasion by American troops would force the British to accept the maritime rights of neutral nations, the Republican objective during three presidential administrations. Even after making the popular decision for war, Madison barely won reelection (by 128 to 89 electoral votes) over DeWitt Clinton, governor of New York, the candidate of Federalists and antiwar Republicans.

THE SECOND WAR WITH BRITAIN

After yielding to pressures for war, the administration learned soon after declaring it that the British government had moved (on June 16, 1812) to eliminate their restrictions on American merchant shippers. In an age in which sailing ships were the only vehicle of transatlantic communications, and crossings usually took three to five weeks, depending on the season and weather, such ironies, or accidents of history, were always possible. Warfare with Britain, however, was not averted. After years of grievances the dispute now encompassed questions about the nature of American independence and national destiny. The treaty that settled the conflict did not resolve many of the outstanding issues with Britain, but by the time fighting in America, and the wars in Europe, had concluded, less tangible national objectives had been achieved.

The Field of Battle

The war fever that had forced Madison to abandon the policy of "peaceable coercion" did not translate into congressional support for increases in expenditures required to outfit and support a credible army and navy. Congress rejected proposals for direct taxes to support the war effort and grudgingly voted basic appropriations. New England opposed the war and ignored strictures against trading with the British during the conflict.

LACK OF PREPAREDNESS

The country was utterly unprepared to fight a war against a world power. The weakness of American forces quickly became apparent, although until Napoleon suffered a massive defeat in his attempt to conquer Russia, Great Britain concentrated its war effort on the European continent. Although Jefferson had effectively deployed the navy against the Barbary states and established the U.S. Military Academy at West Point (1802), he put in place a policy that relied almost exclusively on volunteer militia of citizens to defend the nation against invasion. The regular or "standing" U.S. army was kept purposely small so as to discourage its role in domestic affairs, and not suprisingly it was poorly equipped. In early engagements, the volunteer militia proved largely unreliable; they were handicapped by incompetent leaders, in most cases politicians confidently expecting opportunities for glory.

THE "OFFENSIVE" AGAINST CANADA (1812–1813)

Reflecting the rhetoric of the War Hawks, America military strategy first focused on Canada. A three–pronged attack in the summer of 1812, however, ended disastrously. General William Hull, appointed governor of the Michigan Territory, was forced to surrender Detroit and its fort; Generals Smythe and Van Rensselaer failed at Niagara; General Dearborn never crossed the border in his attack on Montreal. Fort Mackinac (at the juncture of Lakes Michigan and Huron) and Fort Dearborn (modern Chicago) fell to the British and their Indian allies.

Naval Action on the Great Lakes. In 1813, the U.S. navy managed to gain control of Lakes Ontario and Erie. Having gained command of the former, American troops again pushed northward, landing at York (modern Toronto), the capital of British Canada, in late April. The poorly organized action amounted to little more than a raid but resulted in the burning of public buildings as well as ships and materiel, destruction that would not be forgotten by British forces.

The hard–won victory of Admiral Oliver Hazard Perry (sailing under the banner "Don't Give Up the Ship") in the Battle of Lake Erie caused the British to abandon Detroit. This permitted the American army in the west, now assigned to General William Henry Harrison, to mount an overland invasion of the peninsula of upper Canada. Harrison defeated the British and Indian forces at the Battle of the Thames in September 1813. While this clash contributed to no substantial American objective, it was a demoralizing blow to the Indian forces. Tecumseh, now holding the rank of brigadier general in the British army, died in the fighting.

THE WAR AT SEA

American naval victories at first compensated for the disasters on land. In the first six months of the war American frigates forced five British ships to "strike their colors" (lower their flags) in surrender; American privateers captured three hundred British merchantmen. The nation's spirits rose with the impressive victory of Captain Isaac Hull's *U.S.S. Constitution* over the larger British warship *Guerrière*. However, with the turn of the war in Europe, Britain directed its superior sea power against the United States and its commerce in 1813. By the spring of the following year the Royal Navy had put in place an effective blockade of the chief American ports (except those of New England, which traded openly with the British).

THE BRITISH OFFENSIVE OF 1814

After the defeat of Napoleon in Europe, British forces orchestrated an elaborate three-part invasion of the United States in a concerted attempt to defeat and punish their American foes. The plan called for an invasion from Canada and attacks on the Chesapeake Bay and at the mouth of the Mississippi.

Defeats on the crucial northern front—at Niagara and on Lake Champlain, where Captain Thomas Macdonough won an important naval victory (Battle of Plattsburgh) in September 1814—undermined the strategy. The British gained a full measure of revenge, however. Admiral Sir George Cockburn's fleet easily penetrated American defenses surrounding the Chesapeake Bay, scattered the feeble force of American militia charged with defending the national capital, and, under General Robert Ross, torched the public buildings of the "Federal City" (justifying their action as retaliation for the burning of York). The gallant resistance Ross's men encountered at Fort McHenry prevented them from entering Baltimore. This event inspired Washington lawyer Francis Scott Key, who watched the battle from a British ship in Baltimore harbor, to compose the words to "The Star-Spangled Banner."

In the southwest, Sir Edward Pakenham's seasoned British regulars (who had been with the duke of Wellington in Spain) were unimpeded until they reached the outskirts of New Orleans in early January 1815. Between them and the city was a force of frontier militia, local residents (including blacks and "people of color"), and pirates under the command of General Andrew Jackson. Jackson had won a complete victory over the hostile Creek Indians at the Battle of Horseshoe Bend (Alabama) in March, then defeated the Spanish at Pensacola, Florida. From behind well-constructed earthen fortifications before New Orleans, his troops stopped a series of frontal assaults by British forces with their long frontier rifles. Although it was actually fought after the signing of a treaty of peace, Jackson's overwhelming victory at the Battle of New Orleans proved to be the most celebrated and memorable military engagement of the war. His small force suffered but eight deaths and thirteen wounded; Pakenham lost his own life, as well as those of 700 British troops (with 1,400 wounded; 500 captured).

THE HARTFORD CONVENTION

Opposition to the war was widespread in New England, which identified in it and the Madison administration's objectives a calculated hostility to northern and commercial interests. The state legislatures of the region refused to furnish militia for the Canadian campaigns; the banks and businesses boycotted the government's efforts to sell bonds to finance the war; New England farmers and merchants supplied British armies in Canada with meat and grain. Led in Congress by Daniel Webster, then a Federalist representative from Massachusetts, New Englanders attacked Madison's war as unnecessary; they thwarted the administration's efforts to increase revenues and raise additional troops.

Reflecting increasing dissatisfaction with the war and frustration with their minority position in the union, Massachusetts, Connecticut, Rhode Island, Vermont, and New Hampshire sent delegates to a convention in Hartford in October 1814 to consider their options. Secessionists failed, however, in their attempt to gain control of the meeting. Still, the Hartford Convention issued a report recommending seven constitutional amendments that delegates considered necessary to New England's interests. The report endorsed the doctrine of state nullification and proposed amendments: (1) to eliminate slaves from the population count in determining representation in the House of Representatives; (2) to require a two–thirds vote of Congress to admit new states, impose commercial restrictions, or declare war; (3) to limit the president to a single term and prohibit the election of two persons from the same state in succession.

Had the war continued badly, as Federalists expected, the convention might have exerted influence on national events. However, the news of Jackson's victory at New Orleans and then of the signing of a peace treaty ending the war made the gathering appear to be a pointless and discordant (to some a treasonous) episode. It was regarded then as now to be the last gasp of the dying Federalist party.

The Treaty of Ghent

The negotiations that produced the agreement that concluded the war with Britain began in Ghent, Belgium, in August 1814. John Quincy Adams, son of the president and recently minister to Russia (1809–14), was appointed by Congress to head the United States delegation (of five), the most notable of whom were Henry Clay and Albert Gallatin. The British government, primarily concerned with negotiations to settle the European war, sent a less distinguished delegation.

CONFLICTING DEMANDS

The British negotiatiors were instructed in August 1814 to demand (1) cession to Canada of land in Maine and northern New York; (2) British control of the Great Lakes; (3) exclusion of American ships from the Newfoundland fisheries; (4) the creation of a northwestern buffer state for the Indians south of the Great Lakes. They prolonged the negotiations as long as prospects for British troops in the field appeared favorable.

American representatives initially attempted to gain all or part of Canada and British assistance in securing Florida from Spain. They resisted British demands and pressed for acceptance of the administration's position on neutral rights. Their position was weak at the outset, but news of American victories, especially that at the Battle of Lake Champlain (Plattsburgh), considerably strengthened their hand.

Terms of the Treaty. The agreement as finally signed provided merely for the cessation of hostilities and a return of both nations to the *status quo ante bellum* (conditions that existed before the war). Such questions as boundaries and fisheries were referred to commissions for future adjustment. No mention was made of maritime issues.

POSTWAR NATIONALISM

Although the peace treaty with Great Britain reflected an inconclusive result, Americans for the most part considered the outcome of the war favorable to the United States. The news of Jackson's remarkable victory became public before the signing of an agreement at Ghent was known, strengthening the impression that the Battle of New Orleans had been significant. The fact that the republic had survived its greatest peril and that the British military machine, which had finally conquered the great Napoleon, was unable to subdue much smaller contingents of determined Americans appeared to confirm the nation's claim to a special destiny.

Jefferson's election put an end to the ideological struggle that had brought the new nation to the brink of civil war. In power he fulfilled his promise to reduce government expenditures, taxes, and the national debt. He also broadened his consensus and moved it to the moderate center, gaining support from Adams Federalists and further isolating the "high" Federalists. Faced with challenges to his leadership and opportunities of national import, he demonstrated flexibility, making full use of the mechanisms of the central government to assert control and achieve what he regarded to be worthy republican ends.

Jefferson, and Madison after him, believed they could alter hostile British policies toward the United States by using American commerce and trade as a peaceable weapon, an "alternative to war." The efforts they took to resolve America's dependency on and vulnerability to British commercial supremacy, which can be traced to the American Revolution, were ultimately defeated by events in Europe and the ironies of history. Their failed policy did have the positive, if not entirely intended, effects of allowing the new nation time to grow, of stimulating American manufacturing, and of generating a new spirit of nationalism.

Selected Readings

Adams, Henry. *History of the United States of America During the Administrations of Jefferson and Madison* (9 vols., 1889–91) (1967)

Brown, Roger H. *The Republic in Peril: 1812* (1964)

DeConde, Alexander. *This Affair of Louisiana* (1976)

Ellis, Richard E. *The Jeffersonian Crisis: Courts and Politics in the Young Republic* (1971)

Fischer, David Hackett. *The Revolution of American Conservatism: The Federalist Party in the Era of Jeffersonian Democracy* (1965) deVoto, Bernard. ed. *The Journals of Lewis and Clark* (1953)

Horsman, Reginald. *The Frontier in the Formative Years, 1783–1815* (1970)

Malone, Dumas. *Jefferson and His Time* (6 vols., 1948–1981)

Perkins, Bradford. *Prologue to War: England and the United States, 1805–1812* (1961)

Peterson, Merrill D. ed. *The Portable Thomas Jefferson* (1975)

Sheehan, Bernard W. *Seeds of Extinction: Jeffersonian Philanthropy and the American Indian* (1974)

Stagg, J.C.A. *Mr. Madison's War: Politics, Diplomacy, and Warfare in the Early American Republic, 1783–1830* (1983)

8

The Awakening of American Nationalism

1810	Supreme Court rules in *Fletcher v. Peck*
1812–1821	Six western states admitted to the union (Louisiana, Indiana, Mississippi, Illinois, Alabama, Missouri)
1813	Waltham manufacturing system introduced by the Boston Manufacturing Company
1815	Jackson wins Battle of New Orleans; U.S. navy defeats Algiers and Barbary States
1816	First steamboat operates on the Mississippi; Congress charters the (second) Bank of the United States and passes protective tariff legislation
1817	James Monroe inaugurated president; Bonus Bill of 1817 vetoed by President Madison
1817–1825	Construction of Erie Canal in New York State
1818	Jackson's raids in Florida (ending the First Seminole War, 1817–1818); settlement of Anglo–American Convention of 1818
1819	Adams–Onis Treaty results in acquisition of Florida; financial panic and depression begins; Supreme Court rules in *McCulloch v. Maryland* and *Dartmouth College v. Woodward*
1820	Missouri Compromise legislated; Maine admitted as a free state
1821	Missouri admitted as a slave state
1820s–1830s	Revisions to state constitutions introduced
1821	Monroe, having won the popular vote in the election of 1820, receives all but one electoral vote
1822	United States recognizes Latin American republican governments
1823	President Monroe proclaims the Monroe Doctrine in his annual presidential message (December)

1824 Supreme Court rules in *Gibbons v. Ogden*; Lafayette revisits the United States (1824–1825)

1825 Andrew Jackson wins plurality in electoral college; John Quincy Adams elected president by the House of Representatives (February)

1826 Death of John Adams and Thomas Jefferson (July 4, fiftieth anniversary of the Declaration of Independence)

1828 Congress passes the Tariff of Abominations (May); Jackson wins presidential election

After the War of 1812, the new nation seemed to explode in movement and activity. The perception that the war had ended favorably, with the memory of the Hartford Convention, reduced the political opposition of the Federalist party to meaninglessness. The victory of James Monroe, last of the "Virginia Dynasty" of presidents, in the election of 1816, was followed by a period of relative political tranquility, causing many to herald an "Era of Good Feelings." However, Congress's implementation of the American System, advocated by those eager to promote the emerging national market economy, soon revived what President John Quincy Adams called the "baneful weed of party strife." More ominously, owing to differences in the economic development of the country, the economic nationalists' legislative agenda also roused dormant sectional interests.

EXPANDING NATIONAL INTERESTS

In the aftermath of the War of 1812, Congress took action to improve the defenses of the nation. It defiantly determined to rebuild the public buildings in Washington rather than relocate the national capital. The national mood was buoyed by Jackson's victory at the Battle of New Orleans, his raids in Florida, and Decatur's dramatic exploits in the Mediterranean.

Postwar Military Establishment

Reflecting a new sense of military preparedness, Congress made provision for a standing army of 10,000 men in March 1816. President Madison, who had asked for a force twice that number, appointed Jacob Brown and Andrew Jackson to the rank of major general, to command, respectively, the northern and southern departments. Congress put the navy's gunboats up for sale and "mothballed" the warships used on the Great Lakes but otherwise did not reduce the navy significantly. Coastal defenses were improved, the coast guard was enlarged, and new warships were built.

DECATUR'S VICTORIES

After the treaty with Britain had been ratified in 1815, Congress declared war on Algiers, which had resumed its attacks on American shipping and declared war on the United States. Captain Stephen Decatur, commanding one of two squadrons sent to the coast of North Africa in 1815, won a series of engagements with the Barbary corsairs. He imposed a blockade on Algiers and dictated terms to its ruling dey. By treaty, Algiers ended its demands for ransom and tribute and agreed to pay reparations to the United States. Decatur exacted similar agreements from the rulers of Tunis and Tripoli. The U.S. navy's actions in establishing American principles of freedom of the seas were widely celebrated as a great national victory and encouraged American merchants in their overseas ambitions.

The Advancing Frontier

A new pulse of westward migration began at war's end, bringing waves of settlers into the interior. This movement brought renewed pressure for expansion of the nation's borders and the opening of the frontiers for settlement. In Washington, President Monroe, who took office in March 1817, envisioned a continental destiny for the United States. He was encouraged in this by his secretary of state, John Quincy Adams.

RISE OF THE NEW WEST

The population of the United States grew dramatically in the first twenty years of the nineteenth century—more than 80 percent, from 5.3 million to 9.6 million. By 1820 almost 2.5 million Americans, or 25 percent of the total population, lived in regions west of the Appalachians; that number would more than double in the next ten years. Six new western states joined the union between 1812 and 1821—Louisiana, Indiana, Mississippi, Illinois, Alabama, and Missouri. After reapportionment in 1822, the new west held 47 of 213 seats in the House of Representatives, 18 of 48 seats in the Senate.

There were many reasons for the great westward migration across the mountains, all in some way related to the fact that there were rich and abundant lands in the interior. Knowledge of their availability at cheap prices became a factor in the older and more settled areas of the eastern seaboard, where the growth of towns and cities caused land to increase significantly in value (producing a profit for some, impossible prices for others). In many areas of the older plantation South, where farmland had been exhausted by staple crop agriculture, whole families (including slaves) migrated to the new states of the southwest territory, today the Deep South.

THE ROUTES OF WESTWARD MIGRATION
1815 – 1825

INDIAN REMOVALS

Following General William Henry Harrison's victories over the Indians of the Northwest Territory during the War of 1812, several treaties were concluded to open lands in Michigan, Indiana, and Illinois for settlement. The Indians were forced to migrate to lands west of the Mississippi River. In the southwest, action was taken in July 1816 against hostile Seminoles and runaway slaves, who were in possession of Fort Apalachicola in Spanish East Florida; this precipitated the First Seminole War (1817–18).

FLORIDA AND THE TRANS–CONTINENTAL TREATY

Command of American forces in the region was given to General Andrew Jackson in late 1817. He pursued the Seminoles into Florida, capturing Spanish forts in the process. During this campaign he also court–martialed and executed two British traders for having aided the Seminoles. Jackson's raids were popular at home, the cause of outrage abroad. They enabled Secretary of State Adams, who defended American actions as self–defense, to convince the Spanish that they could no longer effectively hold their colony.

Pressured by Adams, Spain agreed to cede Florida on condition that the United States assume unpaid claims of American citizens against Spain up to $5 million. The terms of the Adams–Onis Treaty of 1819 also provided for Spain to transfer its claims to the region north of California and west of the Rocky Mountains to the United States. The United States abandoned claims to Texas that it had derived from the Louisiana Purchase.

ANGLO–AMERICAN CONVENTION OF 1818

American interests in the Pacific Northwest were safeguarded in an agreement with the British government providing (1) that the northern boundary of the United States west of the Lake of the Woods was the 49th parallel to the Rockies; (2) that the Oregon country was to be held in joint occupation for ten years. At this time the region was principally of interest to companies engaged in the fur trade.

THE EMERGING NATIONAL ECONOMY

The economy of the United States before the War of 1812 was largely shaped by geography and its extensive river systems. Time and space worked against the creation and expansion of interregional markets, crucial to the prosperity of new inland settlements. In the years after the war, transportation projects and innovations, funded by private and public funds, refashioned nature and laid the foundations for a national market economy. To encourage this development, Congress passed legislation to regulate banking and encourage domestic manufacturing.

The Transportation Revolution

By cutting off the overseas and coastal trades, the embargo and the blockade put in place by the British in 1813 had demonstrated the inadequacies of the nation's roads and waterways for economic and military purposes. The economic premium placed on improvements in transportation stimulated private and public schemes for roads, canals, and related technological improvements.

INTERNAL IMPROVEMENTS

The rapid growth of the nation's population, particularly in the new western and southwestern regions, increased pressure for direct government support of internal improvements. Most championed were turnpike and canal projects. Funds for such improvements had been budgeted during the Jefferson administration and used to construct the National or Cumberland Road, from Cumberland, Maryland, to Wheeling on the Ohio River (1811–18).

The Bonus Bill of 1817. Despite sectional rivalries and states' rights prejudices, Congress passed a bill proposed by John C. Calhoun to set aside the bonus ($1.5 million) owed the government by the Bank of the United States to create a permanent fund for internal improvements. "Let us bind the republic together with a perfect system of roads and!canals," he implored. "Let us conquer space" In the last days of his presidency, Madison, though supportive of internal improvements, vetoed the bill, believing, as Monroe would after him, that such measures required a constitutional amendment.

State–Supported Improvements. Most of the new roads and canals that were constructed were financed by state appropriations and private capital. New York started work on the Erie Canal in 1817. Upon its completion in 1825, the Great Lakes were linked to New York City and the flow of trade redirected. The project was a financial success well before work was finished. Traffic on completed upstate sections was heavy.

The example of the Erie Canal stirred other states, mercantile interests, and entrepreneurs to frenzied action. They realized that they were in competition for the nation's trade and wealth—only by improving roads and waterways could they hope to bring the produce of the interior to their depots. Pennsylvania aided turnpike companies and canal promoters, notably to extend the Lancaster Pike, connecting Pittsburgh to Philadelphia—but with less success, largely because of geographical factors. New Jersey, Maryland, Virginia, Ohio, and Indiana supported similar projects.

Toll roads and canals made travel much easier and more comfortable, but freight still had to be transported by cart (or barges on canals) and animals. Inland freight transportation, particularly for heavy finished goods, made little progress against river currents. The solution of this grudging problem in the ongoing assault on space was left to the railroad.

STEAMBOATS

Since it was common knowledge that, for farmers and merchants alike, prosperity depended upon how fast producers could get their goods to market, it is not surprising that inventors and entrepreneurs made many efforts to improve travel by horsedrawn stage and sailboat. The financial rewards for increased speed were substantial.

Steam–powered carriages and vessels had lived in inventors' dreams for more than a century before the steamboat was first made practicable by John Fitch in Philadelphia in 1790. The invention was improved by the trials and errors of several others and commercially developed by Robert Fulton and his wealthy backer Robert R. Livingston. The steamboat proved difficult to perfect owing to the different requirements of the several river systems and the ocean. No one before Fulton had the capital and entrepreneurial skills required to make it a financial success. Steamboats were most noticeably a factor in the quickening economic activity on the western waters of the Ohio and Mississippi valleys, where (after their introduction in 1816) some seventy boats were in operation by 1820.

EFFECTS OF THE TRANSPORTATION REVOLUTION

Expansion and improvement of roads and waterways, aided by the development of new and faster vessels, made it possible for farmers and merchants to reach new and more distant markets. Greater and easier access to markets led in turn to regional specialization and interregional interdependency. Southern planters concentrated more and more on supplying cotton to British (and New England) textile producers. New England turned more and more to manufacturing. The northwest sold foodstuffs to both regions. By modern standards each region remained to a considerable extent self–sufficient.

National Finance

For the national economy to expand productively, it had to have an adequate supply of currency and credit. During this period the Treasury did not issue paper money or certificates—financial sources for expansion had to be gained elsewhere. Commercial and business investment depended on paper bank notes issued by state banks (redeemable for hard currency on demand) and on the credit extended by mercantile firms for commercial and business transactions. To resolve these inadequacies the nationalists, much like Hamilton before them, sought to establish a national system of finance.

THE BANKING SYSTEM

After Congress failed to recharter the Bank of the United States (1811), state–chartered banks increased rapidly, from 88 in 1811 to 246 in 1816. Only Massachusetts exercised control over the quantity of bank notes such banks were permitted to issue. The demand for credit in the first years of peace was enormous. By 1816 the amount of currency in circulation was twice as large as it had been five years earlier.

Second Bank of the United States. To curb what were perceived to be loose banking practices by the state banks and to check further inflation of the currency, Calhoun and Clay joined in securing a congressional charter for a second Bank of the United States (1816). One fifth of its capital stock was subscribed by the federal government, while more than 31,000 citizens purchased the remaining four–fifths. Through the issue of its own notes, the national bank (the B.U.S.) managed to compel state banks to limit their issues and to honor them at full face value.

THE PANIC OF 1819

Alarmed by the high level of speculation in the purchase and sale of western land, which state banks fueled with easy credit, the Bank of the United States took steps to contract the supply of paper bank notes in circulation. This action increased demand for redemption of bank notes in hard currency, which drained the undercapitalized resources of many state banks. The resulting deflation in prices set off a financial panic that produced a long and severe depression, with many losses, failures, and bankruptcies.

In the western and southern states, which were particularly hard hit, the B.U.S.'s action was bitterly resented. Antibank and debtor relief movements grew, transforming state and local politics. Congress provided some relief in 1820 and 1821. Prices for new land were reduced to encourage outright purchases. Distressed purchasers were credited with reductions in price and given extensions for installment payments.

The Growth of American Manufactures

The restrictions on the carrying and overseas trade under the embargo and the wartime blockade forced the United States to become more self–sufficient economically. Demand for domestically produced manufactured goods diverted capital investment from trade into industry and stimulated technological innovation. Without foreign competition, prices for such American goods had remained artificially high throughout the war. Manufacturing, particularly of textiles in New England, grew rapidly.

DEMANDS FOR PROTECTIONISM

Following the Treaty of Ghent and the reopening of trade, the British merchant fleet returned to American ports. In an effort to take back the business they had lost, British merchants engaged in the practice of "dumping" their exports on the American market—they sold manufactured goods at prices below production costs so as to regain customers at the expense of American producers. Since British goods were also in many cases superior to their American counterparts, such predatory pricing threatened doom for fledgling American businesses.

Domestic manufacturers lobbied Congress for protection, demanding that a high tariff or duty be placed on certain foreign goods entering the home market. Manufacturers of textiles in New England and of iron and metal goods in the middle Atlantic states were joined by growers of hemp in Kentucky and by sheep raisers in Ohio, New York, and Vermont to form a protectionist coalition. Farmers and those tied to commercial agriculture—who either exchanged their produce for, or purchased, finished goods, and consequently preferred the lowest prices possible—generally tended to oppose tariff protection.

The Tariff of 1816. Protectionism enjoyed wide support in Congress immediately after war, even among southerners, notably John C. Calhoun. The development of the home market, it was believed, would make the United States economically independent of Europe, benefitting all regions of the country.

The tariff legislation that passed in 1816 set high duties on selected woolen and cotton goods. New England's cotton manufacturers were thus able to retain domination of the market for coarse cotton fabrics. Still, woolen and cotton goods remained the nation's principal imports (amounting to 29 percent of the total in 1821).

BEGINNINGS OF THE FACTORY SYSTEM

The stimulus given to manufacturing also had an effect on methods of production. The domestic system of assembling products, whereby different components or processes were "put out" to workers in their homes, gradually died out. The various manufacturing functions were brought to a single site, the factory or mill.

The movement to a factory system of production was made possible by two innovations. Eli Whitney, of Connecticut, introduced the system of interchangeable parts (a concept of mass production) to manufacturing. By 1799 he was making pistols by assembling component parts (fabricated by machine tools). In 1813 three merchants, Francis Cabot Lowell, Patrick Tracy Jackson, and Nathan Appleton, who had formed the Boston Manufacturing Company, brought cloth production into one factory in the town of Waltham, Massachusetts. Here the entire process of spinning and weaving was accomplished by machines, driven by water power.

The Lowell Experiment. Although some of the new manufacturing concerns recruited whole families as factory workers, the methods introduced by the Boston Manufacturing Company proved to be the most widely influential. The new mill they established at Lowell, Massachusetts, was operated by young unmarried women, who lived closely regulated lives, residing in well–managed boardinghouses. These "factory girls" worked long and tedious hours for relatively low wages, but, except for the nature of the grouping, the conditions they encountered at Lowell and similar sites were probably not much different (and in some ways better) than those they knew on the New England farms. The decline of farming in New England caused many farm boys to go to sea or look for work in towns. The choices for their unmarried sisters were few, usually domestic service of some kind.

At this stage in the development of the American factory system, when labor was scarce, manufacturers sought to attract workers and provide them with a better alternative. Work conditions in Britain and Europe were decidedly different. There, where labor was not scarce, workers were generally exploited and not infrequently brutalized.

THE MARSHALL COURT

During John Marshall's long tenure as chief justice of the Supreme Court, the judicial branch became coequal with the legislative and executive branches. The decisions reached by the Court during this period enhanced the power of the national government and expanded the realm of property rights. The Court's rulings reduced the authority of the state governments, eliciting resentment from those who subscribed to the states' rights philosophy of the Kentucky and Virginia resolutions.

The Chief Justice's Influence

A Virginia Federalist, the disciple and biographer of George Washington, Marshall came to the high court at a time when the judiciary was weak and its constitutional role still in doubt. The Court's powers had barely been sketched in the final version of the Constitution (article III); an attempt made during the Constitutional Convention to specify its right of judicial review had been defeated. Like Hamilton, Chief Justice Marshall saw the Constitution as a framework for the construction of a nation, not as a sacred document that delimited the sphere of government. He also used the powers of the federal judiciary to prevent national economic development from being hindered by the several state legislatures and court systems.

Marshall was a dominating intellect and figure on the Supreme Court, serving from 1801 to 1835. Although Republicans held the presidency continuously during his tenure, and Jefferson and Madison made six appointments to the Supreme Court, the chief justice continued to win over his colleagues to his views. He wrote 519 of the 1,106 opinions the Court handed down during his time on the bench.

Asserting the Court's Jurisdiction

Marshall rejected states' rights theories, repeatedly holding that the Constitution was not a mere compact among sovereign states. His decisions effectively established the principle of judicial review and the Supreme Court's preeminent role as interpreter of the Constitution and arbiter of disputes in the American court system.

In *Marbury v. Madison* (1803), the Court struck down a provision of the Judiciary Act of 1789. In effect it asserted its authority to review Congress's use of its constitutional power to define the functions and jurisdiction of the federal judiciary (Article I, section 8).

In *Fletcher v. Peck* (1810), the Court struck down an act of the Georgia legislature, finding it conflicted with the Constitution's mandate that the states make no laws "impairing the obligation of contracts." Although it had previously stated its opinion concerning the constitutionality of state laws, this was the first time the Court had rendered such an act void. In *Martin v. Hunter's Lessee* (1816), the Court strongly maintained its appellate jurisdiction over the state courts when decisions were challenged on the basis of conflict with the federal Constitution. The principle was reasserted in *Dartmouth College v. Woodward* (1819) and, particularly forcibly, in *Cohens v. Virginia* (1821).

The Power of the Federal Government

In its review of state and federal legislation the Marshall Court regularly applied the doctrine of "implied powers," first invoked by Hamilton. The Court used the doctrine with great consistency to sanction the national government's powers to act in matters not specified in the Constitution.

In *McCulloch v. Maryland* (1819), Marshall, speaking for the Court, upheld the constitutionality of the second Bank of the United States, finding that it fell within what was "necessary and proper" for Congress to do in fulfilling its responsibility to coin and borrow money. He denied the right of the states to restrict the Bank's activity by taxing it, stating, in words borrowed from the argument of counsel Daniel Webster, that the power to tax contained the "power to destroy."

In *Gibbons v. Ogden* (1824), Marshall, for the Court, declared invalid a monopoly granted by New York State for the operation of steamboats. His far-reaching decision defined Congress's power to regulate so broadly that it embraced a large part of intrastate as well as interstate and foreign commerce. Commerce was not simply "traffic" but "every species of commercial intercourse." This decision was particularly significant for the growth of the nation's economy, permitting the development of regional and national markets and denying the states the ability to direct the flow of business.

The Protection of Property

The Marshall Court carefully scrutinized legislation that seemed hostile to property interests, particularly the acts of the states. State legislatures, tracing their origins to the colonial assemblies, had continued to be active in economic matters. For example, they continued to make grants of monopolies, or exclusive rights, to inventors after Congress had passed federal patent legislation (1790, 1793).

Fletcher v. Peck (1810) had effectively established the principle of the "sanctity" of contracts, also holding that "a grant is a contract." In the *Dartmouth College* case, the Court held that the charter of Dartmouth College, granted by King George III, was a valid contract and therefore could not be altered by the state of New Hampshire against the will of the college. In *Craig v. Missouri* (1830), Marshall offered a strict interpretation of the constitutional provision prohibiting the states from issuing bills of credit, thereby protecting creditors from an inflationary scheme.

THE "ERA OF GOOD FEELINGS" AND ITS AFTERMATH

After the War of 1812 the Federalist party's opposition to Republican administrations completely collapsed, giving the appearance of an "Era of Good Feelings." In 1820 President James Monroe was reelected with only one dissenting vote in the electoral college—that of William Plumer of New Hampshire, who believed the first Monroe administration had indulged in wasteful extravagance.

A strong nationalist, Monroe continued to be guided by precedents established in the Washington and Jefferson administrations, in which he had served; he even continued to dress in eighteenth–century "small clothes." The president consciously worked to promote harmony, still believing, like his predecessors in office, that political partisanship was dangerous to the republic.

The Missouri Compromise

Sectional differences related to the institution of slavery had been a major obstacle in the Constitutional Convention and a source of friction in the first Federal Congresses. After a period of dormancy, they reemerged in 1819 like "a fire bell in the night," as former President Jefferson put it.

THE TALLMADGE AMENDMENT

The territory of Missouri having applied for admission to statehood and a bill to that effect having been introduced, James Tallmadge of New York rose in the House of Representatives in February 1819 and proposed an amendment that threatened to disturb the numerical balance between slave and free states in the union. Slavery had been established in Missouri since its early settlement, and the proposed state constitution provided for the protection of property (implying property in slaves as well). Tallmadge proposed the gradual emancipation of slavery in Missouri by prohibiting the introduction of additional slaves and specifying that all children born to slave parents within the state would be free at the age of twenty–five. The House passed the amendment; the Senate rejected it. The Tallmadge amendment touched off a heated controversy, which the few remaining elected Federalists and some northern Republicans attempted to exploit at the expense of the "Virginia Dynasty."

Sectional Compromise. The Missouri question was resolved in 1820 after Maine (then a part of Massachusetts) applied for statehood. Engineered by Henry Clay, the Missouri Compromise provided for the admission of Missouri to the union as a slave state and of Maine as a free state, thus keeping the number of slave and free states in balance. Congress also legislated the principle that slavery was excluded from all of the territory embraced by the Louisiana Purchase north of latitude 36 30, except in Missouri itself. The nationalist mood of the country contributed to the desire for a resolution of the question by compromise.

The Monroe Doctrine

A renewal of European interest in the western hemisphere and a revival of European colonial ambitions caused the administration to adopt a vigilant nationalist foreign policy. In his presidential message of 1823, the president declared the position of the United States on European interference in the Americas, which over time became known as the Monroe Doctrine.

THE DIPLOMATIC BACKGROUND

Following the end of the Napoleonic Wars in Europe, Spain's colonies in Central and South America took up arms in attempts to win their independence. The United States adopted a policy of neutrality but, with public sentiment in America supportive of the patriot cause, took positions that had the effect of favoring the new republics. The federal government did not, for example, restrict the revolutionaries from purchasing armaments and matriel in the United States. Monroe and Secretary of State Adams attempted to enlist Great Britain's support for recognition of the Latin American governments, but, failing in this, the administration in 1822 gave official recognition to Colombia, Argentina, Peru, Mexico, and other states.

At the Congress of Verona (1822) the representatives of the Quadruple Alliance (Russia, Austria, Prussia, France) had considered a scheme that had as its goal the recolonization of Spain's former colonies in America. They had previously united to reestablish monarchies in Europe. Great Britain, which enjoyed a lucrative trade with the former Spanish colonies, refused to participate in such a policy. George Canning, the British foreign minister, suggested in 1823 that the United States join Great Britain in opposition to the intervention in Latin America—a proposal that gained the support of former presidents Jefferson and Madison. Britain's refusal to extend official recognition to the new republics remained an obstacle to such a collaboration. Canning began to back away from his proposal after the French government pledged not to intervene in Latin America.

Adams's Recommendations. Throughout his long career in diplomacy, Secretary Adams had been a strong nationalist and ardent expansionist. He and Monroe subscribed to the policy declared by President Washington (and his successors) against entangling alliances and disliked the idea of putting the United States in the position of appearing a "cock–boat in the wake of the British man–of–war."

Adams took the threat of the Quadruple Alliance seriously. He particularly feared that its intervention in Latin America might provoke Britain to take Cuba, which he believed in the natural course of things would join the United States ("an apple severed by the tempest from its native tree cannot choose but fall to the ground"). He was also alarmed by the Russian Czar's edict of 1821, in which the boundary of Russian Alaska was extended southward to the 51st parallel (within the Oregon country) and the western coast of North America was identified as a possible field for future Russian colonization. He believed the British proposal for collaboration presented the administration with an opportunity to make a bold statement concerning the differences between the New World and the Old. Confident that the British government would support the United States in any event, he urged Monroe to independent action.

MONROE'S MESSAGE TO CONGRESS

Monroe heeded Adams's advice and chose to announce the Monroe Doctrine in his presidential message of December 1823. In this communication he advised the European powers (1) that the North and South American continents were not to be considered fields for future colonization; (2) that the attempt by any European monarchy to extend its political system to the western hemisphere would be regarded as dangerous to the peace and safety of the United States; and (3) that the United States had no intention of interfering "in the internal concerns" of the European powers. Although the Monroe Doctrine was in fact merely a presidential proclamation of the national right of self–defense, it had important implications for American foreign policy. After years of indecision and vacillation in matters relating to the Latin American republics, the United States had found a clear and understandable basis for defining its national and hemispheric interests.

The ability of the United States to enforce the Monroe Doctrine in this period was limited; however, it did have an effect on the weaker European powers. In 1824, only months after the publication of Monroe's message, the Czar backed away from his earlier position and abandoned Russia's claim to the Oregon country.

Revival of Party Strife

Beneath the surface calm of the Era of Good Feelings, there were growing divisions. New political factions were forming, primarily in response to the depression caused by the Panic of 1819 but also in reaction to the centralizing and activist policies of the national government. A variety of interests began to coalesce under the banner of states' rights.

THE ELECTION OF 1824

The congressional caucus system had generally determined the nominees in presidential elections prior to 1820 (when Monroe was virtually unchallenged). In 1824, however, the nominee of the Republican caucus, Secretary of the Treasury William H. Crawford, of Georgia, who fell ill shortly after his nomination, was opposed by three other candidates put forward by their respective states: Andrew Jackson of Tennessee, Henry Clay of Kentucky, and John Quincy Adams of Massachusetts.

Crawford had the support of states' rights advocates. Jackson had served in both houses of Congress and was celebrated as a military hero, but he took no clear stand on political issues. Clay ran on his proposals to revive the nation's economy and build a domestic market. His American System called for spending on internal improvements, protection of domestic manufacturing by means of the tariff, and support for the Bank of the United States. Adams had an impressive record as a diplomat and statesman but no broad political appeal; like Clay he was strong on economic issues.

The Decision of the House. Jackson won a plurality of the popular vote, but he fell short of a majority in the electoral college, receiving 99 votes (Adams won 84, Crawford 41, Clay 37). The election was thus thrown into the House of Representatives, where Clay gave his support to Adams. When Jackson learned that Clay had been named secretary of state (by tradition the "heir apparent" to the president), he was persuaded that a political deal between Adams and Clay had robbed him of the presidency. His supporters decried the arrangement as a "corrupt bargain" and determined to insure his election in 1828. Jackson obliged them by beginning his campaign during Adams's first year in office. No evidence was presented to document the charge of corruption, but both Adams and Clay continued to be haunted by it.

DEMOCRATS AND NATIONAL REPUBLICANS

The Jacksonian leaders promoted a cult of personality for their hero, Old Hickory. A coalition that gradually resembled a political party formed around his candidacy. The great house of the Republican party began to fall apart. Calhoun, now vice–president, Crawford, and Martin Van Buren joined the anti–Adams forces after 1824, and, using the name Democrat, emphasized their return to fundamental Jeffersonian principles. Republicans who continued to support the administration called themselves National Republicans and embraced the nationalistic program of Clay and Adams.

THE SECOND PRESIDENT ADAMS (1825–1829)

John Quincy Adams was perhaps the most intelligent and learned man ever to serve as president of the United States. However, he lacked the attractive personal qualities that increasingly formed a requirement for popular support. His strongly nationalist agenda included proposals for spending on roads and canals and the construction of warships to strengthen national defense. He also revived Enlightenment ambitions in advocating measures to promote information, knowledge, and learning, to improve and enrich the nation culturally by means of legislative and administrative initiatives directed from Washington.

Adams had an array of political enemies in Congress and within the executive branch before he took the oath of office. Nevertheless, he refused to remove government officeholders and clerks who owed their appointments to his political opponents if they were competent. His sincerity and seriousness of purpose sounded a high but discordant note in the new age of rough–and–tumble politics and increasingly bitter partisanship.

The Adams administration never enjoyed good relations with Congress. The Senate fell into extended bickering over his proposal to send two delegates to the Panama Congress of Latin American republics, called by the patriot leader of Venezuela, Simon Bolivar (1826). It narrowly approved the mission, although the American representatives failed to reach the Congress before it adjourned due to delaying tactics employed by Jackson's supporters. The campaign to discredit the Adams administration played a large role in the political maneuvering that brought about the tariff of 1828 (also called the Tariff of Abominations; see chapter 9). The rates were set at extraordinarily high levels, in part to create a dilemma for the president. He nevertheless signed the bill.

Adams took a particularly unpopular stand in opposing the state of Georgia's effort to remove the last Creek Indians from lands within the state. He determined to uphold the good faith of the federal government, which had guaranteed the Indians' possession of their land under a 1791 treaty. Georgia had gained their approval to another agreement in 1825, but Adams believed it had been obtained by fraud. The confrontation, a unique episode in early Indian relations, ended in 1827 when the Creeks signed an enforceable agreement with the state.

*P*rior *to the War of 1812, Americans perceived their republican experiment as an international event, a manifestation of the Enlightenment values and ambitions that shaped the culture of the late eighteenth century. Significantly, the principal front of the first United States capitol (designed 1793) had faced east, toward Europe. The expectation that America's experiment would inspire a new republican order in Europe was disappointed, however—first by Napoleon and, after his defeat, by the revival of the European monarchies.*

Not suprisingly, after the happy conclusion of the War of 1812 and in the face of Europe's exhaustion, a new sense of American independence arose. The nation's attention shifted to the settlement and development of the interior; its thinking became more continental, its culture and speech more Americanized. The visit of the marquis de Lafayette in 1824 and the death of both Adams and Jefferson on July 4, 1826, confirmed Americans in their belief that the United States had a special destiny.

Selected Readings

Bemis, Samuel Flagg. *John Quincy Adams and the Foundations of American Foreign Policy* (1949)

Billington, Ray Allen. *Westward Expansion* (1974)

Dangerfield, George. *The Era of Good Feelings* (1963)

Dublin, Thomas. *Women at Work: The Transformation of Work and Community in Lowell, Massachusetts, 1826–1860* (1979)

Green, Constance McLaughlin. *Eli Whitney and the Birth of American Technology* (1956)

Horwitz, Morton. *The Transformation of American Law, 1780–1860* (1977)

Hunter, Louis T. *Steamboats on the Western Rivers* (1949)

Jeremy, David J. *Transatlantic Industrial Revolution: The Diffusion of Textile Technologies Between Britain and America, 1790–1830* (1981)

Mayo, Bernard. *Henry Clay: Spokesman of the New West* (1937)

Nevins, Alan. ed. *The Diary of John Quincy Adams, 1794–1845* (1951, 1969)

Scheiber, Harry N. *Ohio Canal Era* (1969)

Taylor, George Rogers. *The Transportation Revolution, 1815–1860* (1951)

Turner, Frederick Jackson. *The Rise of the New West* (1906)

Ware, Caroline F. *The Early New England Cotton Manufacture* (1931)

Wiltse, Charles M. *John C. Calhoun: American Nationalist, 1782–1828* (1944)

9

Jacksonian Democracy and Whig Opposition

1828 Tariff of Abominations passes (May); Calhoun writes South Carolina Exposition and Protest

1829 Jackson inaugurated president

1830 Hayne and Webster debate the nature of union (January); Congress passes Maysville Road bill (vetoed by Jackson) and Indian Removal Act

1831 Anti–Masonic party holds first national party convention (September)

1832 Congress votes recharter of the Bank of the United States (vetoed by Jackson); Democrats hold their first national nominating convention and reelect Jackson for a second term

1832 Congress passes tariff of 1832, which South Carolina nullifies, along with the 1828 tariff (November); Black Hawk War results in defeat of Sauk and Fox Indians

1833 Congress passes Force Bill (January) and Compromise Tariff of 1833 (March); South Carolina rescinds tariff nullification (March)

1833–1834 Jackson orders removal of federal funds deposited in the Bank of the United States and its branch offices and transfers to "pet banks"

1835 Chief Justice Marshall dies; Jackson names Roger B. Taney to succeed him

1836 Jackson issues Specie Circular (July); Van Buren wins presidency

1837 Supreme Court rules in *Charles River Bridge v. Warren Bridge*; financial panic precedes a depression (1840–1843)

1840 Congress passes Independent Treasury Act (July, repealed August 1841); presidential election contested by Van Buren and Whig candidate General William Henry Harrison of Indiana

1841 Harrison inaugurated (March) and dies (April); Tyler succeeds to the presidency

1842 Webster–Ashburton Treaty negotiated; Treaty of Wanghia, opening China to American trade, is concluded

The politicians who managed Andrew Jackson's campaign for the presidency in 1828 were the first to recognize the implications in the shift to direct elections—in that year only two states still chose presidential electors indirectly, in their state legislatures. The rule of "King Caucus," the selection of presidential candidates in closed congressional caucuses, had ended. Popular participation dictated a new political order. Jackson's men perceived that political theater had become an integral part of the election process.

The Republican consensus collapsed in the mid–1820s, giving rise to the second party system and intense party rivalries. However, competition between the Democrats and the Whigs, unlike that between the Federalists and the Republicans, served to strengthen the bonds of union. While it flourished the second party system effectively contained or masked the sectional differences that grew and intensified in response to regional patterns of economic development.

THE AGE OF THE "COMMON MAN"

During the 1820s and 1830s property requirements for voting and holding office were either eliminated or lowered. These and related changes encouraged a new era of participatory politics.

Political Reforms

The growth of the New West and consequent shifts in population soon had effects on state and national politics. By the late 1820s most states had drafted or modified their constitutions and laws so as to permit more direct popular participation in the electoral process.

GEOGRAPHICAL INTERESTS

The struggle between western and eastern interests in American politics, present from the colonial period, reemerged after the War of 1812. In Congress politics increasingly reflected the rise of the New West and political issues relating to its growth and development. In 1820, eighteen of the forty–eight members of the Senate represented western states. In the next decade the population of these states rose from 2.2 to 3.7 million.

The inhabitants of the western counties and frontier regions of the established eastern and southern states generally shared the outlook of the New West. They pressed for direct popular sovereignty, reapportionment of electoral districts, and greater representation in the legislatures of their states.

CHANGING STATE CONSTITUTIONS

Most of the eight new western states that entered the union before 1820 drafted constitutions that provided for frequent elections, removal of religious and property qualifications for the suffrage, and effective popular control of the executive and the judiciary. The older states followed, gradually loosening or eliminating property qualifications for voting and holding office during the 1820s and 1830s.

CHANGING ROLE OF THE POLITICAL PARTY

Coincidental with the expansion of the electorate were increases in the number of elected offices and more frequent elections. By the end of the decade a new attitude emphasizing the positive benefits of permanent political parties had emerged. The leading exponent and practitioner of the idea was Martin Van Buren, head of the popular Bucktail faction that wrested control of the Republican party in New York from the entrenched Governor DeWitt Clinton. Van Buren organized the first modern political "machine" in America, the Albany Regency, which after 1824 worked for the election of Jackson.

The Election of Andrew Jackson

The politicians who ran Jackson's campaign organized supporters and formed alliances on the state and local levels well in advance of the election of 1828. They were careful to subordinate specific issues to political image–making, to find the broadest basis for support in casting their appeal. The growing circulation of inexpensive newspapers enabled them to reach wide audiences.

In Jackson the new party managers had an ideal candidate—a popular military hero, western Indian fighter, and outspoken nationalist with few ideas. He was effectively portrayed as "Old Hickory," the "farmer from Tennessee," the "second Washington," the "friend of the common man." An elaborate ceremony celebrating the victory of the "Hero of New Orleans" was staged in that city in January 1828. The candidate was present to deliver ghostwritten speeches. Although effective, little of the image–making had much basis in fact. Jackson had been born in poverty in western North Carolina, to be sure, but those days were well behind him. He was a lawyer and successful land speculator, a rich cotton planter, squire of the Hermitage plantation, outside Nashville, Tennessee, which was worked by more then one hundred slaves. His political managers shamelessly directed a negative campaign against President Adams, portraying him as a corrupt aristocrat. Friends of Adams struck back with personal attacks of their own directed at

Jackson, but their attempts backfired. Adams himself practiced the old politics, remaining above the political fray. Jackson won a big victory in the election of 1828, carrying all of the southern and western states, Pennsylvania, and most of the electoral votes of New York—his margin in the electoral college was 178 to 83.

REMOVALS AND APPOINTMENTS

Expressing contempt for the trained expert and a belief that government could be made "plain and simple," Jackson declared his intention to remove competent as well as incompetent government clerks and officeholders. Despite his endorsement of the spoils system and the pressures to reward his supporters, the new president removed only about one-tenth of government employees who served under him during two presidential terms.

Jackson appointed Van Buren to what was considered the top post in his administration, that of secretary of state. His other cabinet appointments were made to satisfy the various factions of his party. The president never established close contact with Congress, and he surrounded himself with personal friends. This "Kitchen Cabinet" contained his principal political advisors and managers: William B. Lewis (who lived in the White House), Amos Kendall, Francis P. Blair, and Isaac Hill.

A feud quickly developed between the President and Vice–President John C. Calhoun, who had presidential ambitions and several friends in the cabinet. Calhoun's support of his wife, who with others engaged in a social campaign to ostracize Peggy Eaton, wife of the secretary of war (and a favorite of Jackson), angered the president. Calhoun's fall was complete after the President was told by his advisors that at the time of the First Seminole War (1818), Calhoun, as secretary of war, had recommended that he be court–martialed for his raids into Florida. Jackson removed the Calhoun supporters from his cabinet in 1831.

Democracy and Opportunity

Eager for rapid growth and expansion, the Jacksonians portrayed established economic interests as the bastions of "aristocracy." They called their new political party "the Democracy." Although Jackson's managers and supporters made effective use of the rhetoric of egalitarianism, the new administration pursued policies that expanded economic opportunities for the common man rather than measures to promote social reforms (civil liberties were still confined to white male citizens) or to regulate economic activities for the public good.

WESTERN LANDS AND INDIAN REMOVALS

Jacksonian Democrats pushed to lower the sales price for government land in the western regions and to gain easy terms for purchasers. Southern planters in particular coveted Indian lands for expansion of cash crop agriculture. Jacksonians in Congress attempted to legislate a progressive reduction in the price of public land unsold after a given period. The administration opposed Henry Clay's proposal to distribute the proceeds from the sale of public lands to the states.

In his first annual message to Congress, Jackson urged a speedy and complete removal of Indian tribes to the region beyond the Mississippi. As a consequence of the Removal Act of 1830, more than ninety treaties were concluded during his eight years in office to compel the remaining 60,000 Indians to surrender some 25 million acres in the states east of the Mississippi. Jackson did not mask his personal hatred for "savages"; he refused to recognize Indian lands guaranteed by previous treaties with the federal government. He even went so far as to support actions against the Cherokees taken by the state of Georgia in defiance of federal authority. He also refused to enforce the Supreme Court's ruling against the state's unilateral action in *Worcester v. Georgia* (1830).

Several tribes resisted. The Sauk and Fox under Chief Black Hawk, who had returned to Illinois, were crushed by the Illinois militia in what became known as the Black Hawk War (1832). The Cherokee nation, which had adopted a republican form of government and taken up agricultural ways, resisted the attempt to infringe on their treaty rights. Jackson dispatched troops to force them to move westward to lands considered deserts; most Cherokees followed the "Trail of Tears" (on which many died) to Oklahoma in 1838.

The Seminoles likewise refused to accept a treaty of removal, and their chieftain, Osceola, fought to keep their lands. The Second Seminole War, in which the Seminoles, joined by their black allies (who had run away from the plantations of the deep south), fought a guerilla action that lasted from 1835 until 1843, when the government gave up the effort to defeat Osceola's surviving forces. Against this background, the Bureau of Indian Affairs was formed in 1836 to administer the western reservations (which the U.S. army was to oversee).

JACKSONIANS AND THE SUPREME COURT

When John Marshall died in 1835, Jackson appointed a loyal political lieutenant, Roger B. Taney, to replace him as chief justice. Though Taney was by no means a dominating figure, there was an increasingly Jacksonian direction, a bias in favor of expanding economic opportunity, in the Supreme Court's decisions while he was on the bench. This trend was made clear in the case of *Charles River Bridge v. Warren Bridge* (1837), which concerned the state charters of two companies operating toll bridges over the Charles River, in Massachusetts. The Court found that the first–issued charter could not exclude the competition of a second company and bridge. In his opinion, Taney modified the Marshall Court's doctrine on the sanctity of contracts, finding that the states could amend or void contracts when the public good required it.

STATES RIGHTS AND THE UNION

The personal quarrel between President Jackson and Vice–President Calhoun reflected a growing constitutional crisis over the question of states' rights and federal authority. Led by South Carolina, the states of the old South became increasingly outspoken in reaction to the high tariff duties on imported goods. Jackson shifted course in attempts to maintain his political strength in the South, but when Calhoun and South Carolina threatened to leave the union, he acted decisively.

Jackson and Internal Improvements

Although Jackson had favored federal support for internal improvments prior to taking office, he altered his position once in office to gain support from states' rights advocates of the South and inflict a blow on his rival, Clay. In 1830 he vetoed a bill authorizing the federal government to subscribe to the stock of the Maysville and Lexington (Kentucky) Turnpike, intended as an extension of the National Road. Echoing the veto messages of Madison and Monroe on similar subjects, he called for a constitutional amendment to resolve questions about such legislation; he asserted that the Maysville Road (to be constructed within Kentucky) was more properly a state than a federal project. Despite this stricter standard for federal funding, total expenditures on federal internal improvements increased during his administration.

Calhoun and the Tariff

Calhoun had vigorously supported the protective tariff of 1816, expecting that South Carolina would benefit from it and share in the industrial expansion of the nation. The economy of the state, however, grew more and more dependent on cotton growing, its lands steadily exhausted for lack of crop rotation or fertilization. With the opening up of the rich lands of Alabama and Mississippi, which many South Carolinians left to work, cotton production dramatically increased, causing prices to fall. South Carolina's population growth dropped to insignificant levels and, unable to compete with the better lands of the southwest, its agricultural production declined.

Ignoring these economic factors, planters of the old South blamed their plight on the protective tariff, which increased the cost of the imported goods they bought from abroad (principally Britain). While South Carolina's economic position declined, protectionist sentiment in New England and the middle states grew.

THE TARIFF OF ABOMINATIONS (1828)

The tariff legislation of 1828 had been the product of election-year politics. Jacksonians in Congress had attempted to persuade both protectionist and low–tariff men that their leader was "safe" on the tariff question. Southern supporters of Jackson, led by Calhoun, permitted rates to be pushed to excessive levels in certain schedules in the hope that the Adams men in New England would find the bill unpalatable and vote it down. The tactic backfired, however, leading embarassed southern politicians to blame northern interests for the outcome.

THE SOUTH CAROLINA EXPOSITION AND PROTEST

Fearful that his state's hostility to the tariff might result in secession, Calhoun turned to the Virginia and Kentucky resolutions of Madison and Jefferson (1798–99) to devise a constitutional mechanism to check the rule of the majority. He adopted and expanded upon Jefferson's concept of nullification and put forward a systematic states' rights theory of the union. The South Carolina Exposition and Protest was published by the state legislature, without indicating Calhoun's authorship, in 1828.

Calhoun began his tract by asserting that the Constitution was a compact between the states (or "principals"). The union they had created was merely their "agent"; they had retained sovereignty. When the constitutionality of specific legislation was in question, therefore, the states had the recourse of "interposing" themselves and nullifying or voiding a measure they found to be unconstitutional. A specially called state convention, embodying the state's sovereignty, could apply the remedy of nullifying and preventing the enforcement of an act of Congress within the state. The objectionable legislation could then be enforced only by ratification of an amendment to the Federal constitution, which required the approval of three–fourths of the states. If an amendment were ratified, the objecting state had the choice of submitting or seceding from the union.

Following the procedure outlined by Calhoun, the South Carolina legislature passed a series of eight resolutions declaring the 1828 tariff unconstitutional. But Calhoun, then a candidate for reelection as vice–president on the ticket with Jackson, urged his state not to attempt nullification until it could be determined what course the new administration would take in tariff matters.

THE WEBSTER–HAYNE DEBATE (1830)

A major controversy erupted in the Senate in January 1830 when Senator Samuel A. Foot of Connecticut proposed that Congress investigate the desirability of temporarily limiting public land sales. This provoked Thomas Hart Benton of Missouri to charge that eastern manufacturing interests wished to restrict the growth and prosperity of the new western states. Eager to form a sectional alliance to defeat the tariff, Senator Robert Y. Hayne of

South Carolina supported Benton, declaring that the South and the west were victims of New England's manufacturing interests.

Daniel Webster, senator from Massachusetts, took the floor to reply to Hayne's remarks, the argument moving from the question of public lands to the constitutional basis of the union. Hayne presented Calhoun's views on state sovereignty and the doctrine of nullification. Webster, in his famous reply, rebutted them—the states were sovereign only in their sphere. The Constitution, "erected by the people," had granted the federal government superior authority in certain specified powers.

Who was to decide the constitutionality of federal laws? Webster asked. The Supreme Court, the judicial branch created by the Constitution. Webster then shifted the question from what the framers had intended, in effect admitting the historical basis for the compact theory; he elaborated on the consequences of acceding to South Carolina's theory, which he suggested would be disunion and civil war. He concluded with the ringing words "liberty and union, now and forever, one and inseparable."

Webster's text was widely reprinted, acclaimed by former presidents Madison and Monroe as well as by the public. President Jackson, who had sent a message of congratulations to Hayne after his speech, took note. At a political dinner celebrating Jefferson's birthday a few months after the debate, at which Calhoun was also present, he stunned states' rights advocates with the carefully calculated toast: "Our federal union: it must be preserved." Calhoun's reply: "The union—next to our liberty most dear."

The Nullification Controversy

South Carolinians closely followed the deliberations of Congress on tariff matters. In his presidential message of December 1830, Jackson recommended a decrease in tariff duties to conciliate the South but observed that the protective tariff of 1828 was constitutional.

THE TARIFF OF 1832

On July 14, 1832, Jackson signed a new tariff act, which reduced duties to levels slightly below those set by the legislation of 1828. The reaffirmation of protectionism, however, strengthened the pronullification party in South Carolina, which won control of the state's legislature and quickly issued a call for a state convention to consider the momentous question of nullification.

THE ORDINANCE OF NULLIFICATION

South Carolina's state convention convened in November 1832. It passed an ordinance declaring the tariff acts of 1828 and 1832 null and void, prohibiting the collection of customs duties within the state and threatening secession if the federal government used force. The legislature made provisions for raising and arming troops and elected Calhoun, who then resigned from the vice–presidency, to the U.S. Senate. Its invitation to other state legislatures to meet in a general convention elicited only denunciations of its actions.

JACKSON AND THE FORCE BILL

In December 1832 President Jackson issued a proclamation to the people of South Carolina, declaring that federal laws could not be disobeyed, that secession was illegal, and that "disunion by armed force is treason." He stationed warships in Charleston harbor, transferred artillery to Fort Moultrie, and held troops in readiness. In January 1833 he asked Congress to endorse the use of military action to enforce federal laws.

The Compromise of 1833. Calhoun, aware of his state's isolated position, and Clay, seeking to defuse the crisis, cooperated in pushing through a compromise. On March 2, 1833, Congress passed a new tariff law, providing for a gradual reduction of tariff rates over ten years until they reached 20 percent ad valorem (that is, of the value of an item). The Force Bill, authorizing the president to use the army and navy to collect duties, was enacted on the same day. Following the lead of Calhoun, South Carolina suspended and then (in convention) rescinded its ordinance of nullification. However, the convention reasserted the legitimacy of state action by nullifying the Force Bill.

THE "BANK WAR" AND PARTY POLITICS

During the same week that he signed the tariff of 1832, Jackson vetoed a bill that would have renewed the charter of the Bank of the United States. The fight over his presidential veto played into the skillful hands of Jackson's advisors, who successfully transformed the contest into a symbolic popular campaign against monopoly and special privilege.

Jackson and the Bank

Jackson had signaled hostility to the Bank of the United States in his first annual presidential message, citing questions about its constitutionality and effectiveness. A substantial portion of the Democratic party represented the interests of state banks, which coveted federal deposits in the Bank's branch offices and wished to be free of their supervisory interference. Others such as Jackson himself, particularly southerners and westerners, expressed provincial distrust of banks and corporations of all kinds, believing only hard money had real value. Van Buren, the mastermind of the Bank war, realized that the destruction of the B.U.S. would benefit the financial interests of New York City and reduce those of Philadelphia.

BIDDLE AND THE B.U.S.

Under the leadership of Nicholas Biddle, a member of a wealthy Philadelphia family who became its president in 1823, the Bank of the United States had brought order to the nation's financial system, generally pursuing conservative banking policies in the national interest. The B.U.S., though a private institution, was closely connected to the U.S. government, which owned 20 percent of its stock. It was the only bank to hold deposits of federal monies. With headquarters in Philadelphia and twenty–nine other branch offices in other cities around the country, the B.U.S. exercised wide influence in the national economy. Since it regularly used its financial powers to limit the supply of bank notes issued by state banks and served to check easy credit, the Bank was hated in expanding frontier regions and opposed by entrepreneurs and debtors.

The Bank had been chartered for twenty years in 1816 and did not require congressional reauthorization until 1836. It had generally remained neutral in politics, but Jackson's outspoken hostility to the institution (and the prospect of his reelection) irritated Biddle and caused him to take a new and dangerous course. He began to lend money and extend favors to members of Congress to strengthen support for the Bank. On the advice of Daniel Webster and Henry Clay, Jackson's principal opponent for reelection, Biddle chose to push for recharter legislation before the presidential election of 1832.

JACKSON'S VETO MESSAGE

The Bank bill passed both houses of Congress but was vetoed by the president in a strong message prepared by his advisors, calculated for use in the presidential campaign.

Jackson's message described an institution that had become too large and independent, too powerful to be given control of banking and finance in the states. He denounced the B.U.S. and its practices, accusing Biddle and the Bank's stockholders of being "a favored class," "opulent citizens" advancing their own interests at the expense of "humble members of society—the farmers, mechanics, and laborers." Even worse, Jackson observed, was the fact that "more than a fourth part" of the Bank's stock was held by foreign investors, a fact he whipped up into a threat to the nation's liberty and independence: "If we must have a bank with private stockholders, every consideration of sound policy and every impulse of American feeling admonishes that it should be purely American."

The Election of 1832

With the Bank veto message, Jackson's advisors had again accurately measured popular sentiment, providing the president with a ringing, if demagogic, popular issue. By exaggerating the role of the common enemy, the "Monster Bank," they also managed to keep their coalition of often conflicting component groups (such as those of "hard money" and state banking interests) together.

THE NATIONAL PARTY CONVENTION

In September 1831, the Anti–Masonic party had held the first national nominating convention—delegates met as representatives to nominate William Wirt of Maryland as their presidential candidate, and drafted the first national party platform. In December the National Republicans met in Baltimore to nominate Henry Clay for president and draft a platform. In May 1832, the Democratic party held its first national convention in the same city and renominated Jackson for a second term, without a platform. The adoption of the party nominating convention further increased the role of popular participation in national politics. But at the same time, it justified the role of the party leaders and managers, increasingly professional politicians, and provided an enlarged arena for the political machine.

THE JACKSON–CLAY CAMPAIGN

Henry Clay, the popular "Spokesman of the West," overlooked the new power of public opinion in the presidential campaign of 1832. Misled by the passage of the recharter legislation, the great parliamentarian confidently expected to defeat Jackson with the Bank issue. Biddle directly aided Clay's campaign and used his patronage and influence to buy newspaper endorsements. Nevertheless, Jackson was reelected by a wide margin, with Van Buren (whom the Senate had refused to confirm as minister to Great Britain) as vice–president.

The Bank and Federal Deposits

Jackson interpreted his reelection as a mandate to destroy the Bank. Infuriated by Biddle's use of the Bank's resources in support of Clay's candidacy, he determined to "kill" the institution by removing federal deposits from its control. He had to dismiss two treasury secretaries (who feared the financial consequences of the action) before a third, the loyal Roger Taney, dutifully drew out the governmental surpluses. Federal funds were then deposited with selected state banks, called the administration's "pet banks" (on one of which Taney served as a director).

Biddle responded to the removal of federal funds by taking measures to reduce the B.U.S.'s lending and by raising its interest rates on new loans. He believed that the move was required by the reduction of the Bank's capital, but extended and prolonged the tightening in the hope that the inevitable recession (which indeed came, 1833–34) would be blamed on Jackson. While the opposition to Jackson's policies grew, Biddle's action served only to strengthen Jackson's claim that the Bank and its president were too powerful and independent.

The Second Party System

By the late 1830s a new two–party political system structured American politics. This second party system was profoundly different from the first in its emphasis on grass–roots organization and party loyalty. Democrats and Whigs, reflecting different concepts of growth and expansion, contested elective offices on the national, state, and local levels.

FORMATION OF THE WHIG PARTY

Hostility to the methods and policies of President Jackson eventually produced a coalition that formed a permanent opposition party. The Whigs declared opposition to "King Andrew I," recalling the political tradition of the era of the American Revolution and opposition to King George III. The party took form between 1834 and 1836. Its nucleus was one part of the old Republican party, the National Republicans of the Clay–Adams school. Other groups joining the Whig ranks included (1) fiscal conservatives who opposed Jackson's attacks on the Bank and the financial system; (2) native–born Americans hostile to the growing numbers of foreign immigrants (who more frequently became Democrats); and (3) states' rights advocates who had broken with the Democrats because of Jackson's handling of the nullification controversy.

PARTY CREEDS AND LOYALTIES

The Democrats and the Whigs presented two quite different visions of the future to American voters during what became annual campaigns on the state and local levels. Still, the parties shared many ideas and beliefs, and both were continuously engaged in efforts to harmonize radical and conservative elements.

Whigs. Whigs advocated steady growth through careful nurturance. They wished to develop the national economy of the country as an integrated domestic market. They thus encouraged manufacturers and subscribed to Clay's American System. They embraced the idea as well as the political issue of internal improvement. For this reason they for some time opposed territorial expansion of the nation, believing it scattered the nation's wealth and resources and hampered economic growth. Those in the manufacturing sector, capitalists and workers, tended to support the Whig program. Whigs disputed the idea that there was an innate conflict between capital and labor (which their protectionist policies, by reducing foreign competition, tended to mute).

The Whigs believed in institutions, professed faith in church (they were overwhelmingly Protestant) and family, and decried the lack of order and stability in Jacksonian society. They were stronger in the settled communities of the nation and among the older British stock of inhabitants, but they were not in fundamental terms conservative. They generally embraced the idea of progress, accepted technological innovation, and were active in many social reforms.

Democrats. Democrats feared the consequences of "consolidation" of power and believed the Whig program, by increasing the value of land, would raise prices beyond the reach of the common man. Whig measures, they believed, would be detrimental to the worker and small landholder and only further enrich the monied class. Their hopes lay in a continuing process of westward expansion, a constant supply of cheap land and a safety valve for those who wished to retain their independence. In an age of boom and bust economic cycles (and no government "safety nets"), this remedy for hopes and disappointments had tremendous appeal.

The Democratic rhetoric of unlimited freedom attracted many groups within the rapidly expanding American population—such as those with entrepreneurial ambitions and most, but not all, non–British immigrants. To prevent the entrenchment of power and privilege, Democrats advocated a small and relatively passive national government and rotation in office. In practice, however, they pursued many of the measures advocated by Whigs, such as internal improvements, on the state level. Their rhetoric also masked their own injustices—the opportunities presented by cheap western lands, for example, were more often than not seized by land speculators and developers, who sold small portions to new settlers at marked–up prices. Democrats were not an antibusiness party—they enjoyed the support of commercial, manufacturing, and farming interests that were opposed to protection and centralizing policies.

Party Factions. Both parties contained discordant elements. Democrats were divided on fiscal and currency matters. The majority supported an expansionist monetary policy, "soft money" or easy credit through state banking systems. However, a significant number of Democrats (such as Jackson himself) distrusted all banks. The Workingman's party, or Loco-focos, which emerged in 1834–35 in New York and other northern cities, believed that banks fostered inflation (robbing the worker of the value of his labor) and insisted that workingmen's wages be paid only in hard currency. They also resisted technological change, fearing that new machines would eliminate jobs.

Whigs had equally contradictory elements within their coalition. Southern Whigs were advocates of states' rights and tended to be strict constructionists. The Whig party also absorbed the Anti–Masonic, which had formed with surprising strength in opposition to secret and privileged societies. (Their principal concern was with the secret Society of Freemasons, of which both Jackson and Van Buren were members.)

THE ELECTION OF 1836

Jackson's influence was strong enough to gain the election of his hand–picked successor, Vice–President Martin Van Buren. The Whigs adopted a regional strategy, devised by Biddle, in attempts to throw the election into the House of Representatives. They ran three candidates—Daniel Webster (northeast), William Henry Harrison (west), and Hugh Lawson White (south). Still, Van Buren won by a small majority of the popular vote and received 170 votes in the electoral college to 124 for the three Whigs.

The Panic of 1837

The last years of Jackson's presidency were marked by rapid economic expansion, flush times fueled by the activity of the state banks (some eitghty-nine of which had begun to receive government funds under the new deposit system). The excesses contributed to the financial panic and economic depression that began in 1837.

SPECULATIVE BOOM

The rapid growth and extension of the population of the United States, in a period of largely unregulated economic activity, made a boom and bust cycle of some proportion inevitable. The effects of Jacksonian policies, however, exaggerated the phenomenon.

The construction of turnpikes, canals, and railroads by private investors and state governments had stimulated new settlements and the formation of new markets. Prices of town lots as well as farm lands rose, reflecting the exuberant confidence in the future of the nation. The steady increase in government land sales reached boom proportions in 1835 and 1836; the government's receipts in 1836 ($24 million) were ten times those of 1834. Faced with huge surpluses in government revenues, the Congress and the president agreed in 1836 to distribute large sums (based on congressional representation) to the states, which were quickly expended on transportation projects.

The expansion of credit more than accommodated the requirements of economic growth and new settlement. The issuance of bank notes and credit by state banks, the growth of foreign investment in state bonds and the stocks of railroad and canal companies, combined with the elimination of the B.U.S.'s restraining influence, contributed to a speculative mania in 1835–37. Prices spiked to levels that overconfidently discounted (or anticipated) future successes.

THE SPECIE CIRCULAR (1836)

By July 1836, Jackson and his advisors had become alarmed by the extent to which payment for federal lands was being made with largely unsecured bank notes (resting upon inflated land values). In order to check inflation and to protect the government revenues, the president issued the Specie Circular, requiring federal land offices to receive only gold and silver in payment for government lands. This order curbed speculative land ventures but, together with the payment of the federal surplus (out of the "pet" deposit banks) to the states, set in motion a violent deflation.

FINANCIAL CRASH

The market value of the state bank notes dropped sharply. Panicked European investors, already worried by economic troubles in their own countries, attempted to liquidate their American securities on the open market. Eastern banks, which were pressed to meet foreign obligations, called in the loans they had advanced to banks in the South and west.

The nation's credit system collapsed. Excessive demand for gold and silver caused banks across the country to suspend specie payments (or redemption of paper bank notes). Debtors defaulted on loans. Several states repudiated their state bonds. During the next few years many banks and businesses closed their doors; factories and shops shut down. Crop failures, especially in 1837, further worsened conditions.

VAN BUREN'S REMEDIES

Government revenues from customs and land sales fell off so rapidly that the Van Buren administration approved the issue of $10 million in Treasury notes as an emergency measure. Some 20 million acres of public land had been sold in 1836; only 3.5 million in 1838. The distribution of the surplus funds to the states was suspended. After a long fight in Congress, the Independent Treasury Act (1840) was signed, whereby the government was divorced from the banking system and "subtreasuries" were created in the important cities as depositories of government funds.

THE WHIGS AND THE ELECTION OF 1840

In 1840 the country was still in a depression. The Whigs had little difficulty blaming the Panic of 1837 on Jackson's policies and Van Buren's failure to find solutions.

The "Log Cabin and Hard Cider" Campaign

The Whig party was grounded in deep differences over political and economic issues. But, remembering how the Democrats had manipulated the Bank issue, delegates to the Whig nominating convention passed over the party's leader, Henry Clay, and selected General William Henry Harrison as their candidate for president. The capture of the presidency was the sole objective of party professionals like the powerful Thurlow Weed of New York.

Whigs skillfully exploited the Jacksonian formula for electioneering success—winning a great popular majority with a military hero and Indian fighter (noted for his victory at the Battle of Tippecanoe), clever images and slogans, and a well–organized political machine. They presented Harrison as the log–cabin candidate (though he had been born in a mansion in tidewater Virginia) and the "man of the people." In a manner reminiscent of Jacksonian characterizations of John Quincy Adams, they succeeded in portraying Van Buren as an aristocratic, Europeanized dandy.

In a campaign remarkable for noise and the constant display of coonskin caps, cider barrels, and miniature log cabins, the Whigs outshouted and outvoted the Democrats. Harrison took 53 percent of the popular vote, the electoral college by 234 to 60. Clay, still the Whig leader, confided that he lamented "the necessity, real or imaginary, which had been supposed to exist, of appealing to the feelings and passions of our countrymen, rather than to their reasons and their judgments."

"Tyler too."

To strengthen their party in the South, the Whigs had nominated John Tyler, a states' rights Virginian, who hated Andrew Jackson but was really no friend of the policies championed by Clay and Webster. This had given them a jingle–like ticket—"Tippecanoe and Tyler too"—but it soon became a taunt. Harrison died of pneumonia five weeks after his inauguration. Tyler became the first vice–president to succeed to the presidency in this way.

THE WHIG LEGISLATIVE AGENDA

With majorities in both houses of Congress, the Whigs called a special session in 1841 to enact their party's national legislative program. Their agenda included (1) repeal of the Independent Treasury Act and the charter of a new Bank of the United States; (2) the enactment of a protective tariff; (3) the "log cabin bill" (the Preemption Act of 1841), originally put forward by the Democrats, which provided easier terms for obtaining western lands; and (4) a measure to distribute the proceeds from the sale of public lands to the states. This was in essence an updated version of Clay's American System.

The Independent Treasury Act was quickly repealed, but the Whigs in Congress could not convince President Tyler to approve legislation (he vetoed two bills) to form a new national bank. After much wrangling, Tyler did sign the moderately protective tariff act of 1842, but he refused to permit the tariff to go into effect unless Clay abandoned his plan to distribute the land sales to the states.

Tyler's Cabinet. Tyler's refusal to accept Clay's program brought about open war between the Whig leaders in Congress and the president (whom they dubbed "His Accidency"). Clay's followers in the cabinet resigned. Following the recapture of the House of Representatives by Democrats in the 1842 elections, Clay left the Senate. Tyler's new cabinet and policies reflected an unmistakable states' rights and pro–South bias, which cut across established party lines. The change in direction was punctuated by his appointment in 1844 of Calhoun, now again a Democrat, as secretary of state.

Whig Diplomacy

Daniel Webster, secretary of state, did not resign from the Cabinet with other Harrison appointees, choosing to proceed with negotiations he had begun with Great Britain on several difficult issues, which had in fact brought the two nations close to war.

ANGLO–AMERICAN CONTROVERIES

The chief questions were the dispute concerning the boundary between Maine and New Brunswick and the unsatisfactory joint occupation of the Oregon country. Minor but irritating grievances included (1) the *Caroline* incident, in which British authorities in Canada had destroyed an American ship hired to supply Canadian rebels during the country's 1837 rebellion; (2) the *Creole* case, involving American slaves who mutinied and sailed to the Bahamas, where they were freed by British authorities; (3) British interference with American merchant ships suspected of engaging in the slave trade; and (4) complaints against several states that had repudiated their debts to British investors.

The Webster–Ashburton Treaty. When Robert Peel replaced Lord Melbourne as prime minister of Great Britain in 1841, his new government sent the friendly Lord Ashburton to Washington to negotiate differences. The treaty he and Secretary Webster signed in August 1842 (1) settled the Maine–New Brunswick boundary by defining a compromise line, which gave the United States 7,000 of the 12,000 square miles in dispute, and (2) provided for American ships to join British patrols off the coast of west Africa to police slave traders flying the American flag. The *Creole* case and the Oregon question were not resolved, but Ashburton conveyed "regret" for the attack on the *Caroline*. The treaty averted war and improved relations between the two countries.

THE CHINA TRADE

American, principally New England, merchants had been trading with China, through Canton, since 1785. The typical voyage to the Orient included a stop in the Pacific northwest to obtain furs to exchange with the Chinese. Following Great Britain's success in forcing the Chinese to expand trade with foreigners in 1842, the United States, through its commissioner Caleb Cushing (backed by four U.S. navy warships), negotiated a commercial treaty that gave American merchants privileges identical, and in some particulars superior, to those gained by the British. The Treaty of Wanghia marked the beginning of a period of expanding trade with China and renewed interest, especially on the part of northern Whigs, in the strategic importance of the Oregon country and the Pacific Coast.

In the 1820s and 1830s constitutional checks on the direct popular vote, originally believed necessary to prevent the tyranny of the majority, were gradually eliminated. The founding fathers' views on political power—and their fears of its abuse—seemed out of date in the new democratic age. The people chose a popular military hero as national leader. From the White House he embarked on a "dismantling operation" of the federal government to check concentrations of power and privilege and expand opportunities for the common man. The apparatus that his lieutenants employed to capture the presidency, the political party and machine, introduced a new if extraconstitutional mechanism of national cohesion.

Jackson's policy of weakening the power of the national government, and of interests that coalesced around it, however, had its dangers. His victory in the Bank war led to instability in the financial system, which led to a panic that took back the gains his supporters had realized from their expanded opportunities. Faced with an extreme expression of states' rights, the nullification movement, he was forced to define the limits of his dismantling principles. He acted decisively once he perceived a threat to the corporate union. The states' rights theory that underlay his politics on the national level would not be permitted to obstruct the principle of majority rule. And yet Old Hickory could not arrest the deepening divisions created by economic and social forces.

Selected Readings

Cole, Donald B. *Martin Van Buren and the American Political System* (1984)

Debo, Angie. *And Still the Waters Run: The Betrayal of the Five Civilized Tribes* (1973)

Freehling, William V. *Prelude to Civil War: The Nullification Controversy in South Carolina* (1966)

Hammond, Bray. *Banks and Politics in American from the Revolution to the Civil War* (1957)

Howe, Daniel Walker. *The Political Culture of American Whigs* (1979)

Meyers, Marvin. *The Jacksonian Persuasion: Politics and Belief* (1960)

Pessen, Edward. *Jacksonian America: Society, Personality, and Politics* (rev. ed., 1979)

Prucha, Francis Paul. *American Indian Policy in the Formative Years* (1962)

Rohrbough, Malcolm J. *The Land Office Business: 1789–1837* (1968)

Tocqueville, Alexis de. *Democracy in America* (1st ed., 1835; trans. George Lawrence and ed. J.P. Mayer and Max Lerner) (1966)

Ward, John W. *Andrew Jackson: Symbol for an Age* (1955)

Wilson, Major L. *Space, Time, and Freedom: The Quest for Nationality and the Irrepressible Conflict, 1815-1861* (1974)

10

American Society at Mid–century

1793 Cotton gin invented by Eli Whitney, of Connecticut

1800 Gabriel Prosser, a slave, attempts to lead an insurrection of some 1,000 slaves near Richmond, Virginia; he and thirty-five others are executed

1801 Revival meeting at Cane Ridge, Kentucky, marks beginning of Second Great Awakening

1817 Formation of the American Colonization Society

1822 Plans of Denmark Vesey, a free black, for a slave insurrection in Charleston, South Carolina, are discovered

1823 Publication of James Fenimore Cooper's first "Leatherstocking" novel, *The Pioneers*

1824 New Harmony experiment begun by Robert Owen

1826 The American Temperance Society is founded

1829 David Walker, a free black of Boston, publishes his *Appeal to the Colored Citizens*, urging slaves to "kill, or be killed!"

1831 Insurrection of slaves in Virginia led by Nat Turner results in death of some sixty whites; William Lloyd Garrison begins to publish the *Liberator* calling for "immediate and complete emancipation"

1832 Key vote in the Virginia legislature defeats hopes for gradual emancipation

1833 Founding of the American Antislavery Society

1834 Patent issued to Cyrus H. McCormick for his reaper

1837 Mob attack kills abolitionist editor Elijah Lovejoy in Alton, Illinois

1837 Ralph Waldo Emerson delivers his "The American Scholar" address at Harvard University

1839 Patent issued to John Deere for his steel plow

1844 Telegraph successfully demonstrated by painter and inventor Samuel F. B. Morse; organization of Brook Farm community near Roxbury, Massachusetts; Millerites assemble to witness the end of the world

1845 Frederick Douglass publishes his autobiography Edgar Allan Poe his The *Raven and Other Poems*

1846 Richard M. Hoe invents the rotary printing press

1847–1848 Migration of Mormon community to Utah

1848 Women's Rights Convention held at Seneca Falls, New York (July); John Humphrey Noyes establishes Perfectionist community at Oneida, New York

1851 Nathaniel Hawthorne publishes *The House of the Seven Gables*; Herman Melville publishes *Moby Dick*

1851–52 First serial publication of Harriet Beecher Stowe's *Uncle Tom's Cabin* (book issued in 1852)

1854 Publication of Henry David Thoreau's *Walden* and George Fitzhugh's *Sociology for the South*

1857 Publication of Hinton Rowan Helper's attack on slavery, *The Impending Crisis in the South*; panic and depression of 1857 begins; cotton continues to boom, prices for the commodity peaking in 1860

1859 John Brown raids Harper's Ferry arsenal; celebrated by Emerson, Thoreau, and others

*M*id-century America was predominantly rural—five times as many Americans lived on farms as in towns and cities. The landscape, however, was changing. The population of the north and northwest was swelling as unprecedented numbers migrated from Europe to escape famine, war, and poverty. Rails and telegraph wire were criss-crossing the natural features of the North American continent, especially in the northern latitudes.

The evidence of progress and prosperity in the North and old Northwest territory raised expectations and stirred anxieties, contributing thereby to a broad and powerful impulse for reform. Technological and social changes, as well as a deepening sensitivity to the slavery question among white southerners, tended to isolate the South. In the North the movement against slavery increasingly took on the qualities of a crusade. American culture responded to the nation's growth and expansion but reflected the deepening sectional divisions as well as the increasing readership and patronage of the prosperous middle class.

THE DYNAMIC NORTH

In the decades before the Civil War, the northeast and the old Northwest territory were transformed by rapid growth and technological change. Advances in manufacturing, transportation and communications—the component forces of what is identified as the Industrial Revolution—created a dynamic, rapidly industrialized economy. As the controversy over slavery grew, the northeast and the northwest were increasingly thought of as a single section, the North.

Population Trends

The census of 1850 revealed the remarkable growth of the nation's population and its sectional distribution. The nucleus of 3,929,000 in 1790 had grown to a total population of 12,866,000 in 1830; 23,191,000 in 1850; and over 31,000,000 in 1860.

IMMIGRATION

Early population growth was due chiefly to the rapid reproduction of native–born stock. Between 1820, when statistics were first accurately kept, and 1830, less than 500,000 foreigners came to American shores. But five times as many came in the next two decades—over 4 million in all—most from Great Britain, Ireland, and Germany. By 1850, 12 percent of the population was foreign–born. The United States became an asylum for those who fled from unsatisfactory labor conditions in Great Britain, famine in Ireland, and political revolutions and economic depression on the continent. Few immigrants—only half a million by 1860—settled in the South.

Over 1.5 million native Irish were living in the United States in 1860, most in the cities of the northeast. Some one million native–born Germans were entered in the census of that year, most of them on farms or in the new cities of the old northwest.

URBAN GROWTH

At the close of the American Revolution only five cities in the country had more than eight thousand inhabitants. In 1850 there were 141 such cities, representing every section of the nation. They contained 16 percent of the total population. Already they were struggling with such problems as sanitation, transportation, public health, fire protection, and public safety. Most of the cities of the northeast more than doubled in population between 1840 and 1860. This rapid urban growth reflected the decline of the farming population in many areas of the northeast as well as sharp increases in foreign immigrants.

Nativism. There was a pronounced reaction among native–born Americans to the enormous increase in foreign immigration that began in 1840. While many business owners welcomed the new influx of willing workers (labor costs had been high), others viewed the human wave as a threat to their lives and work. "Native Americans," overwhelmingly Protestant in religion, blamed the new, largely Catholic, immigrants for perceptible increases in political corruption and social disorder. More fundamentally, they feared that the rising tide of immigration would bring with it economic competition, radical politics, and a role in American life for the pope, the head of the Roman Catholic Church.

Significantly, efforts to organize and manipulate "nativist" fears for political purposes proved short–lived and largely ineffective. Several organizations joined in 1850 to form the secret Order of the Star–Spangled Banner, which advocated citizenship tests and restrictions as well as new, tighter immigration laws. The American (or "Know Nothing") party scored some striking victories in state and local elections between 1854 and 1856 but quickly faded into oblivion.

Industrial Expansion

In 1840 the nation's mills and factories had produced goods valued at less than $500 million. By 1850 their annual output had reached more than $1 billion, surpassing the value of agricultural products. In the next decade manufacturing output would almost double.

Southern New England, southern New York, New Jersey, eastern Pennsylvania, and eastern Maryland comprised the first industrial area. After 1840 industrialization spread to western New York, western Pennsylvania, Ohio (along the Ohio River and on the south shore of Lake Erie), Indiana, and Illinois. By 1860 only half of the nation's mills and factories were located in the northeast; however two–thirds of the nation's output of manufactured goods were still produced there. Except in Maryland and sections of Virginia, manufacturing made little progress in the South prior to 1860.

SPREAD OF THE FACTORY SYSTEM

After its introduction in the New England textile industry, the factory system proved adaptable to the production of other goods—notably woolens, iron goods, shoes, clocks, guns, and sewing machines. Mass production of goods lowered their prices, making them affordable to larger numbers of consumers. It did not necessarily improve the quality of goods, however. New England textiles, for example, remained predominantly coarse goods; in spite of the growth of that industry, foreign–made cottons and woolens were the principal imports to the United States, amounting to some 20 percent of the total (as opposed to 29 percent in 1820).

The financing for new factories and mills was increasingly provided by merchant capitalists, redeploying profits from overseas mercantile ventures. With few exceptions the early factories and mills were small establishments

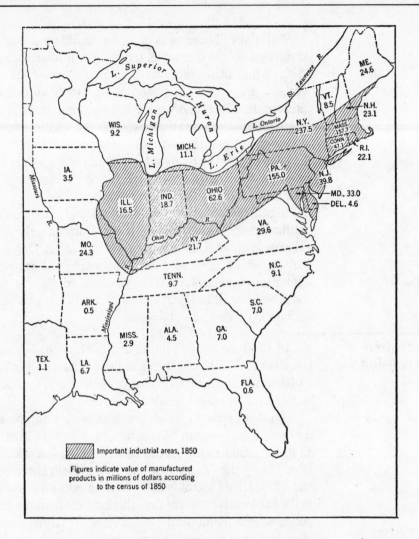

Fig. 10.1 Industrial United States in 1850

owned by individual proprietors, partners, or joint–stock companies. By mid–century, however, the corporate form of organization, under which a few or many holders of shares or stockholders owned an enterprise, was used more widely, particularly in the textile industry in New England.

Innovation. Beginning in the late eighteenth century, early industrialization had relied on imported technologies, such as the spinning and carding machinery used in England. By the mid–nineteenth century, however, as a consequence of growing manufacturing expertise and technological advances, Americans had already achieved superiority in key areas. The excellence of American machine toolmaking—exemplified in the turret lathe and the vernier caliper—was widely acknowledged. New industries were created by several inventions: Charles Goodyear's process for vulcanizing rubber

(1839); Elias G. Howe's sewing machine (1846); Elisha G. Otis's invention of the first passenger elevator (1851); Gail Borden's method for processing food, permitting products such as condensed milk (1856).

New Forms of Power. Oliver Evans converted the low–pressure steam engine of James Watt into a more effective high–pressure engine (1803). But steam replaced water power slowly as the motive force in American factories. In 1830 more than one third of the plants in Pennsylvania used steam; yet in New England less than 10 percent had abandoned water power. Wood remained the principal fuel until the Civil War. However, after 1820 the use of coal increased rapidly (production rose from 50,000 tons in that year to over 14 million tons in 1860).

Changing Working Conditions. Several factors contributed to a deterioration of working conditions in American factories and the failure of idealistic enterprises such as the Lowell experiment. Huge increases in the pool of unskilled laborers made it unnecessary for manufacturers to attract workers—high levels of foreign immigration in the 1840s and 1850s kept pace with the industrial capitalists' needs to expand output.

Additionally, reductions in the protective tariff allowed foreign exporters to sell goods at lower prices in the United States—forcing domestic manufacturers to either reduce production costs or face the prospect of declining profits, losses, and bankruptcy. Many employers reacted by extending the workday and saving money in ways that adversely affected labor conditions. In response to changing work and market conditions, some unions were formed in the 1850s (such as National Typographic Union, Hat Finishers, United Cigarmakers, Iron Molders). However, the constant influx of laborers from Europe made organization difficult.

Transportation and Communication

The development of the steam–powered locomotive in the 1830s and the rapid extension of railways in the 1840s and 1850s dramatically altered patterns of economic development in the North.

THE RAILROAD AGE

Innovations in transportation, permitting space to be traversed more rapidly, were crucial to the industrial expansion of the North. The great spaces that separated producers from consumers in the United States placed a high premium on speed, especially in the movement of perishable freight.

At the height of the canal craze, the railroad became practicable and held out the promise of even faster transport. The first railroad venture was sponsored by Baltimore merchants and bankers who incorporated the Baltimore and Ohio Railroad in 1827. In 1830 there were 32 miles of rails in the country; in 1840 there were 2,818 miles; by 1850 more than 9,000. The rapid extension of rail mileage enabled the railroads to significantly reduce their costs for shipping freight and carrying passengers—thus allowing them to price their services more cheaply and competitively. The extension of trunk lines, into which short or local lines fed, further tightened the east–west flow of commerce and bound the northeast and the old northwest together with bands of steel.

The railroad companies received generous grants of land and stock subscriptions from the various states as well as from the federal government (both directly and indirectly). By 1860 some 30 million acres of federal land had been assigned to the states for such purposes.

Other Modes of Transport. River and canal transport continued to be significant in moving goods to market, especially for bulky freight not susceptible to spoilage. The widespread use of steamboats, especially on inland waters, persisted—in 1860 there were more than a thousand plying the waters of the Mississippi and its tributaries. Canals, notably the great Erie Canal, continued to bring freight from the interior to eastern cities—by 1850 more than 3,200 miles of canals had been dug in the United States. Nevertheless, the railroad, which could more easily surmount geographical barriers and had the advantage of speed, gradually replaced the established modes of commercial transport.

On the high seas, the sleek and swift clipper ships, introduced in the mid–1840s, enabled American merchants to expand their position in, and briefly dominate, international commerce. They allowed American captains to sail around the Cape Horn and reach California in three rather than the usual five weeks' time; however, the completion of a railroad across Panama in 1855 and competition from British ironclad ships caused their rule of the seas to be a brief one.

THE TELEGRAPH

The invention of the electric telegraph gave birth to the first communications industry. Although Samuel F. B. Morse succeeded in making the invention practicable in 1837, the first telegraph line of consequence was not constructed until 1843. By 1860 more than 50,000 miles of lines united the country east of the Rocky Mountains; the next year, San Francisco was brought into the network. The national telegraph network strengthened the ties between northeast and northwest and also, by providing an efficient means to monitor schedules and routes, contributed to the rapid expansion of the railways.

News Media. The extension of the telegraph, combined with the invention of the steam–driven rotary printing press by Richard M. Hoe in 1846, revolutionized the world of journalism. The business of news–gathering, previously dependent on the mails and hand–operated presses, was greatly accelerated. The formation of the Associated Press, a central wire service founded in 1846, punctuated the advent of a new era of journalism and further expanded the amount of information that the individual newspaper could supply.

Agriculture

Growth and technological change also transformed American agriculture. The establishment of a rail link between Chicago and New York in 1853 accelerated the flow of commodities from the old northwest to the northeast, diverting the north–south pattern of river transport through the Mississippi River Valley.

SHIFTING PATTERNS OF AGRICULTURE

The grain–producing and livestock–raising regions shifted to the old northwest. The south came to rely upon the west for its grain and livestock. New England and other parts of the east, in order to meet the competition of western farms, turned to stockraising, dairying, and truck farming. Demand for farm products (and farm prices) increased steadily from the rapidly growing cities of the northeast and from Europe, creating a period of prosperity. The nation's production of staple commodities such as corn, wheat, cotton, tobacco, and wool, as well as other crops, more than doubled between 1830 and 1860.

NEW FARMING METHODS

Although the abundance of cheap and fertile land was responsible for careless and wasteful methods among American farmers, significant improvements in land fertilization, crop rotation, and scientific stockbreeding were introduced throughout the nineteenth century. Many societies for the promotion of agriculture sprang up in the years following the establishment of the first such American organization at Philadelphia in 1785. Institutions dedicated to the advancement of agricultural education and opportunities for competitions, such as the country fair, increased.

Agricultural Machinery. From the earliest colonial settlements, American agriculture had suffered from labor shortages (a circumstance that had contributed to the spread of slavery). Not surprisingly, labor–saving devices were a subject of keen interest to American farmers; they formed a significant portion of the patents issued before 1860. Mechanization became increasingly vital to the farms in the North during the 1840s as a consequence of migration from the farms to the northern cities and the great exodus of settlers to the west. Among the many important labor–saving inventions of this period were John Deere's steel plow (1839) and Cyrus H. McCormick's reaper (1834). These machines, together with horse rakes, mowing machines, seed planters, cultivators, and mechanical threshers and separators, lightened the farmer's labor and helped increase farm production.

THE SOUTH AND THE "PECULIAR INSTITUTION"

Economic and social development in the South had been shaped from the earliest settlements by large–scale plantation agriculture. The decline of staple crop production in the more settled areas of the upper South after the American Revolution led many to question the desirability of retaining a slave economy. However, after the opening of the southwestern frontier, the institution was perceived differently. The "flush times" in the Cotton Belt, as well as fears of slave rebellions and the growing abolition movement in the North, closed the mind of the South on matters of race and slavery. The region remained overwhelmingly agricultural, dominated by large holdings and barely affected by industrial and technological changes.

Slavery and Plantation Agriculture

The South's principal enterprise, the large–scale production of staple or cash crops, had become during the course of the eighteenth century almost totally dependent upon the forced labor of slaves. At the time of the Revolution, the principal cash crops were tobacco in the upper South and rice, sugar, and long–staple cotton in the coastal plains of the deep South.

DECLINING FORTUNES OF THE UPPER SOUTH

Shortly after the War of 1812, a long decline began in tobacco farming. The large profits that tobacco planters had reaped during good growing years in the eighteenth century were rarely seen in the nineteenth. Fluctuations in world supply made market prices unpredictable, while the uninterrupted cultivation of the plant in the tidewater regions of Maryland, Virginia, and North Carolina led to severe soil exhaustion. Tobacco cultivation spread into inland regions, notably to Kentucky, but was increasingly replaced by wheat–growing and other less intensive (or labor–dependent) agriculture in the upper South.

Criticism of Slavery. This shift, at least initially, led many to question the desirablility of retaining the institution of slavery. The inhabitants of western districts of the upper South had long opposed it. Planters such as Washington, Jefferson, and George Mason of Virginia had openly questioned the economic value of the institution and feared its divisive influence in national affairs, as well as the social evils it bred. Such views led Virginia to call a constitutional convention to discuss the abolition of slavery in 1829. The news of a bloody insurrection led by the slave Nat Turner in that state in 1831 initially strengthened support for emancipation in the Virginia legislature; but, after a key vote was lost the following year, discussion of the question ceased. While changing economics caused many to consider some form of emancipation, the South, it should be emphasized, never envisoned a social alternative to slavery or civil rights for the large number of blacks in the region.

The Cotton Kingdom

Slavery would likely have continued to decline in the South were it not for the rapid expansion of the cotton culture after the War of 1812. Expectations of huge profits from raising cotton gave new life to the plantation economy.

COTTON CULTURE AND WHITNEY'S GIN

Cotton had been cultivated along the coasts of South Carolina and Georgia since colonial times. It was in great demand in Great Britain; there the textile industry had been industrialized since the mideighteenth century and was manufacturing ever–increasing supplies of finished cotton goods. The long–staple or sea–island variety grown in the Atlantic coastal plain could not be raised successfully further inland, however. The hardier but coarser short–staple cotton plant grew well in soils from the mid–South to the Gulf of Mexico, although it was difficult to extract seeds from the bolls of the plant without damaging the fibers.

Eli Whitney's invention of the cotton gin (1793), a machine that removed the seeds from raw cotton without injuring the fiber, thus transformed the nature of cotton culture. Cotton plantations spread inland, transforming the landscape of the frontier South. By the 1820s the upland regions of South Carolina and Georgia had been given over to cotton production. The success of the short–staple variety increased land values in the interior. Not coincidentally, it also led to increased pressures for the removal of the Creek and Cherokee Indians from their tribal lands.

EXPANSION OF THE SLAVE ECONOMY

The opening up of rich new lands in the southwest territory and the Louisiana Purchase lured thousands from the established states. The promise of quick profits from cotton production and the abundance of uncultivated land on which the plant could be grown also brought a sharp rise in the demand for black slaves. Gang labor was required to clear the newly formed cotton plantations of what became the states of Alabama, Mississippi, Texas, and Arkansas and the new sugar plantations of Louisiana. The slave population of the new region grew more than tenfold between 1820 and 1860: in Mississippi, it grew from 32,000 in 1820 to 436,000 in 1860; in Alabama, from 41,000 in 1820 to 435,000 in 1860.

The Domestic Slave Trade. Many settlers from the upper South migrated with their entire families and slaves. Those slaveholders who remained behind in the older states often took advantage of the rising market for slave labor and sold some of their slaves. Slave traders, though a despised group, operated freely in the upper South. They purchased and transported slaves to new masters in the deep South or sold them at auction in public markets.

About 400,000 slaves were conveyed there from the upper South, by one means or another, in the two decades before the Civil War.

"COTTON IS KING!"

The enormous growth of the cotton culture in the South, which gave rise to much boasting in the 1850s, is easily measured. In 1792 the South produced some 13,000 bales; in 1820, 500,000; in 1840, 1.35 million bales; in 1850, some 3 million; in 1860, 4.8 million. By midcentury southern planters were producing 75 percent of the world's annual harvest of raw cotton, generating more than 50 percent of the nation's total income from exports. The price of the commodity rose steadily, even defying the Panic of 1857. Significantly, cotton culture, with enterprises related to the production and marketing of the crop, formed the nation's leading business sector prior to the Civil War.

Southern manufacturing, however, did not grow significantly. Despite the efforts of proponents of a diversified (and thus more independent) economy, such as J. D. B. DeBow of *DeBow's Review*, the South remained in many ways a colonial economy. Some industrial concerns enjoyed considerable success, however, notably the Tredegar Iron Works in Richmond, Virginia. Urban growth in the South increased only slightly before the Civil War—the population of southern cities showed growth at the rate of only 6 percent in the census of 1840, 10 percent in that of 1860.

The Rule of the Planter

The compilations of the 1860 census indicate that the households of planters (agriculturists owning twenty or more slaves) composed roughly 4 percent of the white population of the South. The most affluent planters, those owning fifty or more slaves, were a mere 1 percent of the region's white population.

This small group, however, dominated the politics, wrote the laws, and defined the social standards of the old South. With few exceptions, they preferred to see themselves and their society in romantic terms, distinct from the commercial hustle and bustle, the get–and–gain life they identified in the industrializing North.

THE PLANTERS' WORLD VIEW

Southern planters subscribed to a code of chivalry that placed certain notions of honor and duty above self–interest and indeed life itself (dueling not infrequently resolved disputes). By this process of romanticization, the plantation "lady" was elevated to a lofty but isolated postion, not unlike that of a statue on a pedestal. She was nevertheless required to confront the unpleasant facts of farm life every day, often serving as the only dispenser of medical care on the plantation. Although the aristocratic, "cavalier" ideals to which the planter society aspired were in many ways at odds with the harsh realities of life in the old South, these ideals remained nevertheless powerful social forces.

Most of the large and prosperous plantations were established by those who rose from humble origins. The great planters were intensely ambitious men, often like William Faulkner's Thomas Sutpen (of his novel *Absalom! Absalom!* [1936]). Fine manners and the accoutrements of great house living were usually acquired after, not before, a fortune was made. Having made their "killing," such men indulged their pride, seeking acceptance in the ranks of the older order, the descendants of the great figures of the eighteenth century. Wealth and standing in the planter's society were measured in terms of political and social influence, family connections, and, always, the amount of land and number of slaves one owned.

Plantation agriculture was, if successful, a capitalist enterprise, even if operated, ultimately, by the threat of physical violence. The production of the cash crop was all important, and therefore the planting, nurturance, and harvest of the crop required wise planning. Although they conceived of themselves as landed gentlemen, the great planters also had to be tough businessmen. The world market for commodities fluctuated sharply. Overproduction in a bad year, or, conversely, underproduction in a good year could mean the difference between prosperity and bankruptcy. The more substantial planters hired overseers to handle work gangs and enforce discipline but kept a close eye on their accounts. Small planters directed the work of their own slaves.

"PLAIN FOLK" OF THE OLD SOUTH

The majority of the white population in the old South, according to the 1860 census fully 75 percent of white families, held no slaves at all. Of those who did own slaves, most (some 88 percent) owned less than twenty. Despite their numerical superiority, these whites—mostly small farmers who raised grains and livestock—exercised slight influence in southern society. They differed with the large planters on some political issues (notably political representation), but they did not oppose the institution of slavery and the measures that protected it. The planters maintained authority over the white majority by skillfully manipulating their racial and economic fears and by promoting the planter ideal, to which many small holders and farmers aspired. Enough "self–made" men achieved great wealth to make the promise of upward mobility believable.

THE PROSLAVERY ARGUMENT

Open debate about the feasibility of slavery came to an end in the aftermath of Nat Turner's rebellion in Virginia (1831). The aggressive rhetorical attacks of abolitionists eliminated what flexibility remained in the South. Southern publicists and statesmen were soon defending slavery as a sound and humane basis of social organization. Their arguments, derived from the writings of intellectuals such as Thomas Roderick Dew, president of the College of William and Mary, stressed (1) the historical and scriptural justification of slavery; (2) the economic advantages of the institution; and (3) the social benefits that it conferred upon the dominant white population.

The most clever defender of the institution, George Fitzhugh, author of *Sociology for the South, or the Failure of Free Society* (1854) and other works, went so far as to argue that slaves enjoyed better living conditions than the "wage slaves" of northern factories. While there continued to be opponents of slavery—none so outspoken or courageous as Henry Clay's cousin Cassius Marcellus Clay of Kentucky, who for a time even printed an abolitionist newspaper in Lexington—the South became increasingly intolerant of criticism on the subject. The defensive view that slavery was a "necessary evil" was replaced by the affirmation that it was, as John C. Calhoun expressed it in 1837, "a positive good."

The "Gag Rule". Reacting to the literature circulated by northern abolitionists, southern congressmen demanded that abolitionist material be barred from the mails. In 1836 they succeeded in persuading the House of Representatives to refuse to hear or consider antislavery petitions that were regularly sent to Congress. This "gag rule" was finally rescinded in 1844, largely as a result of the persistence of a small group of northern congressmen led by John Quincy Adams and Joshua Giddings, who defended the civil rights of the abolitionists. (The former president served as member of the Massachusetts delegation in the House of Representatives from 1831 to 1848, when he died shortly after suffering a stroke on the floor of the House.)

"Human Property"

The predicament of slaves in the old South is summed up by the contradictory phrase "human property." Transported against their wills from Africa (and later the West Indies), black slaves were powerless before their white owners under the laws of the slaveholding states. They had no standing as "persons" under the United States Constitution. By law, and under the slave codes that elaborately governed their behavior and movements, the slave was chattel, the category of property to which the law assigned horses and cows. Most states had laws that made the murder of a slave by a brutal master a capital crime—but instances of attempts to enforce these laws were few, convictions rarer still.

There is abundant anecdotal evidence of the physical abuse of slaves in the old South, some exaggerated by incensed abolitionists who felt compelled to rouse the men and women of the free states to action. However, because human beings are always capable of it, there were also many examples of kindness and humanity in the strange world of masters and slaves. The gentlemanly code and paternalistic values subscribed to by the leading planters held the scoundrel and abuser of inferiors in the highest contempt. And while the pressure to produce a successful crop led many to drive their field hands to the breaking point, this tendency was counterbalanced by the fact that the financial capital of the planter was almost totally invested in his slaves (the average cost of a field hand was $800)—an economic incentive, among those who heeded reason, to care for their human property.

Nevertheless, as Harriet Beecher Stowe so powerfully reminded the readers of *Uncle Tom's Cabin* (1852), the horror of slavery was not ultimately measured by assessments of the number or degree of severity of abuses—the evil was that the potential for physical abuse always existed under the slave system.

SLAVE LIFE AND LABOR

The majority of slaves lived on sizeable plantations and were forced to work long hours, performing bone–tiring crop labor under close supervision. Those who went to the fields in gangs were put to the hardest toil; the fortunate ones assigned "task" work could look forward to some free time after a job was done. A few were permitted to learn skills and were hired out to earn cash for their masters.

Most slaves could rely on their masters for basic welfare. They were provided coarse work clothing, sufficient food to keep them at work, and shelter. On many plantations they grew their own gardens, enjoyed a few holidays, and received small rewards. On the large plantations, only the privileged few, the house servants, had any significant contact with the master's family. The small number of slaves who were owned by town residents lived more varied and interesting lives.

Subjugation and Resistance. The slaveholders took great pains to tightly circumscribe the world of the slaves. They had to carry passes with them when off the plantation and were forbidden to be out at night. Only those who were very light–skinned could evade this constant surveillance. Slave patrols were vigilant in finding offenders, and punishments were severe and swift. As a means of preventing communications, the slave codes made it illegal to teach slaves to read and write. However, there were masters and mistresses willing to overlook this stricture, and it is estimated that roughly 10 percent of the slaves risked punishment to achieve literacy. The ability to read and write was understood to be the key to freedom, and thus cherished.

The degree to which slaves accepted or resisted their subjugation has been discussed at great length by twentieth–century writers, often reflecting their own political convictions about protest and rebellion. Considered from the perspective of the black slave, especially that of the field worker, however, it is remarkable that a few substantial rebellions did in fact occur. After Nat Turner's rebellion in 1831 no slaveholder needed to be reminded of the possibility of a slave insurrection.

In addition to the discipline enforced by the slave system, the physical geography and sheer extent of the slaveholding states reduced the odds for successful escape. Still, despite the regimen of their lives—the predictable, if minimal, comforts as well as the constant threat of punishment—there were always runaways or fugitives willing to take the chance of reaching the world of limited freedom blacks enjoyed in the northern states. The South's insistence on a tough new fugitive slave law in the agreements that formed the Compromise of 1850 bears this out. Small acts of resistance, in the form of sabotage of plantation property, abuse of farm animals, and feigned sickness were everyday occurrences. Slaves did on occasion murder their master or members of his family.

Afro–American Culture. While the area of their personal freedom was circumscribed, black slaves expressed their humanity in other ways. Even though the slaves' marriages were not recognized by law, they maintained a strong sense of familial community and consciousness. Continuity with African culture and earlier forms of worship was retained in their practice of Christianity. The source of their endurance, and of much of their sense of identity as a community and people, was their religion. It gave them an emotional release from their hard lives and dim prospects and provided moments of rapturous joy that no one could take away. Spirituals, the rich song legacy of their religion, lifted the worshipers and provided opportunities for commentary about everyday life. During the antebellum period, several slave spirituals and songs were adapted by the composer Stephen C. Foster, beginning a new and important influence on American popular culture.

FREE BLACKS

There were some 250,000 free blacks in the South. Many of them (or their parents) had been freed by their masters for acts of nobility or faithful service. They existed independently, held property (some owned slaves), but were denied civil rights. Like the slaves, their lives were increasingly regulated by the slave codes in the years before the Civil War, and they were constantly in danger of being kidnapped, falsely identified as runaways, and forcibly reintroduced to slavery.

REFORMING THE NATION AND ITS INSTITUTIONS

American society during the first half of the nineteenth century was permeated by an optimistic faith in the perfectibility of man. The effort to improve the world as it was went forward in two modes—the impulse to liberate the human spirit, and the call to reform or remake society, which not infrequently were present at the same time.

Social and Religious Experiments

Many radical and experimental proposals for social reform emerged in the 1840s and 1850s. Some emphasized self–realization and the fulfillment of the individual, others strove for new or stronger forms of community and denial of self. Both varieties reflected tensions and strains within northern society.

RELIGIOUS BACKGROUNDS

In the first quarter of the nineteenth century a Second Great Awakening of religious fervor swept first the southwestern and western frontiers and then the east. Evangelical Protestant preachers—principally Methodists, Presbyterians, and Baptists—staged revivals, often in camp meetings out-doors, to win personal conversions to Christ. In sharp contrast to the Calvinist concept of predestination, the foremost Evangelical preacher, Charles Grandison Finney, who drew large audiences in the 1820s and 1830s, preached that the individual could be purged of sin and achieve salvation by an act of "free will." Significantly, Finney also urged his followers to enlist in the cause of moral reform.

While the Evangelicals sought regeneration of the individual through emotional appeals, the rational religious tradition, embodied in Unitarianism (which denied the divinity of Christ), also contributed to the reform impulse. The influential William Ellery Channing and other Unitarian clergymen taught that all human beings contained the capacity for good, advising the faithful to trust their own consciences in ordering their lives rather than church dogma. The cause of humanitarian reforms thus gained strong moral grounding.

Transcendentalism. In the 1830s many nonconformist Unitarians were led to Transcendentalism. It was a spiritualist movement, closely linked to European Romanticism (and thereby influenced by the religions of the East); it appealed mainly to intellectuals. Transcendentalists conceived of God as the "Over–Soul" and believed that human beings contained elements of the divine. Human perfectibility was therefore assumed—they could identify no evil in mankind or nature.

SOCIAL AND ECONOMIC UTOPIAS

In response, or reaction, to changes introduced by the Industrial Revolution and to population trends, some Americans sought to create, or participate in, a new social order. Several idealistic communities were formed, advocating revolutionary economic and social principles.

New Harmony. Robert Owen, the English industrialist and philanthropist, founded a utopian socialist cooperative community at New Harmony, Indiana, in 1824. His fame led to the establishment of a dozen similar ventures. After a formative period, he announced a Declaration of Mental Independence on July 4, 1826—private property, organized religion, and the state of marriage were condemned. While his ideas were controversial, Owen's socialist experiment failed for more practical reasons the next year. His son Robert Dale Owen later observed that New Harmony had failed because of economic factors—land was too cheap and labor too highly paid in America to sustain cooperative action.

The Fourierist Phalanxes. In the 1840s Albert Brisbane and Horace Greeley collaborated in popularizing and promoting the principles of the French philosopher Charles Fourier. Fourierism proposed the organization of society on the basis of phalanxes or cooperative groups, not to exceed 1,800 persons, cooperating in industry, science, and art. More than thirty such phalanxes were established in the northern and midwestern states but only one, the North American Phalanx, in Red Bank, New Jersey, had any real success. It numbered ninety members at its peak and lasted but twelve years. Members of the North American Phalanx were allowed to choose what work they wished to do, the highest wages going to "necessary but repulsive" labor, the lowest to the most pleasant.

Brook Farm. Organized by George Ripley, a Boston Unitarian minister and Transcendentalist, this most famous of communes was organized as a joint–stock company near Roxbury, Massachusetts, in 1841. Its initial mission was to demonstrate the possibilities for self–realization by a communal sharing of labor and leisure—"to combine the thinker and the worker, as far as possible in the same individual."

Toward the end of its six–year existence, it became a Fourierist phalanx. To several members, Brook Farm was an intellectual's paradise, although one of the most notable, Nathaniel Hawthorne, later wrote critically of the experiment, and of the dangers of the egotism he found there, in **The Blithedale Romance** (1852).

RELIGIOUS COMMUNITARIANISM AND RADICALISM

Several Christian sects separated themselves from established Protestant denominations and from conventional society in the early nineteenth century to form new religious communities. These groups built upon a religious tradition that had begun with the first colonial settlements.

The Shakers. Originally a French sect, the Shaker Society (derived from their description as "Shaking Quakers") proved to be the most successful communitarian Christian sect in America. The first Shaker community in America was established at Watervliet, New York, in 1776, and guided by Mother Ann Lee (1736–84), the principal prophet of the church, a refugee from religious oppression in England. By 1825, members had founded more than twenty new communities, most in the northeastern states (there were four in Ohio, two in Kentucky). By the second quarter of the nineteenth century they numbered 6,000.

Following Mother Ann's teachings, the Shakers believed in the dual nature of God, Mother Ann herself representing the feminine side of the divine personality. The sect was fundamentalist in its belief in Holy Scripture—ritualistic dances and, later, hymns united the communities in worship and fellowship. The Shakers believed in the equality (and separation) of the sexes, practiced celibacy, and strove for simplicity and industry in their lives and work. Membership was purely voluntary, but the social and religious order was authoritarian and completely denied democratic instincts. Shakers surrendered individual will for the good of the community; decisions were made by a central ministry, the Head of Influence.

The Oneida Perfectionists. The religious society organized by John Humphrey Noyes at Putney, Vermont, established a famous and financially successful socialist community at Oneida, New York, in 1848. The Perfectionists subscribed to complete equality among the sexes. They also subscribed to the idea of "complex marriage," which horrified the "outside world" and caused them to be branded as advocates of "free love."

In fact they were deeply religious and believed in a responsible concept of mutual marriage—sexual relations were closely monitored. Traditional marriage and family ("special love" unions) were, however, judged to be dangerous to the community. On Noyes's recommendation, the Oneida community bowed to the outside world and abandoned complex marriage in 1879. The following year it abandoned socialism and was reorganized as a joint–stock company.

The Millerites. The religious revivalism of the early nineteenth century had been millennialist, preaching the necessity of conversion and reconversion in anticipation of the second coming of Jesus Christ. In 1832, William Miller, a Calvinistic Baptist minister, predicted that the second coming was imminent. His summons to a new way of life stirred multitudes in all parts of the country, many of whom disposed of their possessions in expectation that the world would come to an end in 1844.

The Mormons. The Church of Jesus Christ of Latter Day Saints took form as a consequence of the religious experience of Joseph Smith in upstate New York in 1820. He believed he was inspired by divine revelation to restore an earlier (but lost) Christian civilization in America, described in *The Book of Mormon* which he published in 1830.

Smith persisted in the effort to found a New Jerusalem in America. The sect's secrecy, unorthodox religious views, and especially its advocacy of polygamy (one husband could marry several wives) caused others to fear and persecute them. In 1844, a mob in Carthage, Illinois, stormed the jail in which Joseph Smith was confined and killed him. Led by his successor, Brigham Young, some 12,000 Mormons left a flourishing settlement in Nauvoo, Illinois, in 1846 to begin a trek into the far west. They established their permanent community, the state of Deseret, on the edge of the Great Salt Lake, in 1847. Like its symbol, the beehive, the Mormons and what became the state of Utah prospered and multiplied.

Mormonism taught that God had once been a human being and that all men and women had the capacity to attain the ultimate perfectibility of divinity, as had Joseph Smith. The Mormon church imposed a strict authoritarian order on its community, rejecting the prevailing American faith in democracy and personal freedoms.

Institutional and Moral Reforms

Although conservative in its social implications, the impulse to reform society was no less fervent than that to liberate the individual. Some of these efforts expressed concerns for the social order, others the growing reach of humanitarianism. Women assumed key leadership roles in these reforms.

EDUCATION REFORM

The push to establish universal public education was the most significant of the social reforms that looked to institutions to implement change and supplement the role of the family. The foundations of the American public school system were laid in the generation before the Civil War.

Secondary Schools. Although the idea of public education was endorsed in the early days of the republic, widespread acceptance by the various states of free, compulsory, tax–supported elementary schools did not begin until the second quarter of the nineteenth century. Public support for such measures reflected increasing concern for the conditions that were shaping the lives of children, particularly those of new immigrants.

Massachusetts, under the leadership of Horace Mann from 1837 to 1848, took the lead in organizing a system of secondary schools. Mann, a firm believer in the shaping power of education, won support for broadening the curriculum and creating professional standards for teachers.

By 1850 there were 80,000 elementary schools with 3,300,000 pupils and 6,000 high schools and academies with 250,000 students in the United States. The quality of the education they provided varied considerably. In 1860 roughly 70 percent of school–age children in the North attended schools; in the South, perhaps 33 percent of white children. School terms and attendance varied; parents who worked on farms and in factories frequently complained that they needed their children to work. Some Roman Catholic immigrants charged that the public schools indoctrinated their children with Protestant values.

SPECIAL EDUCATION

In the belief that all impediments to human progress could be overcome, reformers also focused on the problems of those with disabilities. In 1816 Thomas H. Gallaudet had opened the first school for pupils with hearing impairments at Hartford, Connecticut. The first serious effort to educate those with visual disorders was undertaken by the Perkins Institute for the Education of the Blind, of Boston, founded in 1829.

THE ASYLUM AND PRISON REFORM

The rapid growth of the population, especially in American cities, made previously tolerable conditions for the common custodianship of criminals, debtors, the mentally ill, and the senile appear harsh and inadequate. While understanding of social deviance remained rudimentary, the creation of asylums to deal with particular problems represented a step forward. At least at the outset, the movement to improve conditions also contained the goal of rehabilitation of the individual.

From the 1820s, new penitentiaries or criminal asylums began to be constructed, the first at Auburn, New York, in 1821. Imprisonment solely for debt was abolished; penal codes were modified to remove inhuman punishments. Prison management was organized about the idea that rigid structure and discipline in everyday life (including solitary confinement for contemplation of wrongdoing) would contribute to moral regeneration of the criminal.

Similar principals of organization were introduced to the asylum for the mentally ill—the first was established at Worcester, Massachusetts, in 1833. Progress in the treatment and care of the mentally ill and handicapped owed much to the crusading efforts of Dorothea Dix to inform the American public about inhumane conditions in public facilities.

TEMPERANCE

The crusade against excessive drinking of alcoholic beverages, which had its origins in the eighteenth century, grew noticeably after the creation of the American Temperance Society in Boston in 1826. Local auxiliaries and state societies, supported by the churches, convinced thousands to sign the temperance pledge (close to a million had done so by 1840). In that year the Washingtonian Society was formed and, emphasizing the emotional methods of the religious revival, rapidly spread across the country.

At first these reformers relied upon persuasion to effect their purposes. But in the decade of the 1840s, many began to urge restrictive and prohibitory legislation against the liquor traffic as the best way to promote temperance.

Some of this activity reflected fears of the growing population of new immigrants and the disorder attributed to them. The Maine law of 1851 was the first state enactment forbidding the manufacture, importation, and sale of intoxicating beverages. Women played prominent roles in the temperance movement, documenting the evils that alcoholism visited on the American family.

The Campaign for Women's Rights

The participation of women in the reform and evangelical movements led to the first sustained campaign to remove the political and economic discriminations against them. The demand for civil rights, stressed by Sarah and Angelina Grimké, Frances Wright, Lucretia Mott, and Elizabeth Cady Stanton, brought changes in the laws of several states concerning a woman's control of her property after marriage. The Woman's Rights Convention, held at Seneca Falls, New York, in 1848, was the first of several national conventions to demand the vote for women, equal opportunity with men in education and employment, and an end to legal discrimination against women.

WOMEN IN THE "DOMESTIC SPHERE"

As the industrial and commercial economy grew, there was a corresponding expansion of the middle class, especially in urban communities. More and more women, freed from the burdens of household work (taken up by servants), had time to devote to reading and education, outside activities, and the "home." This economic and domestic change had broad and important implications for social life and popular culture in the antebellum period.

While denied an active role in politics and most business activity, middle–class women effectively used their enhanced authority over the family to exert a stabilizing influence in society. Many were active in educational, humanitarian, and institutional reforms. Others, following the lead of Sara Josepha Hale, editor of *Godey's Lady's Book*, were prominent in the union movement, seeking to avert civil war. The Mount Vernon Ladies' Association of the Union, formed in 1853, worked throughout the decade to raise funds to purchase George Washington's home to serve as a "mecca" of the Union. Their success also laid the foundations for the historic preservation movement.

The importance of the "domestic sphere" in antebellum society is documented by Harriet Beecher Stowe's novel *Uncle Tom's Cabin* (1852) and its extraordinary impact. Her success had much to do with the fact that she relied on middle–class domestic values, rather than mere abolitionist rhetoric, to demonstrate the evils of the slave system.

The Antislavery Crusade

There were many southern sympathizers in the free states, especially among those who had business interests with the South; but hostility to slavery in the North steadily grew. Organized antislavery activity in the South came to an end in the 1830s.

EARLY ANTISLAVERY SOCIETIES

Prior to 1830, the antislavery societies carried on their work in such a moderate spirit that they enjoyed much success in forming units in the slave states. In 1827, in fact, there were more antislavery societies in the South (principally organized by Quakers) than in the North.

The American Colonization Society, founded in 1817, enjoyed wide support in both sections and even received a $100,000 appropriation from Congress. It encouraged a conservative solution to the problem of slavery: gradual emancipation with compensation to masters, and public financing of transportation of freed blacks to colonies abroad. The only colony the society managed to establish, however, was Liberia, on the west coast of Africa, founded in 1822. By 1831 just 1,400 free blacks had crossed the Atlantic to join the settlement.

THE AMERICAN ANTI–SLAVERY SOCIETY

There was a sharp change in the temper of the antislavery movement when William Lloyd Garrison began to publish the *Liberator* in Boston in 1831. The radical Garrisonians, who formed the American Antislavery Society in 1833, scorned "gradualism," arguing that the problem of slavery should be approached from the viewpoint of the slave rather than from that of the master. They demanded the immediate abolition of slavery without compensation to the owners of slaves. The uncompromising nature of their stand gained them support—after five years over 1,300 constituent societies were in existence, with a combined membership above 250,000. One of the society's most noted "lecturing agents" was the black abolitionist and newspaper editor Frederick Douglass, who also advocated temperance, women's rights, and industrial education for blacks.

Abolitionist Tactics

Despite the growth of the American Antislavery Society, the majority of northerners considered the Garrisonian abolitionists to be single–issue fanatics. Fears that they posed a threat to the stability of society, fueled by race prejudice among whites, were widespread and, on occasion, led to hostile mob action. The most notorious anti–abolitionist mob violence resulted in the murder of Elijah Lovejoy, an abolitionist newspaper editor in Alton, Illinois, in 1837.

Garrison's increasingly extreme views, most notably his attack on the Constitution as "a covenant with death and an agreement with hell," coincided with a split in the American Antislavery Society in 1840. More moderate abolitionists moved away from the tactics and rhetoric of confrontation, advocating "immediate abolition gradually achieved." Some chose to work within the political system or their churches—many more joined in petitions to the federal government to abolish slavery in the District of Columbia and other areas under its jurisdiction and in the fight to reverse the "gag rule" in Congress. Still others were active in the Underground Railroad, which sheltered and assisted fugitive slaves.

AMERICAN CULTURE

In the period after the War of 1812 and before the Civil War, the first distinctively American culture took form. American writers began to look within themselves and across their enlarged continental homeland for their subjects and themes. While the nation's primal energies were taken up with territorial expansion, political controversy, business activity, and social and economic reforms, new traditions in literature and the arts emerged to give meaning to the American experience.

Literature

The rise of an American tradition in literature paralleled the expansion of the nation. The great American writers and poets of the period were drawn to universal themes. Local and regional writing also flowered.

THE AMERICAN ROMANCE

While Washington Irving, the nation's first prominent writer, among others, had called for a distinctively American literature, he himself continued to work in the English literary traditions, New York's Dutch past serving as his principal subject. James Fenimore Cooper, of Cooperstown, in upstate New York, dealt with larger American themes. In his "Leatherstocking" novels, or romances, notably *The Pioneers* (1823) and *The Deerslayer* (1841), his frontiersman hero Natty Bumppo (and the Mohican guide Chingachgook) confronted the environment of the American frontier, chronicling the advance of "civilization" and questioning the implications of its impact on the natural world.

The romance proved a useful form for dealing with the large moral subjects and the peculiar circumstances of the American setting. The theme of the individual confronting the expanse of nature was further developed and exploited by Herman Melville and Nathaniel Hawthorne. Melville probed the underside of the natural world, the dangers of democracy's heroic reach, producing the classic *Moby Dick* (1851). In *The Scarlet Letter* (1850) and *The House of the Seven Gables* (1851), Hawthorne dealt with equally difficult questions of inner limits and the individual's responsibilities to society. Hawthorne also chronicled New England's Puritan past and, in the *Marble Faun* (1860), considered the predicament of the American abroad, confronting the moral ambiguity of the Old World.

EMERSON, THOREAU AND WHITMAN

The foremost essayist of the period was Ralph Waldo Emerson, of Concord, Massachusetts, the leading spirit of Transcendentalism. His intellect and learning were grounded in New England Calvinism. But in his effort to transcend that tradition, to chart the life of self–fulfillment and man's place in nature, he became a national spokesman, the poet of human perfectibility. His friend and fellow Transcendentalist Henry David Thoreau gave classic expression to these ambitions in his inner voyage *Walden* (1854).

Walt Whitman, generally regarded as America's finest poet of the period, developed his expansive style while working as a Democratic party newspaper writer and editor. The bombast of the "Young America" movement can be identified in his writings. However, his best and most original poetry, of democracy and self–liberation, collected in *Leaves of Grass* (1855), transcended the superficial and jingoistic.

NEW ENGLAND'S LITERARY FLOWERING

Boston became an important intellectual center in the years after the War of 1812, largely due to the influence of its writers and publishing houses that formed to meet demands of the nation's highly literate reading public (estimated at 94 percent in the North; 83 percent in the white South).

New England's sense of being out of step with democracy and the course of American history gave its literature a distinctive regional tone but also the redeeming qualities of perspective and form. Its stronger sense of English literary background led to the establishment of a New England tradition of poetry and letters, best exemplified in the works of the "Brahmin" poets and essayists James Russell Lowell, John Greenleaf Whittier, Henry Wadsworth Longfellow, and Oliver Wendell Holmes. New England's distinction in narrative history was set by William Hickling Prescott and John Lothrop Motley, who dealt with the moral drama in the western progress of civilization prior to the founding of America. Francis Parkman drew on this tradition in beginning his classic histories of North America, the first of which, *The California and Oregon Trail* (1849) and *History of the Conspiracy of Pontiac* (1851), appeared before the Civil War.

FOUNDATIONS FOR A SOUTHERN TRADITION

The South's literary imagination was deflected by the dilemma of slavery. The "plantation" novels of Nathaniel Beverly Tucker and John Pendleton Kennedy exhibited literary skill but provoked no deeper sentiment than amiability. South Carolina's William Gilmore Simms chronicled the southern frontier with a clear eye in his early career; he later lost focus in defending his section. Much energy was expended in fashioning polemics to justify slaveholding: the works of George Fitzhugh, in particular, displayed much learning if warped brilliance. More enduring was the sharp and raucous humoristic tradition developed by Augustus Baldwin Longstreet and Joseph G. Baldwin, who prepared the way for Mark Twain.

The South's greatest writer of the antebellum period was Edgar Allan Poe. His poetry was highly original, if flavored with the Gothic in the prevailing romantic tradition of the period. His tales of detection and terror (establishing the genre) were placed in Old World settings. However, the psychological episodes that formed them, such as the horrible walling up of the victim of the "Cask of Amontillado," drew on familiar emotions in the South. Southern orators frequently described their fear that an awful "circumvallation" (walling up) of the South by free–soil settlement in the west would eventually lead to racial warfare.

POPULAR CULTURE

Rapid increases in birth rate and immigration, a high level of literacy, and technological advances in publishing contributed to an ever–expanding readership. Book and periodical publishing, as well as newspapers, boomed. Much of what was printed was targeted for mass appeal: sentimental novelists flourished while writers like Melville remained largely unknown. Harriet Beecher Stowe's enormous influence derived from her ability to reach the reading public through the tradition of the sentimental novel. In the theater, melodrama prevailed over serious art, although the classics, such as the works of Shakespeare, were regularly and professionally staged in the principal cities.

A hunger for knowledge and self–improvement among the adult public was perceptible throughout the country. Educational organizations, notably the lyceum and mechanics' institute, penetrated deep into the interior, providing each sizeable town with a forum where traveling lecturers discoursed on mostly serious subjects. Emerson, Greeley, Simms, as well as visiting literary notables such as the English writer Charles Dickens, traveled the circuit, along with hundreds of other lecturers on various subjects. Debating societies also flourished. These existed even on the frontier, in towns like New Salem, Illinois, which contained about 25 families in the early 1830s: one of the New Salem Debating Society's members at that time was Abraham Lincoln.

The Arts of Design

The works of American painters, sculptors, and architects were less self–consciously American, since they depended on European techniques and methods to achieve competence. Most of the best American artists studied in Britain or Europe. The painters of the Hudson River School, notably Asher B. Durand and Thomas Cole, gave moral drama to the representation of the American landscape. George Catlin chronicled the heroic American Indian; John James Audubon, the natural life of North America. The humorous genre scenes of George Caleb Bingham reflected democratic self–confidence and western exuberance. From the 1830s, painting was substantially influenced by the new techniques of lithography and later of engraving, which expanded the artist's audience; the invention of photography in the 1850s had profound effects on the whole world of representational art.

Architecture and sculpture depended to a considerable extent on government patronage; thus classical forms predominated, with decreasing vitality. American sculptors, most of whom secured their training in Italy, were encouraged as a matter of national pride as long as their classicism was literary and abstract, such as Hiram Powers's celebrated *Greek Slave* (1843). Horatio Greenough's ambitious statue portrait of the seated Washington, bare–chested in Roman dress (1832–36), however, was refused a place in the Capitol—indicative, among other things, of the growing importance of middle–class "Victorian" standards. (It is now on display in the Smithsonian Institution in Washington.)

The Greek Revival style, vaguely reflecting democratic antecedents, predominated in the public buildings of the antebellum period. Its use in the construction of residences, large and small, reflected the growing influence of popular culture on American architecture. With technological innovations in publishing and photography, visual images were more accurately and widely reproduced. The design arts as a consequence were increasingly influenced by broad public taste.

In its movement and multiplicity, mid–nineteenth-century American society accurately reflected the enormous, rapid physical growth of the United States. The great natural distances between people and things still distinguished the American experience from the European—technological innovations such as the railroad and telegraph served to reduce them, but the extension of the nation's western boundaries to the Pacific insured that the spatial dimension of American history would remain highly significant.

In the decades before the Civil War the pace of industrialization and urbanization in the North steadily accelerated, with significant consequences for agriculture and consumer industries. In the main, northern society incorporated or adjusted to the powerful changes that were at work in the world. Those individuals who could not do so either headed west or sought to recreate or experiment with the forms of community, following an established American tradition.

The South, however, stood aside from all this. It clung to a much older social structure—of ruler and ruled, of the few over the many—that had not changed since ancient times. That and its dependence on large–scale agricul-

ture and the labor of black slaves set it apart from the rest of the nation and, indeed, from most of the world. By midcentury the stark contrasts between the South and the rest of the nation could not be ignored or viewed as mere cultural variation.

Selected Readings

Dougass, Frederick. *Life and Times of Frederick Douglass* (1845, 1881)

Eaton, Clement. *The Freedom–of–Thought Struggle in the Old South* (1964)

Gates, Paul W. *The Farmer's Age: Agriculture, 1815–1860* (1960)

Genovese, Eugene D. *Roll Jordan Roll: The World the Slaves Made* (1974)

Hansen, Marcus L. *The Atlantic Migration, 1607–1860* (1976)

Kraditor, Aileen. ed. *Up from the Pedestal: Selected Writings in the History of American Feminism* (1968)

McLoughlin, William G. *Revivals, Awakenings, and Reform . . .* (1978)

Myers, Robert Manson. ed. *The Children of Pride: A True Story of Georgia and the Civil War* (1972)

Miller, Perry. *The Raven and the Whale: The War of Words and Wits in the Era of Poe and Melville* (1956)

Rose, Willie Lee. ed. *A Documentary History of Slavery in North America* (1976)

Rothman, David. *The Discovery of the Asylum: Social Order and Disorder in the New Republic* (1971)

Taylor, Joshua C. *The Fine Arts in America* (1979)

Taylor, William R. *Cavalier and Yankee: The Old South and American National Character* (1961)

Tyler, Alice Felt. *Freedom's Ferment: Phases of American Social History from the Colonial Period to the Outbreak of the Civil War* (1944)

Walters, Ronald G. *American Reformers, 1815–1860* (1978)

11

Territorial Expansion and Sectional Conflict

1844 Polk and the Democrats, calling for the "reannexation" of Texas and "reoccupation" of Oregon, win the presidential election over Clay and the Whigs; "gag rule" (1836–1844) rescinded, principally due to efforts of former president Rep. John Quincy Adams (December)

1845 Texas annexed (as a state) by joint resolution of Congress (March)

1846 Treaty with Great Britain settling Oregon boundary is ratified (June); war declared with Mexico (May); David Wilmot introduces his amendment to the military appropriations bill (Wilmot proviso; August)

1847 U.S. forces capture Mexico City (September)

1848 Senate ratifies the Treaty of Guadalupe–Hidalgo, ending war with Mexico and providing for the Mexican cession (March)

1849 General Zachary Taylor, victorious Whig candidate, takes office as President; Gold rush swells population of California, which requests admission to the Union as a free state

1850 Death of Calhoun (March); death of President Taylor, succeeded by Vice-President Millard Fillmore (July); Compromise of 1850 legislated to resolve sectional crisis

1852 First book publication of Harriet Beecher Stowe's *Uncle Tom's Cabin*; death of Clay and Webster

1853 Democrat Franklin Pierce becomes president (March); Gadsden Purchase treaty signed (December)

1854 Kansas–Nebraska Act repeals Missouri Compromise of 1820, enacts popular sovereignty (May); formation of the Republican party

1854–1858 Civil strife in Kansas between proslavery and antislavery proponents

1856 General John C. Frémont, first Republican presidential candidate, loses to Democrat James Buchanan; Charles Sumner of Massachusetts attacked while speaking in the Senate (May)

1857 Supreme Court rules in Dred Scott case (March); publication of Hinton Rowan Helper's *Impending Crisis of the South* and George Fitzhugh's *Cannibals All!*

1858 Lincoln and Douglas debates in Illinois Senate race

1859 John Brown attempts to capture Harper's Ferry armory; is tried and hanged in Virginia

1860 Presidential election contested in two regions by four candidates; Republican Abraham Lincoln elected

The lure of virgin land along the western frontier and the drive for territorial expansion can be traced back to the American colonial experience. The struggle to achieve independence from Great Britain, and to retain that independence against the background of the Napoleonic Wars in Europe, preoccupied the new nation during the Jeffersonian period. At the conclusion of the War of 1812, however, there were for a time no external threats to distract attention from internal development. Increases in wealth and population gave the United States the means to deal decisively to secure its borders, the ambition of all sovereign states.

The immensity of the American frontier, largely unsettled except for seminomadic tribes, as well as the requirements of American politics, caused the United States to identify and achieve its continental ambitions in stages. Territorial expansion was soon perceived as a remedy for the nation's ills: a safety valve for the unfortunate and defeated, a unifying formula for political victory. The process of expansion became a shaping event in the formation of the American nation, as important as the political experiment embodied in the Constitution. But it also provided the means for the nation's social disorder, the institution of slavery, to revive and flourish.

"MANIFEST DESTINY"

Even before North America had been extensively explored and mapped, some Americans persisted in the belief that the boundaries of the United States should extend to extremities of the continent. The French traveler

Tocqueville observed in 1831–32 that a continental vision was "always flitting" before the American mind. The debate over the proposed annexation of Texas and Oregon put American expansionist ambitions into focus. Although many dissented, the majority embraced the idea expressed in 1845 by Democratic journalist John L. O'Sullivan: it was America's "manifest destiny to overspread the continent allotted by Providence for the free development of our yearly multiplying millions."

The Annexation of Texas

Although the Adams–Onis treaty of 1819 with Spain provided for the United States to surrender all claim to Texas, American interest in the territory persisted. Presidents John Quincy Adams (in 1827) and Andrew Jackson (1829, 1835) tried to purchase it from Mexico.

THE TEXAS REPUBLIC

The Mexican province of Texas, which had been largely colonized by emigrants from the United States, declared its independence on March 2, 1836.

American Migration to Texas. After achieving its independence from Spain in 1821, Mexico permitted migration from the United States into its sparsely populated province of Texas. It granted approval to Moses Austin and his son, Stephen F. Austin, to promote colonization by making large grants of land to prospective settlers from the north. Soon other colonizers received generous land grants. By 1830 nearly 20,000 (by 1835, almost 35,000) Americans, chiefly from Tennessee, Mississippi, and Louisiana, had settled in Texas. Many immigrants came to establish plantations and brought black slaves with them; this trend continued even after Mexico had eliminated slavery in 1829.

Texan Independence. Mexico soon became alarmed at the rapid increase of Anglo–Americans and in 1830 prohibited new immigration from the United States. The grievances of Anglo–American settlers against the Mexican authorities mounted. They (1) wanted local self–government in Texas; (2) resented Mexican laws suspending land contracts, imposing duties on imported goods, and forbidding foreigners to enter the province; and (3) feared that the Mexican government would enforce its religious requirement (that all immigrants subscribe to Roman Catholicism) and take steps to free their slaves. Mexico did lift the law prohibiting foreign immigration, but a crisis came in 1835, when, in response to an incident directed at customs officials at the port of Galveston, the Mexican dictator General Lopez de Santa Anna reduced Texas to the status of a military district in the province of Coahuila.

The movement for provincial autonomy in Texas quickly developed into a war for independence. At the Battle of San Jacinto, Texans under General Sam Houston routed Santa Anna's forces and compelled him to acknowledge the independence of the province. The Mexican government, however, refused to honor the agreement and Texan independence.

TEXAS AND THE UNITED STATES

The new republic formally applied for admission to the union. The overwhelming majority of Texans desired annexation, but there was anything but unanimity on the issue in the United States in 1836. Opposition was loudest in the northern states, particularly among antislavery groups, which charged that southern slaveholders were conspiring to create several slave states out of Texas in order to strengthen southern control of the federal government. The controversy, they argued, would end in war with Mexico. Support for the admission of Texas came from (1) Manifest Destiny expansionists; (2) those who feared the potential of an independent Texas and the designs of Great Britain; (3) those eager for new lands, intending to expand the cash crop agricultural model of the South (there was also interest among free–soil settlers); and (4) a small group of speculators in Texas land and depreciated Texas bonds.

Calhoun's Treaty (1844). Jackson recognized the independence of Texas just before he left office, but he left the question of annexation to his successor. Van Buren displayed little interest, primarily because it was too hot an issue and threatened to divide the Democratic party. President Tyler seized on the Texas question after his break with the Whigs, expecting to gain a southern following by promoting it and thereby win the election of 1844. The annexation of Texas became the chief policy goal of the Tyler administration; it carefully conducted a propaganda campaign to "prepare the public mind" for the event, even manufacturing British and abolitionist designs on an independent Texas. Secretary of State Calhoun made no effort at subterfuge, however, and negotiated a treaty of annexation as a measure required for the protection of slavery in the South; it was defeated by a decisive vote in the Senate (June 1844).

Campaign of 1844

Before the election of 1844 Henry Clay, the Whig nominee, and Martin Van Buren, the favorite for the Democratic nomination, opponents of annexation, had agreed to refrain from discussion of the Texas issue in the upcoming presidential campaign. Pro–Texas Democrats, however, upset their plans. They engineered the nomination of dark–horse James K. Polk of Tennessee, formerly speaker of the House of Representatives, at the Democratic convention. An ardent expansionist, "Young Hickory" Polk ran on a platform that called for the "re–annexation of Texas and the re–occupation of Oregon."

Many antislavery Whigs, irritated by Clay's attempt to straddle the Texas issue, cast their votes for James G. Birney, the candidate of the antislavery Liberty party. Polk was elected, polling only 49.6 percent of the total vote, to Clay's 48.1 percent. A shift of a few thousand votes in New York State, which Polk won narrowly, would have given Clay the margin of victory in the electoral college.

ANNEXATION BY JOINT RESOLUTION

President Tyler interpreted Polk's election as an endorsement of his own policy. He sponsored a joint resolution for the annexation of Texas (which, unlike a treaty, required only a majority vote of both houses). Despite the constitutional objections of the Whigs, the resolution passed the Congress just three days before the end of Tyler's term. Texas accepted the terms of annexation and by December 1845 had drafted a constitution under which it was admitted to the union as a new state.

Acquisition of Oregon

In the campaign of 1844, the Democrats attempted to make the annexation of Texas more palatable to northern voters by linking it with the "reoccupation" of Oregon. Expansionists played on residual anti–British sentiment with campaign slogans such as "Fifty–four–forty or Fight" (the northern boundary of the Oregon country.

BASIS FOR AMERICAN CLAIMS

In the late eighteenth century Spain, Russia, France, and Great Britain all set forth vague claims to the Oregon country. Early in the nineteenth century the United States claimed the region on the basis of (1) the explorations of Captain Robert Gray, who in 1792 discovered and named the Columbia River; (2) the Lewis and Clark expedition of 1805–06; and (3) the establishment of John Jacob Astor's trading post, Astoria (1811).

Anglo–American Agreement. British claims to sovereignty in the territory were equally well founded. When attempts to divide the region failed, the United States and Great Britain agreed in 1818 to a ten–year period of joint occupation. The arrangement in effect gave the representatives of the Hudson's Bay Company temporary control of the region. Nevertheless the joint occupation was renewed in 1827 for an indefinite period, with the provision that either nation might terminate the agreement by giving a year's notice.

MIGRATION TO OREGON

Prior to 1830 the contact of the United States with Oregon was limited to the visits of trappers and traders. During the next two decades, and particularly after 1840, migration into the Oregon country was stimulated by (1) propagandists like Hall J. Kelley, who organized a society for the settlement of the territory; (2) the activities of businessmen like Nathaniel Wyeth, who demonstrated by his overland trips (1832, 1836) the practicability of a wagon route to the Oregon country; (3) the missionary activity among the Indians of the Pacific northwest by the Methodists, Presbyterians, and Roman Catholics. By 1845, some 5,000 Americans resided in the Oregon country (the present states of Oregon, Washington, and Idaho, with parts of Wyoming, Montana, and British Columbia).

THE TREATY OF 1846

The steady stream of migrants, which expanded significantly beginning in 1843, encouraged manifest destiny expansionists in their ambitions to gain the entire Oregon country. In his first annual message, in December 1845, Polk asked Congress for authorization to suspend the joint occupation. After much bluster and talk of war, however, he agreed to a treaty that divided Oregon. The northern boundary of the United States (between the Rocky Mountains and the Pacific) was fixed at the 49th parallel of latitude. A diplomatic compromise had become necessary as a consequence of incidents on the Texas border. However, northerners interpreted Polk's willingness to abandon American claims to "All Oregon" as an indication that the President favored southern, slaveholding interests.

THE FRUITS OF WAR

President Polk, a firm believer in manifest destiny, saw the immense opportunity for the United States in a conflict with Mexico. Aware of the strategic value of California and of Great Britain's growing interest, he increased diplomatic and military pressure on Mexico for territorial concessions in confident expectation that the outbreak of hostilities would produce rapid results. Although American victories came, the war was not concluded quickly; opposition to it was strong from the outset.

Polk's Aggressive Strategy

Determined to exploit every advantage to advance American territorial interests in the southwest, President Polk sent troops to defend Texas's claim to the area between the Nueces and Rio Grande rivers in the summer of 1845. He was well aware of the implications of this action. Mexico had cut off diplomatic relations after the United States had annexed Texas and, still refusing to accept the loss of its former province, insisted that the contested region south of the Nueces was Mexican territory.

Polk also positioned a naval squadron off the coast of California and sent a sizeable expeditionary force under Captain John C. Frémont into that Mexican province, ostensibly to make topographical and scientific observations. These forces, and the American consul in the provincial capital of Monterey, were instructed to support a pro–American rebellion in California in the event Mexico declared war.

THE SLIDELL MISSION

In the autumn of 1845 Polk sent John Slidell as a special envoy to Mexico with instructions (1) to offer to assume claims of United States citizens against Mexico if the Mexican government would recognize the Rio Grande rather than the Nueces as the southern boundary of Texas; (2) to offer $5 million for the cession of New Mexico; and (3) to offer up to $25 million for California and New Mexico. Slidell was to conduct his negotiations in such manner as to promote cordial relations with Mexico.

MEXICAN POLICY

Political disturbances in Mexico made Slidell's task doubly difficult. The temper of the country was so hostile to the United States that two Mexican presidents refused to receive Polk's envoy. To patriotic Mexicans it seemed as if the United States, having stolen Texas, was plotting the destruction of their nation. They willingly followed their irate leaders in demanding war against the northern enemy.

The Mexican War

Discouraging reports from Slidell caused Polk to order General Zachary Taylor, "Old Rough and Ready," in command of U.S. army forces in Texas, to advance across the Nueces to the Rio Grande River. When the president learned that Mexican forces had crossed the Rio Grande, he informed Congress that a state of war existed as a consequence of Mexico's action (May 11, 1846).

WAR AND DISSENT

Congress, accepting Polk's statement that Mexico had assumed the role of aggressor, authorized the president to raise an army of 50,000 men and voted $10 million in war appropriations. The western and southern states responded enthusiastically, but the northeast was apathetic. New England abolitionists were particularly severe in their criticism of the administration's policy, warning of the biblical parallels to the tale of King Ahab's coveting of Naboth's vineyard.

CAMPAIGNS IN MEXICO

General Taylor's victories in northern Mexico enabled him to enter the port city of Matamoros in May 1846. Although President Polk thought the pace of his campaign slow, by the end of the year Taylor had captured Monterrey, Saltillo, and Victoria and held a front two hundred miles long.

Anxious for a speedy conclusion to the conflict, Polk in November 1846 ordered a force under General Winfield Scott to move on Mexico City by way of Vera Cruz (on the Gulf of Mexico). Scott's small army (some 14,000 men) encountered resistance but advanced decisively, winning key battles at Cerro Gordo and Chapultepec. It entered the Mexican capital in September 1847.

CAPTURE OF CALIFORNIA AND NEW MEXICO

California and New Mexico, where Mexican control was weak, were easily captured. In June 1846, Colonel Stephen W. Kearney set out from Fort Leavenworth, Kansas, took Santa Fe without opposition, and proceeded to San Diego. Meanwhile Commodore John Sloat and his successor, Commodore Robert F. Stockton, had captured the ports of San Francisco, Monterey, and Los Angeles. The Pacific squadron and Captain Fremont's force provided support to a group of American settlers, who had declared California an independent nation under the "bear flag." Kearney assumed the leadership of these insurgents and other American forces, completing the conquest of California in the fall of 1846.

THE TREATY OF GUADALUPE–HIDALGO (1848)

Despite crushing defeats and loss of territory, the Mexican government resisted American terms for surrender. The frustrated president ordered his diplomatic agent, Nicholas P. Trist, to return to Washington. But, with Polk's aims in sight, Trist continued negotiations with Mexican commissioners and concluded a treaty in February 1848. Under this agreement Mexico agreed (1) to recognize the Rio Grande River as the southern boundary of Texas; and (2) to cede New Mexico and California to the United States in return for $15 million and the assumption by the United States government of American citizens' claims against Mexico (up to $3,250,000). The Senate ratified the treaty by a vote of 38 to 14 on March 10, 1848.

EXPANSION AND COMPROMISE

The sweeping military successes and enormous territorial expanse gained by the United States from Mexico extended the nation's boundaries to the Pacific and altered forever the American mind. The rising nationalistic spirit was expressed in the "Young America" movement in politics, the arts and literature. Not long after war's end, however, the fruits of conquest turned bitter. Disputes arose over whether slavery should be prohibited or permitted in the new territories, reviving the forces of sectionalism and confirming the abolitionists' prophecy.

The Far West   When the Treaty of Guadalupe–Hidalgo was signed, the value of the lands that had been obtained from Mexico by the United States (some 338.6 million acres) was uncertain. Explorers had described vast areas of the new southwest as desert, unfit for settlement.

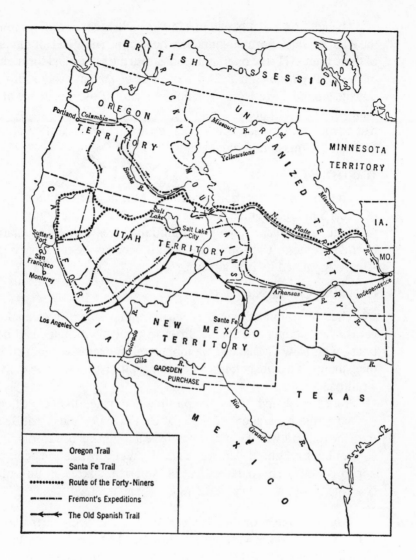

Fig. 11.1 Trails to the Pacific

CALIFORNIA AND THE FORTY–NINERS

By the late 1820s the Hispanic population of Mexican California numbered only 4,000 (several times that number of Indians inhabited the region). In the 1830s groups of merchants from New England and Great Britain began to enjoy growing business in the coastal ports and the provincial capital of Monterey. While their glowing reports of the country sparked some interest in the east, California remained sparsely populated, broken up into large estates. Soon after the transfer of the Mexican cession, however, the news that gold had been discovered in the Sacramento Valley electrified the American public.

The gold rush that began in 1849 brought an extraordinary migration to the Pacific Coast. Fortune–hunters who sought a new El Dorado had a choice of three routes: (1) the overland road across the plains and through the passes of the Rocky Mountains; (2) the Isthmus of Panama route; or (3) the long voyage around Cape Horn. Within two years of the discovery of gold more than 90,000 adventurers, from all parts of the world and every social class, had been drawn to California. The territory, having drafted a constitution, requested admission into the Union.

TERRITORY OF UTAH

The gold rush materially aided the Mormon settlements in the vicinity of Great Salt Lake, which had begun in 1847, when the region still belonged to Mexico. Brigham Young's community was a halfway station on the overland route to California. In 1850 it became the territory of Utah, with Young appointed its first governor.

ISTHMIAN CANAL PROJECTS

The "forty–niners" emphasized the importance of a canal or railroad across the Isthmus of Panama. In 1846 the United States had negotiated a treaty with New Granada (Colombia) for an exclusive right of way across the isthmus. Two years later American capitalists began the construction of a railroad.

Both British and American promoters pursued the idea of constructing a canal across Nicaragua. In 1850 the United States and Great Britain signed the Clayton–Bulwer Treaty, whereby each agreed not to obtain exclusive control over a Central American canal, erect fortifications commanding it, nor to colonize any part of Central America. The neutrality of any canal constructed by private capital was jointly guaranteed.

The Revival of Sectional Debate

From the outset of the Mexican War, it had been clear that the United States would acquire vast new territories when the fighting had been concluded. Disappointed by Polk's decision to compromise on the Oregon question, northern Democrats in the House of Representatives asserted their free–soil principles and pushed for the exclusion of slavery from such lands, thereby breaking the gentlemen's agreement to refrain from debate on the slavery issue.

THE WILMOT PROVISO

In August 1846, with the war going well and some expressing desires to annex "All Mexico," Congressman David Wilmot, a Pennsylvania Democrat, rose in the House with an amendment to the military appropriations bill. He proposed to exclude slavery (or other involuntary servitude) from any territory acquired from Mexico as a result of war or purchase. The resolution reflected the growing resentment of northern Democrats for what they perceived to be Polk's pro–southern policies. The president's willingness to compromise claims to "All Oregon," his support for lower tariff duties, and his veto of internal improvements legislation strengthened this impression.

Wilmot's amendment precipitated a bitter struggle in Congress—it was carried in the House, on largely sectional rather than party lines, but defeated in the Senate. The administration was then able to secure the votes of enough northern Democrats to pass the appropriations bill without it. The principle of the Wilmot proviso, however, would soon refashion the nation's politics.

Presidential Election of 1848. The presidential campaign of 1848 reflected the inability of the second party system to accommodate the burning issue of slavery in the territories. The two national political parties could maintain unity only by ignoring the question. The Whigs, despite their opposition to the Mexican War, sought to retake the presidency with the popular General Zachary Taylor. Their platform merely expressed confidence in their candidate. Polk having declined to run again, the Democrats nominated Senator Lewis Cass, of Michigan. The party adopted the uncertain concept of "squatter sovereignty" or "popular sovereignty"—which left the decision of whether or not to adopt slavery in the territories to the settlers themselves.

In the North, there were defections from both political parties over the slavery issue, but more Democrats fell out of line. The old Liberty party and antislavery Whigs joined dissident Democrats under the banner of the new Free Soil party and nominated former president Martin Van Buren for the presidency. Although Van Buren failed to carry a single state, the Free Soil party won some 10 percent of the popular vote and finished second in the popular vote (ahead of the regular Democrats) in Massachusetts and New York. Taylor defeated Cass in the electoral college, 163 to 127.

The Formula of Compromise

Since the days of the Confederation, the place of slavery in the constitutional order and its role in the future of the new nation had menaced the national politics. At the Federal convention in 1787, the framers had been forced to accept a sectional compromise (see Chapter 6) when disputes over congressional representation could not be resolved. That agreement was reached in large part because it was believed that slavery was dying out. When the rich lands of the Deep South opened up immediately after the War of 1812, the future of the slave economy became more promising.

THE MISSOURI COMPROMISE AND SECTIONAL BALANCE

During the first three decades after the adoption of the Constitution, a rough equivalency of slaveholding and nonslaveholding states was maintained. This occurred more by chance than design. By the time Missouri applied for statehood in 1819, however, the sectional balance was considered a significant component of union. The controversy that ensued over the

Tallmadge Amendment, which proposed gradual emancipation in Missouri, was resolved only after Maine requested admission to the union as a free state. This provided the means to maintain the representational balance between slave and free states.

Congress recognized the idea of sectional balance when it adopted the Missouri Compromise line, which prohibited slavery above 36° 30′ latitude in the territory that composed the Louisiana Purchase. The degree to which this idea had become enshrined in American politics was made evident in the strategy employed by pro–Texas Democrats in 1843–44. They supported the occupation of "All Oregon" to create a coalition for expansion, expecting northerners to go along with the annexation of slaveholding Texas to achieve their own ends.

THE CRISIS OF 1850

The introduction of the Wilmot proviso, which in effect proposed to erase the Missouri Compromise line, turned the floor of Congress into a stage for extended debate over the status of slavery in the territories. How should the new territory won from Mexico be organized? The question dominated the congressional agenda for almost four years. Floor debate became increasingly acrimonious and by 1850 had taken on the appearance of a rhetorical civil war. Sectional loyalties overrode all else. Although they had no illusions that slavery could take hold in Oregon, southern members, for example, held up that territory's admission to the union until 1848, determined to make clear the importance they attached to the sectional balance.

California and the Territorial Question. The congressional dispute over slavery might have continued for years were it not for the discovery of gold in the Sacramento Valley of California in January 1848. By the end of 1849, the territory's population had swelled to 100,000, giving a sense of urgency to the need for local government. Because of Congress's inaction, the Mexican cession was still under military control. In 1849 Californians drafted and ratified a constitution and applied for admission into the union as a free state. It was clear to most Americans that the nation had reached a pivotal moment in its history.

The extension of the nation's boundaries to the Pacific Ocean had brought vast new territories, capable of being organized into many states. The legislative mechanisms devised for their settlement would give shape to the economic and social development of the new region—and thereby profoundly influence the nation's political future. Both northerners and southerners recognized that slave economies could not take hold in the new western regions unless slaveholding were protected by law in the early stages of territorial settlement.

THE COMPROMISE OF 1850

After President Taylor recommended that California be admitted as a free state, southern threats of disunion began to be made with regularity. Moderate members put forward three formulas in an effort to resolve (or defuse) the crisis. The most prominent of these called for (1) the Missouri Compromise line to be extended to the Pacific; (2) Congress to defer the question of slavery in the territories to the federal courts; (3) the decisions on slaveholding to be made by the inhabitants of the territories when they began the procedure to apply for statehood. Most southerners continued to argue that, since slaves were legal property, Congress had the responsibility to provide protection for the slaveholder if he chose to migrate to the new territories with his slaves.

In January 1850, as civil war loomed, Henry Clay, then seventy-two years old, returned to the Senate and attempted to conciliate the sectional conflict and save the union. He introduced a series of resolutions, five of which finally became the basis of the settlement known as the Compromise of 1850. Their introduction marked the beginning of the Great Debate, in which "the great triumvirate," Clay, Calhoun, and Webster, would speak on the Senate floor for the last time. In response to a strong unionist movement that gained popular support in all sections of the country, members gradually moved toward compromise. The Southern Convention, which convened in Nashville in June 1850 to consider whether the South should secede, adjourned without taking any action. The death in the following month of President Taylor, who had insisted that California be admitted before compromise measures were considered, eliminated one obstacle to a broad agreement. Taylor's successor, Vice–President Millard Fillmore, actively contributed to its achievement.

Clay's omnibus bill (one with many provisions) offered something for all. Its most important parts provided for (1) California to be admitted as a free state; (2) the slave trade, but not slavery, to be abolished in the District of Columbia; (3) Congress to enact a more effective fugitive slave law; and (4) territorial governments to be established in New Mexico and Utah with the stipulation that they might be admitted to the union with or without slavery, as they might determine (thus legislating the principle of popular sovereignty). As a single package, the omnibus bill went down in defeat in the Senate in July 1850. Exhausted and in poor health, Clay departed for Kentucky. Others, led by Senator Stephen Douglas of Illinois, completed the compromise by pushing through its principal provisions in separate pieces of legislation.

"Finality" of the Compromise. The compromise measures were opposed by the South's great spokesman and theorist Calhoun, as well as by antislavery men like William Henry Seward of New York. (Seward had spoken of the need to consult a "higher law" on the question of slavery.) In the North, Senator Webster was vilified by abolitionists for having agreed to the new and stricter Fugitive Slave Law of 1850, the one measure southerners had insisted upon in acceding to Clay's compromise package. However, the unionist movement was effective in strengthening the sentimental bonds of union in both North and South. Politicians in both sections endorsed the compromise as the solution of the slavery question.

ELECTION OF 1852

Both national parties pledged to observe the "finality" of the Compromise of 1850 and to refrain from discussing the slavery question. The Free Soil party denounced the congressional agreement. Democrats nominated Franklin Pierce of New Hampshire, who won a resounding victory over the Whig candidate, General Winfield Scott. Pierce strongly endorsed the Compromise, which won him the support of many conservative Whigs, notably Daniel Webster. Suspicions that Scott took guidance from Seward and the antislavery element of the Whig party hurt his candidacy, especially in the South; he received only 42 out of 296 electoral votes.

"A HOUSE DIVIDED AGAINST ITSELF"

The Compromise of 1850, it soon became clear, was a truce rather than a settlement. Still, since most believed that the nation's limits had been reached, the formula for determining the status of slavery in the western territories seemed to be fixed by either the Compromise measures or the Missouri Compromise line. The sectional agreement was broken in 1854, however, when Senator Stephen A. Douglas of Illinois introduced legislation to organize the region west of Iowa and Missouri.

The Limits of Compromise

The flaw in the unionist appeal to the "finality" of the Compromise was that it proposed a static remedy in a dynamic era of growth and expansion. The pledge to refrain from discussion of the slavery issue depended upon restraint. American history had already demonstrated that this formula did not conform to the settlement of the continent.

"YOUNG AMERICA" AND THE EXTENSION OF SLAVERY

In response to a wave of popular revolutions that swept Europe in 1848 and to the United States's new status as a continental power, the eagle of manifest destiny again took to rhetorical flight. A "Young America" movement, reflecting similar movements in Europe, was championed by expansionist Democrats to promote a new cultural as well as political nationalism.

Diplomatic initiatives were undertaken during both the Fillmore and Pierce administrations to expand American interests and territory. While the Whigs were in power, the United States broke with tradition and gave official support to Hungary's movement to gain independence from Austria. In 1854, the efforts of Commodore Matthew C. Perry, at the head of a U.S. navy expedition in the Pacific Ocean, secured a treaty opening Japanese ports to the United States for the first time.

Expansionist activity, however, was no longer a salve for the ills of the nation. In fact, it now became a cause of divisiveness. Any initiative directed toward southern climes was suspected in the North as a ruse by southerners to secure additional territory for its slave economy. Antislavery groups pointed to (1) the private military expeditions of General Narciso Lopez in Cuba (1850–51), which were supported by influential southerners; (2) the Ostend Manifesto, signed in 1854 by Pierre Soulé, James Buchanan, and John Y. Mason (U.S. ministers to, respectively, Spain, Britain, and France), which proposed the idea that the United States would be justified "by every law human and divine" in seizing Cuba; and (3) the military activities, or filibustering, of William Walker in Nicaragua, which seemed to have the support of southern extremists. Southerners, on the other hand, fearing the implications for the sectional balance, opposed renewed efforts to annex Canada. They also blocked a treaty that would have provided for the admission of Hawaii into the union (without slavery).

Expansion, Railroads, and Popular Sovereignty

In the early 1850s western settlement had reached the Missouri River and Indian lands. At the same time pressures were increasing in Washington for the federal government to support the construction of a transcontinental railroad to link the Atlantic and Pacific coasts. A coalition of economic interests secured the opening of Kansas and Nebraska, at the cost of reigniting the sectional conflict.

DOUGLAS AND THE KANSAS–NEBRASKA BILL

Southern and northern interests competed intensively to secure the location of the transcontinental railroad. Aware of the great economic benefits it would confer, the powerful Senator Stephen Douglas of Illinois, chairman of the Committee on Territories, sought approval of Chicago or another northwestern city as the railroad's proposed eastern terminus. He believed the settlement of the Nebraska region would stimulate the population growth that would justify a northern route across the Great Plains, and he mustered his legislative skills to gain the means to insure it.

Repeal of the Missouri Compromise. The Nebraska region was above the Missouri Compromise line, the 36° 30′ line of latitude, where slavery had been prohibited since 1820. Knowing that he had to avoid a protracted dispute over the sectional balance of free and slave states to secure the organization of the area, Douglas worked out a deal with southern members to achieve his ends. He agreed to back a repeal of the Missouri Compromise so that the area west of Missouri would be open to settlement without any restriction against slavery. He also agreed to a division of the region into the Nebraska Territory and the Kansas Territory; it was presumed the latter would be settled by slaveholders.

The Kansas–Nebraska Act (1854). This act thus repealed the Missouri Compromise which, since 1820, had been regarded as the final settlement of the slavery question in the territory of the Louisiana Purchase. Douglas argued that the most democratic way to solve the issue was to allow the people of any new territory to decide whether or not they wished to legalize slavery within their boundaries. He was successful in gaining President Pierce's support for the bill on this basis. His legislation thus had the effect of raising the principle of popular sovereignty, which had been incorporated into the Compromise of 1850, to the level of national policy. The measure ended the sectional truce on the slavery issue and bitterly divided the Congress—southern Whigs and Democrats supported it, northern Whigs opposed it, northern Democrats were evenly divided on the question.

RENEWED OPPOSITION TO THE FUGITIVE SLAVE LAW

Antislavery groups in the North were incensed over the provisions of the Fugitive Slave Law passed in 1850. They denounced it because it failed to provide for a jury trial in the case of suspects, because it applied to slaves who had fled from their masters years before, and because it permitted federal officials to compel any citizen to aid in the apprehension and return of fugitives. Still, in the aftermath of the Compromise of 1850, public sentiment in the North supported enforcement of the new Fugitive Slave Law as the necessary price for preserving the bonds of Union.

The Kansas–Nebraska Act changed all that. Mass meetings were held in northern cities to organize disobedience to the law. Between 1855 and 1859 several state legislatures passed "personal liberty laws" to prohibit the use of local jails for the confinement of fugitives. On occasion mobs formed in northern cities to prevent the apprehension of fugitive slaves. Such actions had the effect of undermining the position of moderates in the South; southerners indignantly accused the North of deliberate intent to violate the Compromise.

THE GADSDEN PURCHASE

Proponents of a southern route for the projected transcontinental railroad were also active. The rapid growth of California helped their cause. However, early surveys indicated rails would have to be laid through a part of Mexico. At the suggestion of Secretary of War Jefferson Davis of Mississippi, President Pierce sent James Gadsden, a South Carolinian and president of a railroad, to Mexico, where he secured the Gadsden Purchase (the southern portions of modern Arizona and New Mexico) for $10 million.

Formation of the Republican Party

The consequences of the Kansas–Nebraska Act were far–reaching. Anti–Nebraska Democrats and Whigs drifted into a new coalition, the Republican party, organized upon the principle of opposition to the expansion of slavery. The Democratic party was increasingly dominated by the South. The Whigs ceased to be a national political party.

"THE SLAVE POWER CONSPIRACY"

The public meetings that were held all over the North to protest the Kansas–Nebraska Act contributed to a reordering of national politics. To the free states, repeal of the Missouri Compromise represented a step backward, a violation of a sacred agreement that had the moral force of a constitutional provision. It seemed to confirm the accusations of abolitionists that the South was engaged in a "slave power conspiracy" of some kind, to make slavery legal in all of the territories or even throughout the settled states. The matter of the territories was enough to cause concern. It was certain that they would have much influence in shaping the nation's future. It was also clear that northern settlers as well as European immigrants would avoid settling in areas that permitted slaveholding. It even seemed possible that slavery might prove adaptable in mining enterprises in the far southwest.

The Republican Coalition. Many northern Democrats abandoned their party in protest against the Kansas–Nebraska Act, further strengthening the moderate and pro–South elements that remained in that party. These anti–Nebraska Democrats, together with groups of northern "Conscience Whigs" and remnants of the Free Soil party, quickly joined in opposition as Republicans. The strongest support for the new party was in the northwest. In the fall elections of 1854, these Republicans joined with the American party (Know–Nothings) to capture a majority of the seats in the House of Representatives. Significantly, the new Republican party made no attempt to win support from the slaveholding South—its organizing principle was opposition to the extension of slavery anywhere within the territories of the United States. It gradually adopted significant portions of the old Whig agenda—the high tariff, support for government–assisted internal improvements, and homestead legislation (also championed by Democrats).

"Bleeding Kansas"

The principle of popular sovereignty, which Douglas had written into the Kansas–Nebraska Act, was quickly put to the test. The Kansas Territory became a battleground, the normal process of settlement transformed into a contest of opposing ideologies. Antislavery as well as proslavery forces recruited, subsidized, and even armed settlers and less permanent representatives in efforts to gain control of the territorial government.

In 1855 the proslavery men, supported by residents of Missouri who rode across the border (Border Ruffians) to influence the outcome, elected a majority of the territorial legislature and established a government at Shawnee Mission, Kansas. Over 6,000 ballots were cast, although perhaps no more than 1,500 were eligible to vote. The newly elected territorial legislators passed measures to legalize slavery in the Kansas Territory. In response, free–soil advocates held a convention at Topeka and framed a constitution barring slavery. President Pierce determined to support the Shawnee government.

Tension within the territory led to civil war in 1856. To arrest free–state leaders, a pro–slavery posse (accompanying a federal marshal) attacked the town of Lawrence, resulting in several deaths. In retaliation for this "sack of Lawrence," the fanatical John Brown led a small band against a settlement near Pottawatomie Creek, where five proslavery men were murdered. Guerrilla warfare continued despite the presence of United States troops in the territory.

The violence in Kansas, grossly exaggerated in many newspaper accounts, had its effect in Washington. On the floor of the United States Senator Charles Sumner of Massachusetts was caned into unconsciousness in the course of making a personal attack on Senator Andrew P. Butler of South Carolina. His assailant, Butler's nephew Preston Brooks, a member of the House of Representatives, became an instant hero in the South.

THE LECOMPTON CONSTITUTION (1857)

Encouraged by Democratic administrations in Washington, proslavery forces in Kansas determined to press for admission to the union as a slave state. Decidedly a minority, they drew the lines of voting districts to offset the free–state majority, who then boycotted the election for convention delegates. The constitution that was written at Lecompton, Kansas, protected slave property within the territory. In a series of tests of that document, it became clear, even to two territorial governors (presidential appointees), that free–state supporters were in an overwhelming majority and that proslavery advocates were manipulating the statehood process for their own purposes. Senator Douglas even denounced the events in Kansas as a denial of popular sovereignty.

Nevertheless, President Buchanan persisted in support for the Lecompton constitution and recommended that Kansas be admitted as a slave state. This was approved in the U.S. Senate but defeated in the House of Representatives. Meanwhile, the free–state majority gained control of the territorial legislature. The Lecompton constitution was defeated in a direct referendum held in January 1858. Kansas entered the union in 1861 as a free state, after several southern states had seceded.

Election of 1856

The strife in Kansas was at its height in 1856 when the presidential contest began. Democrats nominated James Buchanan of Pennsylvania. Buchanan, formerly a member of the U.S. Senate, had served as minister to Great Britain during the Pierce administration. He benefited by having had nothing to do with Kansas. Nevertheless, the party endorsed the Kansas–Nebraska Act and the principle of popular sovereignty. The fact that Buchanan's signature was on the ill–fated Ostend Manifesto did not hurt him; the party platform renewed the call for the acquisition of Cuba.

The platform of the Republican arty vigorously opposed the expansion of slavery into the territories; it denounced the Kansas–Nebraska Act and Democratic policy in Kansas. It also made recommendations for internal improvements legislation. General John C. Frémont of Missouri was nominated for president. The party's rallying cry in its first national election: "Free Soil, Free Speech, Free Men, and Frémont."

Although split by the free–soil issue, the American party once again fielded a candidate, former president Millard Fillmore, who drew support only from procompromise Whigs. The vote it polled may have influenced the election. Buchanan received 1.83 million votes in the popular balloting, to Frémont's 1.34 million and Fillmore's 870,000. The margin of victory for the Democrats was slight in Pennsylvania and Illinois. Republican victories in those states would have won Frémont the presidency, without a single victory in the South. This fact was not lost on southerners.

PANIC OF 1857

Reduced demand for American foodstuffs in Europe after the settlement of the Crimean War (1854–56) led to an economic decline and contraction. Republican politicians effectively used the ensuing business depression, which became evident soon after Buchanan was inaugurated, to discredit Democratic policies. Manufacturers argued that the low–tariff policy of the Democrats (further reductions were made in 1857) had failed to protect them against British competition. The Republican alternative was quickly tested. In the congressional election of 1858 in Pennsylvania, Buchanan's home state, every incumbent Democratic congressman was turned out of office.

The Dred Scott Decision

In an attempt to settle the slavery controversy by judicial decision, the Supreme Court ruled in the case of *Dred Scott v. Sandford* on March 6, 1857, two days after Buchanan's inaugural. The Court's decision, one of the most controversial in its history, only increased the hostile feeling between the two sections.

Dred Scott, a slave residing in Missouri, had been taken by his master into the free state of Illinois and later into the northern part of the Louisiana Purchase, where slavery had been forbidden by the Missouri Compromise. Scott sued for his freedom. In time the case reached the Supreme Court. The principal majority opinion, written by Chief Justice Taney, held that no black slave or descendant of a slave could be a citizen of the United States; therefore Scott had no standing to bring a suit in the federal courts.

More important was Taney's additional ruling on Scott's claim that his residence in the Wisconsin Territory had made him free: the slave was the property of his master, and Congress had no right to confiscate that property in the territories without due process of law. In effect Taney ruled that the Missouri Compromise had been null and void from the day of its enactment.

The decision was denounced in the North. It delighted the South, which now saw slavery protected by constitutional guarantees in every part of the federal territories. The Republican party, however, ultimately gained the most from the outcome. The fact that five of the nine justices were residents of slave states, as well, of course, as the decision itself, seemed to confirm the Republicans' charge that the "slave power" had gained control over the federal government.

The Emergence of Lincoln

Senator Douglas's effort to win reelection to the Senate from Illinois in 1858 was closely contested by Republican candidate Abraham Lincoln. Having broken with Buchanan, Douglas faced challenges from proadministration Democrats as well as from Republicans. He had little choice but to accept Lincoln's invitation to a series of seven public debates. Against a background of "Bleeding Kansas" and the Supreme Court's *Dred Scott* decision, the Lincoln–Douglas debates were widely reported in the nation's press.

Lincoln, a native of Kentucky (who in fact had been born in a log cabin), was a skilled frontier lawyer. He had served several terms in the Illinois legislature but only one in the U.S. House of Representatives (as an antiwar Whig, 1846–48). In accepting the Republican nomination to run against Douglas for the Senate, he made use of a biblical passage to explain the intensifying controversy over slavery: "'A house divided against itself cannot stand.' I believe this government cannot endure permanently half slave and half free. I do not expect the union to be dissolved; I do not expect the house to fall; but I do expect it will cease to be divided. It will become all one thing, or all the other."

Lincoln's prospects for victory were slight. Senator Douglas was the leading figure in the Democratic party, a skilled debater and parliamentarian. Douglas's quarrel with the Buchanan administration over its policy in Kansas had actually won him sympathy in Illinois, causing even some Republicans to endorse his re-election to the Senate.

THE LINCOLN–DOUGLAS DEBATES (1858)

Lincoln was anxious to demonstrate that Douglas and his doctrine of popular sovereignty worked to the advantage of southern extremists; he attacked his opponent's evasiveness on the morality of slaveholding. Sensitive to the moderate political instincts and race prejudice of his region, Douglas retaliated by trying to associate Lincoln and the Republicans with radical abolitionist positions, including racial equality (then perceived as an extreme view). Lincoln responded by distancing himself from the abolitionists. He did not endorse interference with the institution of slavery within the South, where it was specifically protected by the Constitution. Rather, like the founding fathers, he opposed the extension of slavery into the territories.

Douglas won the Illinois election and was returned to the Senate. More important, however, the debates transformed Lincoln into a national figure, one of the leading spokesmen of the growing Republican party. His friends began to organize the campaign that was to bring him the presidential nomination in 1860.

The Freeport Doctrine. The most significant of the debates between Lincoln and Douglas was held at Freeport, Illinois, on August 27, 1858. There Lincoln compelled Douglas to explain how, in light of the *Dred Scott* decision (which the Democrat supported), the settlers of a new territory might exclude slavery. Douglas's reply, which became known as the Freeport Doctrine, was fateful for his political career. He pointed out that although slavery might be constitutionally "legal" in the territories, it could not "exist a day or an hour anywhere, unless it is supported by local police regulations." This explanation, calculated to reassure Illinois voters, further alienated southern Democrats, reducing what chances Douglas still had to win the presidency.

The Impending Crisis

As the presidential election of 1860 loomed, the drift of events seemed to confirm the fears of each section. From the northern perspective, there was additional evidence of the slave power's ambition to control the federal government. The South calculated the possible effects of a Republican victory in the presidential election of 1860.

THE WAR OF WORDS

By the late 1850s the slavery controversy had extended its reach into almost every kind of printed matter. The war of words had been ignited by Harriet Beecher Stowe's novel *Uncle Tom's Cabin* (1852), which sold over 300,000 copies in the first year after its publication. There was a flurry of proslavery responses in fiction, all ineffective but telling evidence of the extent to which Mrs. Stowe had affected the debate.

The Pro–Slavery Argument (1852), a compilation of writings, provided the southern audience with reassuring defenses. In his *Sociology for the South, or the Failure of Free Society* (1854) and *Cannibals All!* (1857), the Virginia lawyer George Fitzhugh went to the attack. He condemned the factory system of the North for reducing workers "to separate, independent but conflicting monads, or human atoms." Southern slavery was presented as a benign social welfare state. Fitzhugh confirmed the free–soil movement's worst fears when he predicted that "slavery will everywhere be abolished or everywhere be reinstated."

More troubling to southern planters than Mrs. Stowe's book was the North Carolinian Hinton Rowan Helper's The *Impending Crisis in the South, How to Meet It* (1857), which was widely circulated by abolitionists. Helper argued that slavery worked against the interests of small farmers and workers. His call for abolition suggested the likelihood that the Republican party would exploit class conflict and pursue an alliance with nonslaveholding southern whites upon taking office. The war of words also continued in Congress. In 1859 Southerners blocked the candidacy of Republican John Sherman of Ohio for speaker of the House because he had endorsed Helper's book.

JOHN BROWN'S RAID (1859)

In mid–October 1859 John Brown, the abolitionist fanatic, and eighteen followers attacked the United States arsenal at Harper's Ferry, on the upper Potomac River (then in Virginia). His goal was to gain enough rifles and ammunition to launch a slave insurrection in the upper South. He was captured, tried for treason against the state of Virginia, and hanged (with six of his group) in December 1859.

Brown's raid seemed a signal event to many southerners rather than an isolated episode of fanaticism. The South was too sensitive to slave uprisings to see such bloodletting objectively. Further, testimony at Brown's trial revealed that his activities had been funded in part by donations from abolitionists. In death, moreover, Brown was transformed into a hero and martyr in the cause of freedom by northern abolitionists and intellectuals, even by writers such as Emerson and Thoreau. Although Lincoln, William H. Seward, and other Republican leaders denounced Brown's act as criminal, southern extremists portrayed it as the logical result of the principles the Republican party was advocating.

ELECTION OF 1860

The strength of the second party system had been the capacity of the national parties to contain disparate regional elements and to unify them in the common cause of winning elections. In 1860 the one surviving national political party could no longer contain sectional conflict in this way, an ominous sign for the union.

Democrats, North and South. At the first of two gatherings of the Democratic national convention, held in Charleston, South Carolina, in early May, southerners demanded a proslavery plank in the party platform. They were able to stop Stephen Douglas from gaining the presidential nomination. However, they could not prevent the convention from endorsing popular sovereignty, and deference to the Supreme Court as remedies to the slavery question. This caused some southern Democrats to bolt the party.

Many more walked out of a second gathering in Baltimore in mid–June when Douglas's supporters won key tests, thereby giving him the regular party's nomination. Southern Democrats formed their own convention and nominated John C. Breckinridge of Kentucky for president. Their platform called for the protection of slavery in the territories and the annexation of Cuba.

Republicans. At their second national convention, held in Chicago in mid–May 1860, the Republicans passed over their most senior leader, Seward, thought by many to be too radical (and unacceptable to the Know–Nothing element of the party). Instead, they nominated Lincoln for president. They drafted a platform that reaffirmed opposition to slavery in the territories but went well beyond that previously all–defining issue. Broad appeals were made to business and agricultural interests—notably endorsement of federal support for a railroad to the Pacific and support for a liberal immigration policy. The party also called for a free homestead act, a high protective tariff, and congressional appropriations for internal improvements.

Constitutional–Unionists. Just prior to the Republican convention, remnants of the old Whig party and of the American, or Know–Nothing, party had united, somewhat in protest, as the Constitutional–Unionist party. Expressing support for a compromise on the slavery question to save the union, their convention chose John C. Bell of Tennessee for president. Their support was concentrated in the border states of the upper South.

Lincoln's Victory. The contest in the free states was between Lincoln and Douglas; in the slave states, between Breckinridge and Bell. Although Lincoln received only 40 percent of the popular vote, he won 18 free states, giving him 180 votes and a majority in the electoral college. Breckinridge won 11 slave states, with 72 electoral votes. Bell took 3 border states, with 39 votes; Douglas only Missouri, and 3 of New Jersey's electoral votes, for a total of 12. Southerners did not overlook the mathematics of the election. In spite of his failure to win a majority of the popular vote and to carry a single southern state, Lincoln would even have defeated a fusion ticket of all three opponents.

*T*he election of 1860 gave the Republican party control of the presidency and the House of Representatives. Democrats still had a majority in the Senate, and the Supreme Court retained its proslavery bias. There was no immediate threat to slavery in the South. The decision for secession and war was by no means a foregone conclusion or inevitable.

The South, however, could not avoid the fact that the handwriting was on the wall. It was increasingly isolated from the rest of the nation by economic developments and cultural differences. The sectional balance had tilted in favor of the North on the admission of California as a free state. It was only a matter of time before the federal government would be completely controlled by free–soil majorities. By 1860, southern leaders could not avoid concluding that their way of life was in jeopardy.

Selected Readings

Barney, William L. *The Road to Secession: A New Perspective on the Old South* (1972)

Campbell, Stanley W. *The Slave Catchers: Enforcement of the Fugitive Slave Law, 1850–1860* (1972)

Fehrenbacher, Don E. *The Dred Scott Case: Its Significance in American Law and Politics* (1978)

Foner, Eric. *Free Soil, Free Labor, Free Men: The Ideology of the Republican Party Before the Civil War* (1970)

Goetzmann, William H. *Exploration and Empire* (1966)

Johanssen, Robert W. ed. *The Lincoln–Douglas Debates of 1858* (1965)

Merk, Frederick. *Manifest Destiny and Mission in American History* (1963)

———. *Slavery and the Annexation of Texas* (1972)

Nevins, Allan. *The Ordeal of the Union* (2 vols., 1947)

———. *The Emergence of Lincoln* (2 vols., 1950)

Potter, David M. *The Impending Crisis, 1848–1861* (1976)

Starr, Kevin. *Americans and the California Dream, 1850–1915* (1973)

Thomas, Benjamin P. *Abraham Lincoln: A Biography* (1952)

Unruh, John D. Jr. *The Plains Across: The Overland Immigrants and the Trans–Mississippi West, 1840–1860* (1979)

12

Civil War

1860 Secession crisis in South Carolina (November–December)

1861 Secession of Mississippi, Florida, Alabama, Georgia, Louisiana,; Texas (January–February); formation of the Confederacy (February); Lincoln inaugurated president (March 4); Confederate attack on Fort Sumter (April); Lincoln proclaims naval blockade of southern coastline (April 19); Secession of Virginia, Arkansas, Tennessee, North Carolina (April–May); First Battle of Bull Run won by Confederates (July 21); the *Trent* affair (November–December)

1862 Confederates surrender Forts Donelson and Henry and the city of New Orleans; McClellan's Peninsular Campaign fails (March–July); Congress passes Homestead Act, Morrill Land Act, Pacific Railway Act, and Second Confiscation Act; Lee's advance into Maryland turned back at Antietam Creek (September); preliminary emancipation proclamation (September)

1863 Emancipation Proclamation (January 1); West Virginia, formed from fifty western counties of Virginia, admitted to the union; French armies occupy Mexico; Confederate invasion stopped at Gettysburg (June–July); U.S. forces take Vicksburg (July 4); first conscription act and draft riots in New York City (July)

1864 Grant invades Virginia; Congress passes second Pacific Railway Act

1864 Sherman takes Atlanta and marches to the sea (September–December); Lincoln reelected president over the Democratic nominee McClellan

1865 Confederate forces surrender at Appomattox (April 9) and in North Carolina and Louisiana (April–May); Lincoln's second inaugural (March 4) and assassination (April 14); Thirteenth Amendment, abolishing slavery, ratified

The civil war that threatened to destroy the United States between 1861 and 1865 profoundly transformed the political, social, and economic life of the nation. It began as a constitutional struggle, became a test of federal authority and of opposing political wills, but soon took on much broader dimensions. The initial belief that it would be short in duration proved tragically mistaken.

The seceding states fought to achieve independence and yet closely modeled the government of their Confederacy on the U.S. Constitution. The Lincoln administration responded with a crusade to preserve the union but, as casualties increased and political pressure mounted, expanded its war aims to include the destruction of slavery and the liberation of black slaves. Thus as the U.S. army extended its occupation deeper into the South, it took on social and economic as well as military responsibilities. In the end, after four years of armed conflict, the union had been preserved. Questions left unresolved since the founding of the republic had been answered—at the high cost of 618,000 lives, still the largest number of American fatalities in any war in the history of the United States. Some 2.5 million men served in U.S. and Confederate forces.

SECESSION

South Carolina reacted to the election of Abraham Lincoln by seceding—or withdrawing—from the union. A special convention, convened to consider the subject, unanimously passed an ordinance of secession on December 20, 1860. In less than six weeks, the other six states of the lower South (Mississippi, Florida, Alabama, Georgia, Louisiana, and Texas) had also seceded. Secessionists justified the act on the grounds that the individual states had not surrendered their sovereignty in forming the union and subscribing to the Constitution (which, however, made no provision for secession). According to this compact theory of union, each state retained the legal authority to withdraw.

Southern "Nationalism"

During the 1850s the idea that the South had its own destiny and the capacity to exist as a separate nation gained increasing acceptance. Southern nationalists argued that their section would prosper more outside the union once free of the taxes and tariffs that increased the cost of their goods to foreign purchasers. They also argued that necessity would compel economic diversification in an independent South. Southern nationalism grew as political events diminished the section's influence within the union.

SOUTHERN FEARS

The extension of "free soil" not only closed possible avenues for southern expansion but raised general fears in the South about the future. Stirred by the fire–eater rhetoric of politicians, the South believed that its loss of voting power in Congress, and consequent reduction in influence in the federal government, placed its institutions and social ways at risk. By 1860 an atmosphere had been created in which conspiracy theories thrived.

Southerners perceived in the growing strength of abolitionism a direct threat to their way of life. The victories of the Republican party, which had elected Lincoln without carrying a single southern state in 1860, seemed to herald their fate. Although Republican politicians maintained that their party would not interfere with slavery in the southern states, such promises were not a guarantee against the possible control of the party machinery by the abolitionists. Furthermore, the Republican party's pledge to exclude slavery from the territories would, if carried out, make the working majority of free states in Congress permanent. In the election of 1860, the Republicans had also championed a protective tariff, a homestead act, and a railroad to connect the Pacific Coast with the old northwest—measures the South had consistently opposed and viewed as hostile to its economic interests and plantation agriculture.

The Confederacy

In February 1861, in Montgomery, Alabama, representatives of the seven states that had seceded from the union organized a new national entity, the Confederate States of America. They selected as their provisional president Jefferson Davis, a Mississippi cotton planter who had served in the U.S. Senate and as Franklin Pierce's secretary of war. He later won a general election for a six–year term. The seceding states quickly seized facilities and property belonging to the U.S. government, leaving but two forts (Fort Sumter, in Charleston, South Carolina, and Fort Pickens, in Pensacola, Florida) under federal control.

EFFORTS AT COMPROMISE

Confusion characterized the general reaction to the secession of the southern states. The abolitionists were pleased to be rid of the "nefarious institution," slavery. There was strong opposition among business interests to the idea of coercion in order to preserve the Union. Sentiment for the Union in both North and South remained strong, and numerous schemes for reconciliation were proposed during the fateful winter of 1860–61.

BUCHANAN VACILLATES

President Buchanan, surrounded by a cabinet in which southern influence was dominant, maintained that there was no constitutional right of secession—but he found no power vested in the federal government to compel the states to obey federal laws. He took no steps to collect customs

THE
UNITED STATES
IN THE
CIVIL WAR

and enforce federal laws in the seceded states. In January 1861 he sent reinforcements to Fort Sumter on board the merchant vessel *Star of the West*, but, after receiving fire from Confederate guns in Charleston harbor, the ship returned to port.

THE CRITTENDEN COMPROMISE

The compromise solution advocated by Senator John J. Crittenden of Kentucky consisted of five proposed "permanent" amendments to the Constitution. The most important of these would have 1) restored the Missouri Compromise line (36° 30′) in the existing (and future) territories of the union—permitting slaveholding south of that line and prohibiting it above; and (2) protected slavery in the states where it was then legal. Southern members who sat on the committee that was to draft the legislation generally approved of these provisions. The Republicans, however, at Lincoln's insistence, refused to endorse a compromise that permitted the extension of slavery into any federal territory.

PEACE CONVENTION (1861)

At the call of the Virginia legislature representatives from twenty–one of the thirty–four states gathered in Washington in February to attempt a reconciliation. The convention produced proposals that differed little from those that formed the Crittenden Compromise. These were submitted to the Senate but attracted no meaningful support.

LINCOLN AND THE UNION

Lincoln's policy reflected his determination to preserve the union, his need to unite the sentiment of the North behind his administration, and his belief that some of the slave states would remain loyal to the federal government. He was guided by the belief that the principle of majority rule, which he considered essential to the functioning and survival of democracy, was under attack around the world.

Lincoln the Politician

Lincoln lacked experience in public office but was a keen judge of character and a supreme political manager. These qualities enabled him to assert the leadership and command required by the crisis. His selection of his cabinet exemplified his political skills. He brought together a varied group of talented and influential individuals, possessed of strong opinions and personal ambitions, and enlisted their best efforts in the cause of managing the union. William H. Seward of New York (state) represented the old antislavery Whigs; Salmon P. Chase of Ohio (treasury) and Gideon Welles of Connecticut (navy) had been anti–Nebraska, free–soil Democrats; Simon Cameron of Pennsylvania (war) and Caleb Smith of Indiana (interior) were leaders of important political machines; Edward Bates of Missouri (attorney general) and Montgomery Blair of Maryland (postmaster general) represented the border slave states. Similarly, Lincoln skillfully used his power to make appointments to lesser offices to strengthen the bonds of union.

FORT SUMTER

President Lincoln considered secession to be illegal and was determined not to surrender Forts Sumter and Pickens, though he indicated he would not attempt to retake the federal installations that had already been seized. He did not wish to alienate the border slave states by making a direct attack on the Confederacy. His decision to send provisions to Major Robert Anderson at Fort Sumter, communicated to Confederate authorities in advance, placed them in the position of having to either acknowledge federal authority or become the aggressor in resisting it. The Confederacy's decision to bombard Fort Sumter (April 12–13), after Major Anderson had refused to surrender without a fight, thus became the precipitating event that marked the outbreak of the Civil War.

On April 15, the day after Sumter fell, President Lincoln proclaimed that an "insurrection" existed in the South. Since U.S. army regulars numbered only 16,000 at the time, he called on the loyal states to raise 75,000 militiamen to serve for three months, soon adding to this a call for 42,000 state troops for a period of three years. Once Congress had been assembled, it authorized the president to enlist 500,000 volunteers for three years' service.

The Border Slave States

The call to arms rallied support for the Lincoln administration in the North but tested the loyalty of the border slave states. Arkansas, Tennessee, North Carolina, and Virginia seceded, considerably strengthening the Confederacy. The capital was moved from Montgomery to Richmond, a clear indication that the upper South (with its more diversified economy) was crucial to the survival of the Confederacy.

In four other slave states—Delaware, Maryland, Kentucky, and Missouri—unionist sentiment proved strong enough to defeat secessionist efforts. In Kentucky, Lincoln's conciliatory gestures overcame the influence of the secessionist governor. In Maryland, his use of martial law was decisive. In Missouri, where civil war broke out between the forces aligned with another secessionist governor and friends of the union, the president's decision to station regular troops in the state affected the outcome. Had one or more of these states joined the Confederacy the union cause would have been greatly complicated.

The Belligerents   The superiority of the Union in human and physical resources was great. The total population of the eleven states that composed the Confederacy was 9,100,000 (of whom 3,500,000 were slaves), while those states loyal to the Union had a population of approximately 20,700,000. The roads and railways, factories and businesses, banking capital and investments, and food supply in the loyal states were vastly superior.

To offset these disparities, the South expected to rely upon its export crops, particularly cotton. Many believed that demand for cotton by European textile manufacturers would cause their governments to support the Confederate cause. The nature of the struggle also gave the Confederacy an early advantage—the Union had to wage war in the South to enforce its authority, while the Confederates, fighting on their own soil, would prove victorious simply by thwarting it. In its defensive strategy, the South could rely on a disproportionately large number of trained military leaders, many of whom had attended West Point.

THE RESORT TO ARMS

In their goal of suppressing rebellion and preserving the union, President Lincoln and his military advisors settled on three principal objectives: the capture of Richmond, the blockade of the ports of the Confederacy, and the control of the Mississippi River. The president's leadership was decisive if at times arbitrary—his objective in the struggle was to inflict defeat on the Confederate armies and to destroy their capacity to wage war.

Early battles were fought according to traditional military tactics and rules and proved indecisive. As the war progressed and casualties rose, military leaders on both sides turned to more daring and unconventional methods in the effort to bring the military struggle to a conclusion.

"On to Richmond"   The proximity of Richmond to Washington (sixty miles by land) encouraged quick strikes by U.S. forces directed at the Confederate capital. Southern commanders—Robert E. Lee, Joseph E. Johnston, and Thomas J. "Stonewall" Jackson—withstood every attempt of the U.S. army to take Richmond during the early years of the war.

THE FIRST BATTLE OF BULL RUN (JULY 1861)

U.S. forces under General Irvin McDowell, eager to seize Richmond, were checked by the Confederates at Bull Run, near Manassas, Virginia. This test of the two uncertain armies resulted in the unexpected rout of U.S. troops.

THE PENINSULAR CAMPAIGN (MARCH–JULY, 1862)

After Bull Run, George B. McClellan, fresh from a successful campaign in western Virginia, was given command of the Army of the Potomac, which he reorganized, drilled, and equipped for the advance on Richmond. Ordered by the president to set his army in motion, he finally decided to approach the Confederate capital by way of Fortress Monroe and the peninsula between the York and James rivers. With much caution he proceeded from Yorktown to within twenty miles of Richmond, where he waited in vain for reinforcements. Faced with stiffening resistance from Confederate troops, now commanded by General Lee, McClellan determined that his position was untenable and abandoned the campaign. Exasperated, Lincoln removed him from his command.

THE BATTLE OF ANTIETAM (SEPTEMBER 17, 1862)

After General John Pope suffered a disastrous defeat at the hands of Stonewall Jackson in the Second Battle of Bull Run, McClellan resumed command of the Army of the Potomac and attempted to stop Lee's move northward. As a consequence of the bloodiest single–day battle of the war at Antietam, Maryland (in which some 4,500 were killed and 18,500 wounded), McClellan forced Lee to retreat. He failed, however, to follow up his victory with a quick pursuit. Lincoln (who said McClellan had "the slows") removed him again, giving the command to General Ambrose E. Burnside.

CONFEDERATE VICTORIES

Lee, with smaller forces, inflicted a disastrous defeat on Burnside at Fredericksburg (December 1862) and at Chancellorsville (May 1863) humiliated Burnside's successor, Fighting Joe Hooker.

Lee's Invasion

During the early summer of 1863 Lee planned another invasion of Union territory, hoping this would serve to relieve pressure on Confederate positions in the western theater of the war and convince the European powers to recognize and give assistance to the Confederacy.

GETTYSBURG (JULY 1–3, 1863)

General George G. Meade, now in command of the Army of the Potomac, managed to engage Lee's forces in the town of Gettysburg, in southern Pennsylvania. This was the greatest battle of the war and a significant turning point for the Confederacy. A daring charge led by General George Pickett almost broke through the center of the Union lines, but reserves finally held the key positions and Lee's bold strategy failed. On July 4, 1863, he gave up

THE PENINSULAR CAMPAIGN

GRANT'S RICHMOND CAMPAIGN

LEE'S INVASIONS of the NORTH

SHERMAN'S MARCH

Civil War Campaigns

his invasion and began a retreat to Virginia. Meade hesitated to take the offensive and lost a chance to destroy the Army of Northern Virginia.

The Blockade

In April 1861 President Lincoln declared a blockade in force around the Atlantic coastline of the Confederacy, from South Carolina to Florida. This naval action was taken to restrict the Confederacy's capacity to wage war and it was calculated to cause shortages in the South's supply of food, medicine, parts, and supplies. The U.S. navy's effective implementation of the blockade had an important cumulative effect on the conduct of the war.

U.S. NAVAL SUPREMACY

At the outbreak of hostilities the South had no navy and virtually no merchant marine from which a navy could be formed. The U.S. navy, on the other hand, continuously expanded its squadrons. It played an important role in controlling the coasts and in supporting the U.S. army in the field. By the close of 1862 the navy controlled all of the important ports in the South except Charleston, Mobile, and Wilmington, North Carolina Blockade–runners, who enjoyed some success at the outbreak of war, found it increasingly difficult to carry on their trade through ports in the West Indies.

IRONCLADS AND SUBMARINES

The Confederates made a bold attempt to break the blockade when they reconstructed the U.S. frigate *Merrimac* as the ironclad *Virginia* and sent it into the harbor at Hampton Roads, Virginia (March 8, 1862), to demolish the wooden ships of the U.S. navy. It might have accomplished its mission had it not been for the appearance of another ironclad gunship, *U.S.S. Monitor*. The duel between the two ships was indecisive, but the attempt to break the blockade was thwarted. The battle was significant from a technological standpoint, heralding a new era of naval design and construction. Desperation later led the Confederates to experiment with torpedoes and submarines. One submarine, the *H.L. Hunley*, blew up the *U.S.S. Housatonic* (as well as itself) in Charleston harbor in 1864.

Opening the Mississippi

Although initial offensives in the upper South had failed, U.S. forces were successful in their efforts to gain control of the Mississippi Valley and to penetrate the lower South.

GRANT'S CAMPAIGNS

Early in 1862, General Ulysses S. Grant secured permission to advance against the Confederate defenses on the Tennessee and Cumberland rivers. With the aid of river gunboats and mortarboats commanded by Navy Flag Officer Andrew Hull Foote, Grant's troops captured Fort Henry on the Tennessee and a few weeks later Fort Donelson on the Cumberland. They then advanced up the Tennessee and withstood a vigorous Confederate attack on the bloody field of Shiloh (April 6–7, 1862).

CAPTURE OF NEW ORLEANS

In the same month Flag Officer David G. Farragut, commanding a squadron of seventeen wooden and ironclad ships, ran past the shore batteries protecting New Orleans and secured control of the city. New Orleans, the South's largest city and financial depot, surrendered April 25. The Confederates were still in possession of the Mississippi River between Vicksburg, Mississippi, and Port Hudson, Louisiana.

FALL OF VICKSBURG

Late in the autumn of 1862, Grant began his long campaign against the heavily fortified river port of Vicksburg. Supported by Admiral David Porter's gunboats, he managed to get his troops in position to besiege the city from the east. For six weeks the Confederates held out, capitulating July 4, 1863. The capture of Vicksburg gave U.S. forces complete control of the Mississippi River and severed Arkansas, Louisiana, and Texas from the other states of the Confederacy.

The Closing Campaigns

After Vicksburg and Gettysburg, Confederate armies fought on but against increasing odds and with declining morale. The Union's superior numbers, resources, and matériel had an increasing effect on the course of battle.

WAR IN THE WEST

Grant, William Tecumseh Sherman, Philip Sheridan, and George "Pap" Thomas cooperated in the autumn of 1863 to rescue the rash General William Rosecrans, who was besieged at Chattanooga, and to win the battles of Lookout Mountain and Missionary Ridge. In the spring of 1864, Sherman began his invasion of Georgia and by September 2 had captured the important terminus of Atlanta. The Confederacy had suffered another major setback the previous month in Alabama when Admiral Farragut was able to penetrate the defenses of Mobile harbor and take the city.

SHERMAN'S "MARCH TO THE SEA"

While Thomas held the Confederates out of Tennessee, Sherman cut loose from his base of supplies and marched across Georgia, devastating all before him (across a line eight miles wide), until he reached Savannah on the Atlantic coast in late December. By waging "total war" and inflicting its horrors on the civilian population, Sherman expected to break the South's will to resist and thereby bring about a quick end to the conflict.

GRANT'S INVASION OF VIRGINIA

With the Army of the Potomac under his direct supervision Grant, now general–in–chief, advanced relentlessly toward Richmond in the Wilderness campaign of 1864. His punishing, if costly, frontal attacks against Confederate lines brought him close to victory in the spring of the following year. He was able to achieve it only after a prolonged siege of Petersburg, Virginia, a key rail center. On April 2, 1865, Lee abandoned Petersburg and Richmond and moved toward Lynchburg, Virginia.

APPOMATTOX

By the spring of 1865 the cumulative effects of the Confederate reverses on land and sea made the outcome of the war inevitable and its prolongation senseless. Lee surrendered his army to Grant at Appomattox Court House, Virginia, on April 9, 1865. General Joseph E. Johnston's surrender to Sherman in North Carolina a few weeks later ended the armed resistance of Confederate forces.

THE CIVIL WAR OVERSEAS

The policies of the European powers had an important bearing on the conduct and the outcome of the Civil War. The Confederacy's strategy depended upon gaining the recognition and assistance of its major overseas trading partners, Great Britain and France. The United States exerted all of its diplomatic influence to prevent such intervention.

British Policy

The Confederacy entered the war anticipating that England's (and France's) need for cotton would bring about a speedy recognition of southern independence. Lincoln, through U.S. minister Charles Francis Adams, son of John Quincy Adams and grandson of John Adams, pressed the British government to observe a strict neutrality. Lincoln's claim that the conflict was a domestic insurrection rather than a war was compromised to an extent by the U.S. navy's blockade of the seceding states. (The imposition of a naval blockade is an act of war.)

FAILURE TO RECOGNIZE THE CONFEDERACY

Although it accorded the Confederate government the legal rights of "belligerent" status soon after the hostilities commenced, Great Britain never formally recognized the independence of the Confederate States of America. There were several factors behind this: (1) the hostility of the British working classes and of British antislavery sentiment to the cause of the South; (2) the failure of the South to win a decisive victory; (3) the failure of "King Cotton" diplomacy, owing to several factors affecting supply and demand; and (4) the successful diplomacy of the Lincoln administration. The other European powers followed Britain's lead—none formally recognized the Confederacy's independence.

THE TRENT AFFAIR

The United States and Great Britain were brought close to war in 1861 by the action of Captain Charles Wilkes, commander of the frigate U.S.S. *San Jacinto*. Without authorization he stopped the British steamship *Trent* off the Cuban coast and removed James M. Mason and John Y. Slidell, who had been appointed Confederate commissioners or envoys to Great Britain and France, respectively. The British government demanded the release of the commissioners and a disavowal of the act. Lincoln tactfully waited to release Mason and Slidell until resentment in the United States over the British attitude had subsided.

BRITISH–MADE CONFEDERATE WARSHIPS

The Confederacy contracted with owners of British shipyards for the construction of six ships (including the *Florida, Alabama,* and *Shenandoah*) designated for service as commerce–destroyers. In 1862 they were delivered to the Confederate government by intermediaries and began destructive attacks upon U.S. merchant shipping. These transactions were vigorously protested by U.S. Minister Adams. Confederate efforts to secure two ironclads (the Laird rams, built by the Laird Shipyards in Liverpool) in 1863 prompted the U.S. government to warn Britain that such transactions might lead to a declaration of war. The British government intervened to detain the ironclads and thereafter was more scrupulous in observing neutrality. The activity of the commerce–destroyers later became the basis for the postwar *Alabama* claims against the British government.

France and Napoleon III

In private, Emperor Napoleon III attempted to persuade Great Britain and Russia to join him in forcing the United States to agree to an armistice. Failing in that, he observed his agreements with Britain and withheld formal recognition from the Confederacy. However, he permitted commerce–destroyers to be constructed in French ports and assisted the Confederate commissioners in borrowing funds. He had his own purposes in aiding the South. Taking advantage of the conflict in America, he ignored the Monroe Doctrine and made his cousin Prince Maximilian of Austria the puppet emperor of a Mexican empire created by French troops. He refused to withdraw from Mexico until the United States sent General Philip Sheridan to the Mexican border at the close of the Civil War.

Powers Friendly to the Union   Russia, Prussia, and the Scandinavian countries were favorably disposed toward the United States during the war. Russia made its policy conspicuous by sending its fleets to visit New York and San Francisco.

THE COSTS OF WAR

The war imposed a wide range of problems upon traditional government structures, the solution of which had far–reaching consequences.

Raising Forces   Both the United States and the Confederacy at first relied on volunteer troops induced by bounties. As it became apparent that the war would be long and hard–fought, both enacted conscription or draft laws. The Confederacy passed the first draft law in April 1862, the United States a similar Enrollment Act in July 1863. Both laws permitted draftees to obtain exemption by hiring a substitute, a provision resented by many of the poor. Opposition to these measures was extensive in both sections. In July 1863, the first draft selections (made in a public drawing of names) in New York City provoked riots that resulted in the deaths of several hundred (mostly black) residents. Troops had to be called from the armies in the field to suppress the disorder.

About 1.5 million men served in the U.S. army and navy during the war; some 900,000 in the Confederate forces. The Confederate ranks dwindled after the course of the war turned in 1863. At their peak in late 1862, Confederate armies numbered no more than 500,000; in 1864–65 more than 100,000 deserted. At the close of the war the Confederate Congress was attempting to impress 300,000 slaves into military service.

Financing the War   Revenues were raised chiefly by means of increases in taxes and customs duties, public borrowings by the U.S. Treasury in the form of short–term notes and long–term bonds, and the issuance of paper money.

The Lincoln administration obtained more than three times as much revenue from loans as from all other sources, some $2.6 billion. Congress passed the Internal Revenue Act in 1862, levying for the first time a tax on incomes. The reluctance of politicians to impose more burdensome taxes led the U.S. Treasury to issue paper currency or "greenbacks," which were made legal tender for all debts, public and private. Some $450 million of these notes, backed by the government but not redeemable in gold or silver, were issued; they depreciated in value as their amount increased, contributing to inflation.

PROSPERITY IN THE NORTH

After a financial panic and business uncertainty in the first months of the war, the economy of the North responded to the stimulus of war production. The general trend of economic activity was reflected in the statistics showing (1) increased production of raw materials by farm and mine, (2) increased mechanization of production in factory and on the farm, (3) unprecedented output of manufactured goods, (4) expansion of transportation facilities, and (5) expansion of trade and commerce. While speculators and war contractors, as always, made fortunes by responding quickly to war–time demands, salaries and wages generally lagged behind prices, resulting in hardship and suffering for many.

Economic Legislation. As a consequence of secession, Republicans enjoyed large majorities in both houses of Congress, permitting them to pass landmark economic legislation that assigned new roles and powers to the federal government. The Homestead and Morrill Land Grant acts provided public lands for settlement (up to 160 acres for each citizen) and public education. Congress steadily raised the protective tariff (to the highest levels in American history). It passed legislation that chartered the Union Pacific and Central Pacific Railroad companies and provided support for their extension of the nation's rail system to the Pacific Ocean. To ease labor shortages caused by the war, Congress (in 1864) relaxed immigration laws to permit employers to transport foreign laborers into the country.

The National Bank Act (1863, amended 1864) promoted the sale of government bonds, but its primary purpose was to establish a uniform, federally regulated banking system throughout the country. It provided for the creation of national banks, each of which was required to purchase federal bonds to the extent of one-third of its capital stock and to deposit them with the Treasury. Against this security the bank might issue bank notes up to 90 percent of the value of the bonds. These national bank notes gradually replaced the many issues of the state banks, which were discouraged by means of a 10 percent tax in 1866.

SOUTHERN FINANCES

Since the blockade largely prevented the collection of customs revenues, the Confederate government resorted to levies on its member states. Most states met their quotas by issuing state bonds or notes. In 1863 the central government passed measures imposing comprehensive excise and heavy income taxes on individuals. A 10 percent tax was also levied "in kind" on agricultural produce. Bond issues, except the first in 1861, failed to produce much hard currency. The most important foreign loan was placed in Paris in 1863 and based upon cotton. The Confederacy financed its war principally by issuing large sums of paper currency (more than twice the amount issued by the U.S. Treasury). Confederate paper money, which was not legal tender for private debts, depreciated in value at staggering rates, contributing to rapid and damaging price inflation (prices rose almost 7,000 percent during the four war years).

Privation in the South. The South's small manufacturing sector found ways to produce ordnance and equipment in the first years of the war. Its plantations and farms, however, were unable to produce an adequate supply of food and provisions. Since the war was conducted almost entirely on southern soil, the devastation of battle had great impact. The blockade further crippled the economy, denying the South necessary replacement parts and matériel and contributing to the disruption in the supply of food and supplies. Shortages in most necessities led to hoarding, black market activity, and food riots.

The Domestic Front

In the North as well as the South, the powers of the central governments were stretched to meet the demands of war. Restraint of civil liberty was deemed necessary in order to quiet criticism of government policies. Spying of various kinds was widespread.

LINCOLN'S WAR POWERS

The president believed that the survival of the union and, to his thinking, the survival of representative government rested on the suppression of the rebellion. The severity of the threat seemed to him to justify extraordinary measures. He frequently made use of martial law and military justice to quash disloyal activities, suspending civil liberties and habeas corpus when he felt that the war effort required it. Decisions of the Supreme Court had held that the writ of habeas corpus (preventing unlawful restraint) could be suspended only by act of Congress.

Even after Congress passed a law (March 1863) providing that suspects could not be kept in prison more than twenty days without indictment by a grand jury, Lincoln continued to authorize political arrests and to uphold sentences by military tribunals. He ignored a ruling of the Supreme Court (in *ex parte Merryman*), which ordered the release of a proponent of secession jailed in Maryland. In 1866 the Court held (in *ex parte Milligan*) that the Lincoln administration had violated the constitutional rights of a civilian by trying him by military justice in a place where the civil courts were open.

CONFEDERATE POLICIES

The administration of Jefferson Davis proceeded more cautiously in its exercise of war powers. The writ of habeas corpus was suspended by authorization of the Confederate Congress (February 1862). So strong was the opposition in many of the states, where the state courts continued to issue the writ, that the Congress in August 1864 withdrew the President's authority. States' rights, which had been the basis of secession, made it difficult for the central government of the Confederacy to enforce its decisions. Since the Confederate constitution forbade political parties, the Davis administration lacked a suitable process by which it could enlist support for, and rebut criticism of, its policies and decisions.

Political Dissent   Opposition to the war, particularly among western Democrats and in the border states, posed problems for the Lincoln administration throughout the war. The president's vigorous use of his war powers and his willingness to overlook legal impediments to executive action prevented dissent from interfering with the war effort

REPUBLICANS

In some regions a sharp division developed within the Republican party between radicals, who demanded the immediate abolition of slavery, and conservative Republicans, who believed that abolition was subordinate to the preservation of the union. Lincoln's conduct of the war was the subject of frequent attack by the radicals, who nearly succeeded in denying him renomination for a second term.

DEMOCRATS

Many of the Democrats, generally known as War Democrats, loyally supported the Lincoln government. The regular party organizations conducted political contests against Lincoln's supporters. A minority of Democrats, called Copperheads, demanded peace without victory and bitterly attacked the president for his despotism. This faction, strong in the states of the old northwest, carried on its propaganda through secret orders such as the Knights of the Golden Circle, the Sons of Liberty, and the American Knights. Lincoln dealt harshly with disloyal elements—most notably by exiling a leading Copperhead, Representative Clement L. Valandingham of Ohio, to the Confederacy.

ADMINISTRATION SUPPORTERS

The Lincoln administration was in fact supported by a coalition of Republicans and war Democrats. This was underscored in 1864 when Lincoln insisted that Andrew Johnson of Tennessee, a war Democrat, be nominated for the vice–presidency on the "Union Republican" ticket. The Democrats made substantial gains in the congressional elections of 1862 as a result of the dissatisfaction with the administration's attitude toward slavery, political arrests, and the conduct of the war. Many political observers believed that Lincoln could not be re–elected in 1864 in a campaign against General George B. McClellan, who had been nominated by the regular Democrats and their Copperhead allies. Timely military victories helped the president to secure 212 electoral votes to his opponent's 21, although he won the popular vote by only 2.2 million to 1.8 million votes.

Freeing the Slaves

Although the Lincoln administration insisted that the war was being waged to preserve the union, the abolition of slavery eventually became an important war aim.

COMPENSATED EMANCIPATION

Lincoln proposed to end slavery by a gradual emancipation, with compensation to masters. Fearing the possibility of racial violence, he initially believed that colonization of free blacks in sites outside the United States was necessary. He tried to persuade representatives of the loyal slave states to accept emancipation with compensation on condition that the federal government bear part of the financial burden—but he failed in this. In 1862 Congress liberated the slaves in the District of Columbia and in the western territories, providing financial reimbursement to their owners.

PROVISIONS FOR CONFISCATION

General Benjamin F. Butler treated slaves who entered the Union lines as contraband of war and, since they were technically "property" used in war service, "confiscated" them. The principle was applied by Congress in the first Confiscation Act, passed in August 1861. A second Confiscation Act (July 1862) liberated all slaves of rebel masters who came within Union lines and authorized the president to enlist free blacks and freed slaves in military and related war service.

EMANCIPATION PROCLAMATION (1863)

As radical pressure for abolition grew, Lincoln concluded that the freeing of the slaves would be useful in the military effort to defeat the Confederacy. Immediately after the Battle of Antietam (September 22, 1862), he issued a preliminary proclamation, giving the Confederate states 100 days to surrender without having to forfeit their slaves. On January 1,1863, he declared "forever free" the slaves in all the states still in arms against the authority of the federal government on that date. Although it did not apply to slaves in the states that remained loyal to the Union or were under military occupation, the Emancipation Proclamation strengthened support for the Union cause at home and abroad and contributed to the collapse of the Confederacy, which to a considerable extent depended on the labor of slaves to continue the fight. Many slaves responded to this additional encouragement and fled from plantations to the Union lines—possibly as many as 500,000 during the course of the war.

COLORED TROOPS

The Bureau of Colored Troops was established within the War Department in 1863 and given responsibility for the recruitment, organization, and service of black soldiers. Black regiments performed well in combat, which served to strengthen support for emancipation. The 54th Massachusetts

Regiment was the first to take the field. Some 180,000 emancipated slaves served in the armed forces of the United States or worked as laborers to support the war effort during the conflict.

THIRTEENTH AMENDMENT

A resolution proposing an amendment to the Constitution to prohibit slavery within the United States or any place subject to U.S. jurisdiction was introduced in the House of Representatives in December 1863. The necessary two–thirds' majorities in Congress were not obtained until January 1865. The amendment was then referred to the state legislatures, three-fourths of which had ratified it by December 1865. Thus the abolition of slavery, only partially accomplished by the Emancipation Proclamation, was completed.

Social and Economic Effects

The experience of the Civil War became the central event in the lives of those who survived it. Veterans (whether physically disabled or not), widows, orphans, and grieving relations; displaced planters, farmers, and freedmen—all suffered losses and endured sacrifices that left deep psychological scars, well documented in the history and literature of the Civil War.

Dislocations to the family during the war, and the consequent need for women to take on new roles and responsibilities, had significant implications for the new modern era. Women, who composed perhaps one–fourth of the nation's factory workers in 1860, were conspicuous in the war effort on both sides, particularly in nursing and related work. They took the jobs and places of men who went off to war, in factories and offices and on the farm. These experiences opened the way for some to pursue new careers and work opportunities in the postwar years.

The conduct of the war, the manner in which it was waged and supported on the battlefield and on the home front, had a decided impact on the postwar economy. The need to deal quickly with large tactical questions set in motion a broad movement to reorganize work and accomplish tasks efficiently. New government agencies and offices, formed in response to pressing wartime needs, often had significant and enduring influence beyond their original purposes. The U.S. Sanitary Commission, for example, formed in 1861 as an auxiliary of the Army Medical Corps, set in motion the public health movement in the United States. The premium placed on rapid response also led to and encouraged consolidation of smaller businesses into larger units in the private sector. Many large American corporations took form during the war years and immediately after. Similarly, shortages of labor and mechanical parts urged the invention of new labor–saving equipment and devices for factory, farm, and home.

*T*he Civil War resolved two important questions that had not been effectively addressed by the framers of the Constitution, by the founding fathers, or by the second generation of national leaders (1) the question of sovereignty and the place of the states in the federal union; and (2) questions that derived from the conflict between fundamental liberty and the constitutional protections given to slavery. After enormous loss of life, in which must be counted that of President Lincoln, a victim of assassination at the close of the war, the union had been determined to be "one nation, indivisible." The contradiction of "human property" was expunged from the Constitution.

There was little to celebrate in military victory and occupation. With the collapse of the Confederacy in the spring of 1865, the federal government confronted difficult issues relating to the readmission of the seceding states and the citizenship of former slaves. The sectional conflict entered a new phase. President Lincoln's objective of "a just and lasting peace" with "malice toward none; with charity for all" was within reach. But it required the exceptional political leadership that only he had proved capable of providing to achieve it.

There are many excellent narratives of the military and social history of the Civil War as well as biographies of political and military leaders. The war was the first to be documented extensively by the new medium of photography, and thus there are many pictures to chronicle the war effort (if not actual battles) at and behind the lines, which have been reproduced in several publications and formats. In addition, the following works are useful in identifying and documenting special subjects:

Selected Readings

Belz, Herman. *The Republican Party and Freedmen's Rights, 1861–1866* (1976)

Boatner, Mark M. III. *The Civil War Dictionary* (1959)

Catton, Bruce. *Bruce Catton's Civil War* (1984)

Cornish, Dudley T. *The Sable Arm: Negro Troops in the Union Army, 1861–1865* (1956)

Crook, David P. *Diplomacy During the American Civil War* (1975)

Esposito, Vincent J. ed. *The West Point Atlas of American Wars* (2 vols., 1959)

Jones, Virgil C. *The Civil War at Sea* (3 vols., 1960–62)

McCardell, John M. Jr. *The Idea of a Southern Nation* (1979)

McPherson, James M. *Battle Cry of Freedom: The Civil War Era* (1988)

Benjamin Quarles, *The Negro in the Civil War* (1953)

Thomas, Emory M. *The Confederate Nation: 1861–1865* (1979)

U.S. Department of War. *War of the Rebellion: Official Records of the Union and Confederate Armies* (70 vols. 1880–1901)

Ward, Geoffrey C. *The Civil War: An Illustrated History* (1990)

Wiley, Bell I. *The Life of Bill Yank* (1952)

———. *The Life of Johnny Reb* (1943)

Woodward, C. Vann, ed. *Mary Chesnut's Civil War* (1981)

13

Reconstruction and Reunion

1863 Emancipation Proclamation (January); Lincoln announces his plan for reconstruction (December)

1864 Congress passes Wade–Davis bill (July); Lincoln refuses to sign it; Arkansas and Louisiana comply with the President's plan; Congress refuses to seat their elected representatives

1865 Assassination of Abraham Lincoln (April 14); Vice–President Johnson assumes office; President Johnson implements his plan for "restoration," Congress rejects it; ratification of the Thirteenth Amendment

1866 Congress passes the Civil Rights Act, Fourteenth Amendment, Freedmen's Bureau Bill; Joint Committee on Reconstruction recommends against seating the representatives of the former Confederate states and asserts Congress's authority over reconstruction; Tennessee readmitted to the union after ratifying the Fourteenth Amendment

1867 Congress passes the Military Reconstruction Act, Tenure of Office Act, and Command of the Army Act over Johnson's vetoes; Alaska purchase ratified

1868 President Johnson impeached and tried before the Senate; Grant elected president over Democrat Horatio Seymour; Arkansas, Alabama, Florida, Louisiana, North Carolina, South Carolina satisfy congressional requirements and regain seats in Congress; ratification of Fourteenth Amendment

1870 Virginia, Georgia, Mississippi, and Texas readmitted; passage and ratification of the Fifteenth Amendment

1870–1871 Congress passes the Enforcement (or Ku Klux Klan) Acts to enforce the Fourteenth and Fifteenth amendments

1872 Grant reelected president, defeating Horace Greeley, the Liberal Republican and Democratic candidate; Congress passes the Amnesty Act

1873 Financial panic sets off an economic recession

1874   Democrats win a majority of seats in House of Representatives

1875   Congress passes the Specie Resumption Act and a civil rights act (based on a bill submitted by Senator Sumner in 1872)

1876   Presidential election betweeen Tilden and Hayes inconclusive

1877   Electoral commission certifies Hayes's victory; Compromise of 1877 brings about withdrawal of remaining troops from South; President Hayes visits the South

*A*s *the nation recovered from its losses and the north and west enjoyed increasing prosperity, the federal government had to deal with the consequences of the Confederacy's defeat. The South and the southern economy was in ruins. Slaves had been liberated but needed protection and assistance if they were to benefit from their freedom and gain a livelihood. Many areas depended on the U.S. army to enforce law and order.*

The sectional animosities that had led to the armed conflict, and intensified in battle, persisted in the postwar era. For a decade after Appomattox the nation bitterly debated the procedures by which the defeated Confederate states should be permitted to regain their former standing in the union. At issue was the meaning of the Civil War and the depth of the nation's commitment to the political and civil rights of its new black citizens.

PRESIDENTIAL RECONSTRUCTION

**The South
in Defeat**

At the conclusion of the war the South was in a state of economic and social collapse. In many areas there was a complete breakdown of the economy. From Virginia to Texas travelers in the first years of peace found evidence of physical destruction, poverty, and hunger. The land between Washington and Richmond was described as a "desert." Atlanta, Columbia (South Carolina), Mobile, Richmond, and many smaller towns had been gutted by fires. Even in areas that had escaped the devastation of battle, the landscape bore evidence of war and privation—in ruined mills, bridges, dams, and railroad tracks and in fields overgrown with weeds.

The war had destroyed the basis of southern society and dislocated much of the population, both white and black. Confederate bonds and money were worthless. Transportation and industry were at a standstill. Having lost their ownership of slaves, southern planters, once affluent and powerful, found that $2 billion in investment had disappeared. Former slaves were now free from bondage but they lacked means of support. Some U.S. army troops remained in the South to maintain order, and Congress created the Bureau of Freedmen, Refugees, and Abandoned Lands within the army to provide assistance of various kinds to freed slaves (and poor whites) displaced by the war.

POLITICAL QUESTIONS

Political reconstruction was imperative for the South, where most governmental processes, except for the U.S. military control, had ceased with the demise of the Confederacy. But readmission of the seceding states had important implications for national politics. After the secession of the seven states and the withdrawal of their Democratic delegations, Republicans had become dominant in Congress and used their majorities to pass Whiggish economic legislation. The return of what would likely be seven solidly Democratic delegations to the House and Senate held out the prospect of a revival of the old political alliance between the South and the agricultural northwest—and of new Democratic majorities in the Congress.

The question of what role freed blacks would play in postwar southern society became the central issue in all political formulations. With the abolition of slavery, representation of the former slave states would no longer be calculated by means of the three–fifths clause of the Constitution. The number of seats allocated to the southern states in the House of Representatives was certain to increase, since it would be based simply on population figures for both blacks and whites.

Framing a Reconstruction Policy

Members of Congress, even before Lee's surrender, had turned their attention to political procedures for bringing the "states of the secession back into the union." However they, as well as their constitutents, were divided over how to deal with them. Some thought an early reconciliation preferable or necessary for the well being of the union; most expected the rebels to pay a heavy price for the consequences of their rebellion. Others demanded that the entire South be treated as a "conquered province," arguing that Congress had the constitutional power to govern with military force if necessary.

LINCOLN'S PLAN

President Lincoln wished to restore the union as soon as possible. Since there was no constitutional right to secede, he argued, the states of the Confederacy had merely been "out of their proper practical relation" to the Union. In December 1863, the president issued a Proclamation of Amnesty and Reconstruction by which he (1) offered to pardon all (with the exception of Confederate leaders) who would swear allegiance to the government of the United States and accept "all acts of Congress passed during the existing rebellion with reference to slaves"; and (2) authorized the establishment of a new government for any state if one–tenth of its qualified voters of 1860 would take the required loyalty oath. Following his formula, three states under the control of the U.S. army—Louisiana, Arkansas, and Tennessee—established new state governments.

CONGRESSIONAL REACTION

Lincoln's conciliatory proposals were supported by moderate and conservative Republicans but opposed by congressional leaders of his party's radical wing. The so–called radicals (given the name by journalists of the day) were unwilling to pass so quickly over the acts of secession. In July 1864, they put through the Wade–Davis bill. This reconstruction legislation (1) authorized the president to appoint a provisional governor and charged him with taking a census of adult males; (2) permitted the governor to call elections to a state constitutional convention when a majority of white male citizens had taken a loyalty oath; (3) excluded from the electorate former Confederate officeholders and soldiers, requiring of voters an "ironclad oath" that they had not taken up arms against the United States; and (4) mandated that the new state constitutions contain language that (a) abolished slavery, (b) denied the vote to former Confederate civil and military officials, and (c) repudiated the debts of Confederate state governments.

Lincoln refused to sign the Wade–Davis bill, giving it a pocket veto. This led some to accuse him of "dictatorial usurpation" of Congress's powers to legislate. Neither Lincoln's plan nor the Wade–Davis bill dealt with the issue of black voting rights.

JOHNSON'S PLAN FOR "RESTORATION"

President Lincoln's unfinished work fell to his successor, Vice–President Andrew Johnson, the Tennessee Unionist and former Democrat. Like Lincoln, he approached the issues of reconstruction by denying that secession had been legal. In his formula for "restoration" of the states, he proposed to grant amnesty to all former Confederates when they took an oath to "support, protect and defend the Constitution." (He excepted certain officers, political leaders, and substantial property holders, requiring them to apply individually for a presidential pardon.) Johnson appointed provisional governors in seven former Confederate states and authorized them to supervise the election of delegates to a state constitutional convention. To complete their restoration to the Union, these states had to repeal the ordinances of secession, repudiate the Confederate state debts, and ratify the Thirteenth Amendment. By the end of 1865 all but one of the states that had seceded (Texas) had met the terms of either Lincoln's or Johnson's plans, established state governments, and elected representatives to Congress.

CONGRESSIONAL RECONSTRUCTION

Congress refused to seat the senators and representatives elected by the provisional state governments authorized by President Johnson. The members of these proposed delegations contained former leaders of the Confederacy, notably Alexander Stephens of Georgia, who had been its vice–president. Also there was evidence that several of the southern states had not fully accepted emancipation. It was clear that the resident's formula could not insure that change would take place in the South.

Support for the Radicals

Opposition to the president's plan steadily grew among voters in the North. Responding to it, the radicals, led by Thaddeus Stevens of Pennsylvania in the House and Benjamin Wade of Ohio in the Senate, created a Joint Committee on Reconstruction in the Congress. This committee, consisting of fifteen members, was empowered to examine conditions in the South and to propose new reconstruction measures to be implemented by Congress rather than the executive.

MOTIVES OF THE RADICALS

High moral purpose and partisan self–interest merged in the plans and strategy of the radical Republican leaders. Their sincere desire to safeguard the interests of blacks in the South existed side by side with their determination to create a Republican party in the South and to prevent their Democratic opponents from regaining majorities and undoing their legislation. Their opposition to what they believed was executive encroachment on the authority of Congress grew with their dislike for President Johnson, who, unlike Lincoln, was inflexible and tactless in dealing with his political opponents.

RECONSTRUCTION LEGISLATION

As details of new black codes passed by the southern states became known in the North, Congress, prodded by radical leaders, took steps to place emancipated blacks under the protection of the federal government. The black codes were similar to the codes that had been established for slaves and free blacks in the old South. They empowered local officials with the means to govern the work and movements of freedmen.

FREEDMEN'S BUREAU BILL (1866)

Early in 1866 President Johnson vetoed a bill extending the life of the Freedmen's Bureau, declaring it unconstitutional. In July 1866, a reauthorization bill was passed over the president's veto, extending the powers of the bureau to protect and assist the emancipated slaves, particularly in contending with the black codes. (The bureau's greatest accomplishment would be its role in establishing schools and providing educational opportunities for the freedmen.)

Civil Rights Act (1866). In April 1866, President Johnson vetoed a civil rights act, conferring citizenship on black Americans and assuring them equality with white citizens under the law. With support from moderate Republicans, the Radicals repassed the bill over a presidential veto.

The Fourteenth Amendment. Also in April 1866, the Joint Committee on Reconstruction proposed the Fourteenth Amendment to the Constitution, which Congress promptly passed and referred to the states for ratification. By its provisions, the amendment (1) conferred citizenship on every person born or naturalized in the United States and prohibited state laws from abridging rights of citizens without "equal protection" and "due process of law"; (2) provided for reductions in the congressional representation of states that denied blacks the right to vote; (3) barred ex–Confederates from holding national and state offices if they had filled similar posts before the war and violated their oaths to support the Constitution of the United States (this could be removed by a two–thirds vote in each house of Congress); and (4) required repudiation of the Confederate debt and affirmation of the validity of that of the United States.

Tennessee quickly ratified the amendment and was readmitted to the union (1866). While approval of the amendment would likely have secured readmission of the other seceding states, all of them, with Delaware and Kentucky, voted against it. President Johnson encouraged the southern states in their opposition. For the moment the amendment failed to gain the required support of three–fourths of the states. In the North, rejection of the amendment, as well as acts of violence directed against blacks in the South, strengthened support for the radicals in Congress.

The Radicals in Control

Radical Republicans increased their majorities in the congressional elections of 1866, thereby securing complete control of both houses of Congress and the margins needed to override presidential vetoes. President Johnson's active support for conservative Republican candidates during the campaign served only to further alienate the radicals.

THE RECONSTRUCTION ACTS (1867)

Congress moved quickly to ratify the Fourteenth Amendment. Over President Johnson's veto, it passed the Military Reconstruction Act, which was supplemented later in the year by acts outlining administrative and legal procedures. This legislation provided for the following formula: (1) the ten unreconstructed states were divided into five military districts, with a major general in command of each; (2) the military commanders were to supervise voter registrations, enfranchising adult black males and loyal white males, who would then elect state constitutional conventions; (3) the conventions were to frame state constitutions, which had to provide for the suffrage of black men and be acceptable to Congress; (4) state legislatures, elected by qualified voters, were expected to ratify the Fourteenth Amendment. Upon ratification of the Fourteenth Amendment, the unreconstructed states could then apply for representation in Congress.

By 1869 most southern states had ratified the Fourteenth Amendment and had been permitted to rejoin the union. The amendment received the necessary majority of three–fourths of the states and became part of the Constitution. Virginia, Georgia, Mississippi, and Texas were not able to satisfy Congress until 1870, when they were readmitted on condition that their legislatures ratify the Fifteenth Amendment, which forbade any state to deny the right to vote to any person on the ground of "race, color, or previous condition of servitude."

Curbing Presidential Power

Fueled by resentment and distrust that had grown during the war years and in the debate over reconstruction, the struggles between the executive and legislative branches produced perhaps the most serious constitutional crisis in the nation's history. Defeated and intemperate, President Johnson attacked Congress for usurping constitutional powers of the executive branch. In an effort to prevent their legislation from being obstructed by him, the radicals took unusual steps to limit his authority. They also indicated their willingness to pass measures to limit the authority of the Supreme Court in the event the Court attempted to interfere with congressional reconstruction (which it did not). In conceiving the legislative the dominant branch of government, congressional radicals, in the opinion of growing numbers, threatened the constitutional principle of separation of powers.

THE TENURE OF OFFICE ACT (1867)

This act required the Senate's consent for the removal of any official, including cabinet members, whose appointment by the president had required Senate approval. At the same time the Command of the Army Act virtually stripped the president of his functions as commander–in–chief, requiring him to issue military orders through the commanding general of the U.S. army (at the time, Grant).

IMPEACHMENT OF PRESIDENT JOHNSON

When Johnson removed a favorite of the radicals, Secretary of War Edwin M. Stanton, the House of Representatives impeached the president for "high crimes and misdemeanors"—specified in nine charges based on the Tenure of Office Act and two others (accusing him of failing to properly execute the reconstruction acts and of giving speeches that encouraged disrespect for the Congress). Andrew Johnson was the first, and remains the only, president to have been formally impeached and tried by the Senate.

Trial and Verdict (March 5–May 26, 1868). The trial resulted in the acquittal of Johnson by one vote. In the proceedings, legal and constitutional issues were largely subordinated to questions of politics and ideology. On the key charges, the vote was 35 to 19 for impeachment, with seven Republican senators resisting radical pressures and joining the Democrats in voting for acquittal. Having failed to obtain the necessary two–thirds majority to convict, the radicals made no further efforts to remove Johnson.

FOREIGN AFFAIRS DURING THE JOHNSON PRESIDENCY

Despite the confusion and bad feeling caused by the constitutional struggles, Secretary of State William H. Seward was able to convince both Congress and the president to support measures that significantly extended the nation's boundaries. Alaska (called Seward's Folly at the time) was purchased from Russia for $7.2 million in 1867; the Midway Islands, one thousand miles west of Hawaii, were annexed the same year.

THE GRANT ERA

After the turmoil of the Johnson years, the Union's best military commander, Ulysses S. Grant, was perceived (initially by both parties) to be a political savior. However, he provided little stability during his two terms in the presidency, during which the element of national purpose in reconstruction politics was dissipated by corruption and scandal.

The Grant Administration

Grant believed that the nation supported the political and economic policies of the congressional radicals and cast his lot with the Republican party in 1868. His victory over the Democratic nominee, Horatio Seymour, wartime governor of New York, was won with three southern states still under military occupation. Although his popular margin was small, he carried all but eight states.

THE CABINET

Grant was unable to translate his abilities as a military commander into effective presidential leadership. He lacked vision and wisdom, and his years in the White House were characterized by political incompetence. He generally relied on the advice of machine politicians, but he did appoint three particularly able cabinet members: Hamilton Fish as secretary of state, Jacob D. Cox (interior) and E. R. Hoar (attorney general).

Secretary Fish skillfully concluded the matter of the *Alabama* claims against Great Britain, the award for which an international tribunal set at $15.5 million. Hoar was forced to resign when he opposed Grant's plan to annex Santo Domingo, defeated largely through the efforts of Senator Charles Sumner of Massachusetts.

CORRUPTION AND SCANDAL

Grant ignored and sometimes contributed to abuses of the "spoils system" by Republican politicians, permitting unscrupulous and dishonest men to use him and his high office for their own purposes. His failure to enforce a standard of public behavior indirectly contributed to a series of scandals and unsavory episodes, which included (1) "Black Friday" (1869), when Jim Fisk and Jay Gould using Grant's prestige, tried to corner the nation's gold supply; (2) the Crédit Mobilier (1872), involving Vice–President Schuyler Colfax, which profited illegally through the construction of the Union Pacific Railroad; (3) the Whiskey Ring (1875), among whom were Grant's private secretary, which conspired to cheat the government of internal revenue taxes on distilled liquor; and (4) the Belknap fraud (1876), in which the family of Grant's secretary of war gained large profits from the assignment of trading posts in the Indian Territory.

The Reformers

By 1872 some leaders in the Republican party were in revolt against the low level of public ethics tolerated by the Grant administration, often referred to as Grantism. A few had been charter members of the party in the years of its organization; others had been close to the Lincoln administration and were eager to persuade their fellow Republicans to return to the principles of the prewar years. They were joined by three larger groups: (1) those who felt that Grant had followed too harsh a line in the South; (2) those who wanted a reform of the civil service; and (3) those who felt that Grant should lead Congress in a systematic reduction of tariff schedules.

ELECTION OF 1872

At a convention of reformers in Cincinnati in May 1872, Horace Greeley, the editor of the New York *Tribune*, was nominated as the "liberal Republican" candidate for president. The Democrats also nominated Greeley in the hope that fusion with the liberal Republicans might enable them to defeat Grant. The president nevertheless went on to an overwhelming reelection victory in the fall.

Postwar Economic Expansion

As the South struggled with its tragic heritage, the rest of the nation underwent a rapid economic expansion. The boom was characterized by the penetration of the western regions beyond the Mississippi River, discovery and exploitation of natural resources, and the emergence of a national market economy.

THE REPUBLICAN PARTY AND THE ECONOMY

During the war years the Republican party passed legislation and pursued policies that made the federal government a promoter and facilitator of economic growth, expansion, and consolidation. It passed a series of measures to stimulate settlement of the west, encourage expansion of the nation's infrastructure, and protect American industry (principally by means of tariffs) from foreign competition.

Extending rail and wire. Eastern business interests, western mining companies, and the growing communities of the Pacific Coast bound the nation together with miles of steel rails. On May 10, 1869, the Union Pacific and Central Pacific railroads met near Ogden, Utah, with two engines "facing on a single track, half a world behind each back." This first transcontinental line was one of five built before 1877. Numerous feeder lines contributed to formation of a national railroad system. This system brought manufacturers closer to the raw materials they needed and to the markets in which they sold their goods, gave the city dweller easier access to the resources of farm and forest, and greatly improved travel.

By 1866, as a result of merger and expansion, the Western Union Telegraph Company had created the first national communications system. The first transcontinental telegraph line was completed in 1861, the first successful trans–Atlantic cable in 1866. A more advanced communications technology was demonstrated in 1876 at the Centennial Exhibition in Philadelphia, when Alexander Graham Bell displayed his electric telephone machine.

Panic of 1873 and the Currency Issue. The boom after the war led investors and speculators to excesses, and, not surprisingly, an economic contraction soon marked the temporary limits of the expansion. It began with a panic caused by failed railroad investments and the Treasury's removal of some $100 million of greenback money from circulation. In the economic downturn that followed, a fierce debate was waged across party lines over whether government bonds should be redeemed in greenbacks or in gold. Debtors generally favored payment in greenbacks, which would have put more paper money in circulation and pumped up the money supply, contributing to a reinflation of the economy. Creditors and banks fought to maintain the gold standard, fearing that an increase in the circulation of greenbacks would result in depreciation of the dollar. Sectional and class antagonisms were heightened as the issue raged. Western, agrarian, labor, and growth–oriented business interests, hard hit by the fall of the economy, tended to be "greenbackers." The capital–rich East and hard–money advocates resisted their demands. The issue was only temporarily settled by the Specie Resumption Act of 1875, which introduced a new specie–backed paper currency to replace the greenbacks.

THE SOUTH UNDER RECONSTRUCTION

The control exerted by Congress over governments in the states of the former Confederacy redirected southern politics in the postwar years. Nevertheless, congressional reconstruction failed to make lasting changes in the social and economic patterns of the South. Continuing federal intervention in state affairs was viewed as tyranny by most southern whites. Despite this intervention, blacks remained largely in a state of economic subjugation; and because of it they were frequently victimized by white terror groups.

Economic Adjustments

The postwar southern economy revived slowly and remained depressed in most regions due to a lack of capital for investment, widespread poverty, and poor agricultural practices.

NEW PATTERNS IN AGRICULTURE

The revolutionary changes effected by the war compelled many landholders of the South to either sell or reduce the size of their plantations. Some sold off surplus acres, but the majority preferred to try a plan of cultivation on shares, striking deals with tenants who were too cash poor to lease land by making regular payments. Owner and tenant entered into a partnership known as sharecropping, whereby one furnished land, the other labor—the proceeds from the sale of the crop were split on the basis of the share arrangement.

The cash necessary to finance these arrangements was generally supplied by merchants or store owners, who took mortgages or liens on the crops as security for credit (on heavily marked–up provisions and supplies) and loans. Planters, sharecroppers, and small farmers often became dependent on these merchants and moneylenders; planters who ran their own stores prospered. Interest rates were high—which almost dictated that farmers pursue the risky course of growing only staple or cash crops like cotton and tobacco. The system was not productive or just, and it resulted in increased debt and many failures.

"Forty Acres and a Mule". Freedmen had initially hoped that a "radical" idea advanced by Congressman Thaddeus Stevens would be adopted. He had called for the government to confiscate the land of former Confederates and redistribute it (also providing a work animal) to former slaves. At the end of the war some 10,000 black farmers occupied small parcels of land that had been assigned to them by either military commanders or the Freedmen's Bureau. Their expectations of gaining title to these holdings were dashed, however, when Congress failed to legislate the necessary grants of land. Many blacks managed to farm as sharecroppers (and enjoy some control over their lives and work); most had to work under the contract labor

Emancipation and Restoration of Southern States

system. A small but significant number of blacks managed to purchase their own lands, and black entrepreneurship, evident in several southern cities before the war, responded to new if limited opportunities.

Political Transition

The Reconstruction Acts of 1867 denied to the planter aristocracy the political power it had enjoyed before the Civil War. Registration lists in the former Confederate states showed that there were 703,000 black and only 627,000 white voters in 1868. As new governments were formed in conformity with congressional measures, however, most whites regained the vote. The Amnesty Act (1872) permitted all except the most prominent ex–Confederates (perhaps numbering 500) to regain full citizenship. In the states of the upper South (notably, Virginia and North Carolina), where the majority of the population was white, the Democratic party quickly gained control of state government.

"RECONSTRUCTED" STATE GOVERNMENTS

The new Republican political majorities in the Deep South were formed by (1) free blacks and freedmen; (2) whites from outside the South who had come to pursue opportunities (called carpetbaggers); and (3) white Southerners—small farmers, enterprising manufacturers, and former Whigs—who hoped to advance themselves by cooperating with the congressional program (called scalawags).

Blacks made up the greater part of the Republican party in the South, but they held few offices during the Reconstruction period—twenty blacks were elected to the U.S. House of Representives, only two were sent to the U.S. Senate (most of these men had been born in freedom and educated outside the South). Blacks formed a majority in only one house of one state legislature (South Carolina); three blacks were elected lieutenant governor, none governor. Only one gained appointment to a state supreme court during the period.

CORRUPTION AND REFORM

The legislatures elected in the southern states in 1868 and 1869 passed many quick fix measures, notably generous subsidies to builders of railroads, hoping to revive the South's prostrate economy. The increases in public spending, largely funded by new taxes and the issuance of state debt, were in general too rapid and poorly thought out, encouraging waste, extravagant expenditures, and fraud. In North Carolina, for example, the public debt more than doubled in two years, while the tax rate in Louisiana during 1870 was three times the rate in the more populous state of Pennsylvania. Many in official positions abused the public trust and engaged in outright fraud and graft. However, such practices also occurred in a number of northern legislatures and, of course, within the federal government itself, especially during the Grant years.

In spite of the excesses and abuses of the Reconstruction governments, some black and white leaders sincerely tried to make life better for the average southerner. During the years 1870 to 1875 they persuaded Republican legislatures to enact laws to provide for more and better courts, new hospitals and asylums, and public school systems.

Restoration of "White Supremacy"

By a variety of means, all relying on grass roots methods of harassment or intimidation, conservative southern whites managed to regain the control of state governments and to reverse the congressional reconstruction program.

ORGANIZED TERRORISM

Southern whites turned to nonpolitical methods in their efforts to defeat the Republicans. Secret societies—the Ku Klux Klan, the Knights of the White Camelia, the Boys of '76—were used as the instruments of a policy of terrorism designed to strike fear into blacks and compel them not to exercise their new political rights. The Klan, the most notorious of these vigilante organizations, was dominated in many districts by terrorists who made use of all forms of violence, including murder, to bring down the Republican state governments. In some areas, notably in the Deep South, such clubs and groups organized and acted openly with impunity.

PEACEFUL COERCION

Southerners who disdained the violent tactics of the Klan and other secret societies turned to more subtle forms of coercion. Freedmen were denied employment and credit, kept from the polls, and intimidated by other means short of force to prevent them from voting for Republican candidates.

THE ENFORCEMENT ACTS

As resistance and acts of violence against Republican state governments grew, they had an effect at the polls. (By 1870 new Democratic majorities had taken control of the legislatures of Georgia, North Carolina, and Tennessee.) In response to these campaigns of intimidation, President Grant asked and received from Congress tough enforcement measures: (1) An act passed in May 1870 imposed heavy penalties for violations of the Fourteenth and Fifteenth Amendments; (2) an act of February 1871 placed congressional elections under the control of the federal authorities; (3) the Ku Klux Klan Act of the same year gave the president military powers to suppress violence in the southern states. (In 1871 President Grant used these powers to subdue the Klan in South Carolina.) These measures had the effect of restraining (but not eliminating) terrorism, and in the elections of 1872 blacks voted in large numbers. In the presidential election, Democrats managed to win only three states in the South: Georgia, Tennessee, and Texas.

REPUBLICAN RETREAT

In the aftermath of the 1872 election, Democrats and conservative opponents of the Republican governments in the South stepped up their efforts to regain power. They abandoned efforts to compete on a variety of issues and focused on winning over white voters with simple racist appeals. This strategy, with continuing intimidation, proved successful and formed a pattern that would maintain white supremacy in the South for several generations.

These developments led Charles Sumner to draft and introduce in the Senate in 1872 a wide–ranging bill to secure the political and civil rights of freedmen. The Massachusetts senator also included provisions to outlaw the system of racial segregation that was spreading in the South. In 1875 Congress approved a civil rights act that only faintly resembled Sumner's first bill, clearly signaling a change in its mood—no provisions were made in the act for its enforcement.

In the congressional elections of 1874 the Democrats won control of the U.S. House of Representatives, thus breaking Republican control of Congress. The following year President Grant acknowledged a shift in national public opinion when he refused to send troops to Mississippi in response to the request of that state's Republican governor. Still he did intervene two years later, dispatching soldiers to South Carolina to quell racial violence that had erupted at a Fourth of July centennial celebration.

The End of Reconstruction

By 1876 only three state governments in the South remained in the hands of the Republicans—South Carolina, Louisiana, and Florida, the first two of which were still propped up by military authority. Most of the South had been reclaimed by southern Democrats and the nation had grown perceptibly weary of conflict in the region.

THE DISPUTED ELECTION OF 1876

After the failure of the liberal Republican movement, Horatio Seymour, defeated by Grant in 1868, had remarked, "Our people want men in office who will not steal, but who will not interfere with those who do." By 1876, however, the leaders of both political parties believed that the time for housecleaning had arrived. The Republicans were anxious to put the scandals of the Grant administration behind them and to stop defections from their ranks over public ethics; their prospects in the fall elections were further dimmed by the severity of the economic decline that had followed the Panic of 1873.

Tilden versus Hayes. Reformers in the Democratic party engineered the nomination of Samuel J. Tilden, who as governor of New York had broken the power of William Marcy Tweed, the corrupt "boss" of New York City's Tammany Hall. Alarmed by the advantage the Democrats appeared to have with the issue of public morality, the Republicans ignored Grant's wish for a third term and turned to the governor of Ohio, Rutherford B. Hayes, whose career had been untouched by any hint of scandal.

The Inconclusive Balloting. Governor Tilden won the popular vote by a comfortable margin (over 55 percent of the vote); but, though he carried New York and several other northern states in addition to the South, he was sure of only 184 electoral votes, one short of the necessary majority. Hayes had 165. Twenty electoral votes were in doubt: one of Oregon's three votes and those of South Carolina, Florida, and Louisiana, where both Republicans and Democrats claimed victories. It fell to Congress to determine the official results, although the Constitution provided no explicit procedure for resolving such a dilemma.

The Electoral Commission. Congress created a special electoral commission to settle the controversy. Three Republicans and two Democrats from the Senate, three Democrats and two Republicans from the House, and five justices of the Supreme Court voted eight to seven (along party lines) in favor of Hayes on every disputed point—he was awarded all twenty of the contested electoral votes and declared elected (by 185 to 184 electoral votes). The commission's report was presented to Congress on March 2, 1877, two days before the new president was to take office.

"The Compromise of 1877"

The decision of the electoral commission would not have been accepted were it not for the fact that Hayes and other Republican politicians had worked out a private political agreement with some practical–minded southern Democrats. Often called the Compromise of 1877, this series of informal understandings assured these southern leaders that Hayes would withdraw U.S. troops from the South and appoint at least one southerner to his new cabinet. In return for their cooperation, they also gained other concessions, including support for federal subsidies for railroads and other public works in the South.

EXECUTIVE ACTIONS BY PRESIDENT HAYES

Hayes (who gained the derisive nickname Rutherfraud) lived up to most of the terms of the agreement. While he expressed support for black political rights and vetoed a bill that would have repealed the Enforcement Acts, he withdrew the troops from South Carolina and Louisiana and clearly indicated that he had no intention of sending them back on similar missions. On a tour of southern cities following his inauguration, he told freedmen that they would be better off if southern whites were "let alone" by the federal government. This remark (let alone, roughly equivalent to the French laissez faire) became a slogan throughout the South and seemed to sum up the Republican party's retreat from *radical reconstruction*.

The "Redeemers"

The withdrawal of U.S. troops from the South placed the states of the former Confederacy under the firm political control of their white citizens. Although Hayes and other Republicans thought they would be able to bring former southern Whigs into their party, most Southerners continued to see them as the party of blacks and corrupt outsiders who wished to exploit the region.

THE NEW RULING COALITION

The new state governments were supported by white majorities, of Democrats and conservatives, principally united by a commitment to "sound" government, by which they meant very limited government and white supremacy. Remnants of the old planter class and new leaders in fields of business and finance joined forces to form the coalition. They skillfully manipulated racial and sectional hatreds to retain support among white farmers and laborers of the South. In reaction to the high level of spending of the Republican state governments, the new majorities cut state budgets, reducing taxes and services, including those for education. "Redeemed" governments, however, were by no means free of fraud and corruption.

The bitter political battles of Reconstruction eventually wore down the nation's will to persist in the effort to restructure southern society and lift former slaves to full citizenship. The measures that were required to enforce federal standards, particularly the stationing of troops, seemed to many Americans at odds with the traditions of local self–government. Similarly, the quite practical idea of providing parcels of land in the South to former slaves depended on confiscations, which, however justified by rebellion, appeared to conflict with constitutional rights of property. In retrospect, it would seem that the nation's commitment to the social ideals of Reconstruction was brief, limited, and never clearly distinct from popular desires to punish the South and its secessionist politicians.

The promise of unlimited economic prosperity in a new modern era, combined with the pain of Civil War memories, contributed to a national desire for sectional reconciliation and reunion. The prevailing view among white Americans, that nonwhites were racially inferior to them, served to provide a rationale for an orderly retreat from radical objectives.

The price of reunion was high. It introduced new inequalities and incongruities to American politics and social life based on race, in direct contradiction to constitutional amendments and legislative provisions. And it required the United States to abandon black freedmen in their day of greatest hope, consigning them to second–class citizenship, with tragic consequences for all Americans.

Selected Readings

Benedict, Michael Les. *A Compromise of Principle: Congressional Republicans and Reconstruction, 1863–1869* (1974)

Brock, W.R. *An American Crisis: Congress and Reconstruction, 1865–1867* (1963)

Hyman, Harold. *A More Perfect Union: The Impact of the Civil War and Reconstruction on the Constitution* (1973)

McFeely, William S. *Grant: A Biography* (1981)

———. *Yankee Stepfather: General O. O. Howard and the Freedmen* (1968)

McKitrick, Eric L. *Andrew Johnson and Reconstruction* (1960)

Perman, Michael. *Reunion Without Compromise: The South and Reconstruction, 1865–1868* (1973)

———. *The Road to Redemption: Southern Politics, 1869–1879* (1984)

Rose, Wille Lee. *Rehearsal for Reconstruction: The Port Royal Experiment* (1964)

Sefton, James. *The United States Army and Reconstruction* (1967)

Sproat, John G. *"The Best Men": Liberal Reformers in the Gilded Age* (1968)

Summers, Mark W. *Railroads, Reconstruction, and the Gospel of Prosperity: Aid Under the Radical Republicans, 1865–1877* (1984)

Trelease, Allen. *White Terror* (1967)

Appendix A

THE DECLARATION OF INDEPENDENCE
(July 4, 1776)
The Unanimous Declaration of the Thirteen
United States of America

When, in the Course of human events, it becomes necessary for one people to dissolve the political bands, which have connected them with another, and to assume, among the powers of the earth, the separate and equal station to which the Laws of Nature and of Nature's God entitle them, a decent respect to the opinions of mankind requires that they should declare the causes which impel them to the separation.

We hold these truths to be self-evident, that all men are created equal, that they are endowed by their Creator with certain unalienable Rights; that among these are Life, Liberty, and the pursuit of Happiness. That to secure these rights, Governments are instituted among Men, deriving their just powers from the consent of the governed, that whenever any Form of Government becomes destructive of these ends, it is the Right of the People to alter or to abolish it, and to institute new Government, laying its foundation on such principles and organizing its powers in such form, as to them shall seem most likely to effect their Safety and Happiness. Prudence, indeed, will dictate that Governments long established should not be changed for light and transient causes; and accordingly all experience hath shown, that mankind are more disposed to suffer, while evils are sufferable, than to right themselves by abolishing the forms to which they are accustomed. But when a long train of abuses and usurpations, pursuing invariably the same Object, evinces a design to reduce them under absolute Despotism, it is their right, it is their duty, to throw off such Government, and to provide new Guards for their future security. Such has been the patient sufferance of these Colonies; and such is now the necessity which constrains them to alter their former Systems of Government. The history of the present King of Great Britain is a history of repeated injuries and usurpations, all having in direct object the establishment of an absolute Tyranny over these States. To prove this, let Facts be submitted to a candid world:

He has refused his Assent to Laws the most wholesome and necessary for the public good.

He has forbidden his Gvernors to pass Laws of immediate and pressing importance, unless suspended in their operation till his Assent should be obtained; and when so suspended, he has utterly neglected to attend to them.

He has refused to pass other Laws for the accommodation of large districts of people, unless those people would relinquish the right of Representation in the Legislature: a right inestimable to them and formidable to tyrants only.

He has called together legislative bodies at places unusual, uncomfortable, and distant from the depository of their Public Records, for the sole purpose of fatiguing them into compliance with his measures.

He has dissolved Representative Houses repeatedly, for opposing with manly firmness his invasions on the rights of the people.

He has refused for a long time, after such dissolutions, to cause others to be elected; whereby the Legislative Powers, incapable of Annihilation, have returned to the people at large for their exercise; the State remaining in the meantime exposed to all the danger of invasion from without, and convulsions within.

He has endeavoured to prevent the population of these States; for that purpose obstructing the Laws for Naturalization of Foreigners; refusing to pass others to encourage their migrations hither, and raising the conditions of new Appropriations of Lands.

He has obstructed the Administration of Justice, by refusing his Assent to Laws for establishing Judiciary Powers.

He has made Judges dependent on his Will alone, for the tenure of their offices, and the amount and payment of their salaries.

He has erected a multitude of New Offices, and sent hither swarms of officers to harass our People, and eat out their substance.

He has kept among us, in times of peace, Standing Armies, without the Consent of our legislatures.

He has affected to render the Military independent of and superior to the Civil Power.

He has combined with others to subject us to a jurisdiction foreign to our constitution, and unacknowledged by our laws; giving his Assent to their acts of pretended legislation:

For quartering large bodies of armed troops among us:

For protecting them, by a mock Trial, from Punishment for any Murders which they should commit on the Inhabitants of these States:

For cutting off our Trade with all parts of the world:

For imposing Taxes on us without our Consent:

For depriving us, in many cases, of the benefits of Trial by Jury:

For transporting us beyond Seas to be tried for pretended offenses:

For abolishing the free System of English Laws in a neighboring Province, establishing therein an Arbitrary government, and enlarging its Boundaries, so as to render it at once an example and fit instrument for introducing the same absolute rule into these Colonies:

For taking away our Charters, abolishing our most valuable Laws, and altering, fundamentally, the Forms of our Governments:

For suspending our own Legislatures, and declaring themselves invested with Power to legislate for us in all cases whatsoever.

He has abdicated Government here, by declaring us out of his Protection, and waging War against us.

He has plundered our seas, ravaged our Coasts, burnt our towns, and destroyed the lives of our people.

He is at this time transporting large Armies of foreign Mercenaries to compleat the works of death, desolation, and tyranny, already begun, with circumstances of Cruelty and perfidy scarcely paralleled in the most barbarous ages, and totally unworthy the Head of a civilized nation.

He has constrained our fellow Citizens taken Captive on the high seas to bear Arms against their Country, to become the executioners of their friends and Brethren, or to fall themselves by their Hands.

He has excited domestic insurrections amongst us, and has endeavoured to bring on the inhabitants of our frontiers, the merciless Indian Savages, whose known rule of warfare is an undistinguished destruction of all ages, sexes and conditions.

In every stage of these Oppressions We have Petitioned for Redress in the most humble terms: our repeated Petitions have been answered only by repeated injury. A Prince whose character is thus marked by every act which may define a Tyrant, is unfit to be the ruler of a free People.

Nor have We been wanting in attention to our British brethren. We have warned them from time to time of attempts made by their legislature to extend an unwarrantable jurisdiction over us. We have reminded them of the circumstances of our emigration and settlement here. We have appealed to their native justice and magnanimity, and we have conjured them by the ties of our common kindred to disavow these usurpations, which would inevitably interrupt our connections and correspondence. They too have been deaf to the voice of justice and of consanguinity. We must, therefore, acquiesce in the necessity which denounces our Separation, and hold them, as we hold the rest of mankind, Enemies in War, in Peace Friends.

We, therefore, the Representatives of the United States of America, in General Congress, Assembled, appealing to the Supreme Judge of the world for the rectitude of our intentions do, in the Name, and by the Authority of the good People of these Colonies, solemnly publish and declare, That these United Colonies are, and of Right ought to be Free and Independent States; that they are Absolved from all Allegiance to the British Crown, and that all political connection between them and the State of Great Britain is, and ought to be, totally dissolved; and that as Free and Independent States, they have full Power to levy War, conclude Peace, contract Alliances, establish Commerce, and to do all other Acts and Things which Independent States may of right do. And for the support of this Declaration, with a firm reliance on the Protection of divine Providence, we mutually pledge to each other our Lives, our Fortunes, and our sacred Honor.

[Names omitted]

Appendix B

ARTICLES OF CONFEDERATION

Adopted by Congress November 15, 1777
(ratified and effective March 1, 1781)

To all to whom these Presents shall come, we the undersigned Delegates of the States affixed to our Names send greeting.

Whereas the Delegates of the United States of America, in Congress assembled, did, on the fifteenth day of November in the Year of our Lord One Thousand Seven Hundred and Seventy seven, and in the Second Year of the Independence of America, agree to certain articles of Confederation and perpetual Union between the States of Newhampshire, Massachusetts-bay, Rhode Island and Providence Plantations, Connecticut, New York, New Jersey, Pennsylvania, Delaware, Maryland, Virginia, North-Carolina, South-Carolina, and Georgia in the words following, viz. "Articles of Confederation and perpetual Union between the states of Newhampshire, Massachusetts-bay, Rhode Island and Providence Plantations, Connecticut, New-York, New-Jersey, Pennsylvania, Delaware, Maryland, Virginia, North-Carolina, South-Carolina and Georgia."

Article I. The Stile of this Confederacy shall be "The United States of America."

Article II. Each state retains its sovereignty, freedom, and independence, and every Power, Jurisdiction and right, which is not by this confederation expressly delegated to the United States, in Congress assembled.

Article III. The said states hereby severally enter into a firm league of friendship with each other, for their common defence, the security of their Liberties, and their mutual and general welfare, binding themselves to assist each other, against all force offered to, or attacks made upon them, or any of them, on account of religion, sovereignty, trade, or any other pretence whatever.

Article IV. The better to secure and perpetuate mutual friendship and intercourse among the people of the different states in this union, the free inhabitants of each of these states, paupers, vagabonds and fugitives from Justice excepted, shall be entitled to all privileges and immunities of free citizens in the several states; and the people of each state shall have free ingress and regress to and from any other state, and shall enjoy therein all the privileges of trade and commerce, subject to the same duties, impositions and restrictions as the inhabitants thereof respectively, provided that such restriction shall not extend so far as to prevent the removal of property imported into any state, to any other state of which the Owner is an inhabitant; provided also that no imposition, duties or restrictions shall be laid by any state, on the property of the united states, or either of them.

If any Person guilty of, or charged with treason, felony, or other high misdemeanor in any state, shall flee from Justice, and be found in any of the united states, he shall, upon demand of the Governor or executive power, of the state from which he fled, be delivered up and removed to the state having jurisdiction of his offence.

Full faith and credit shall be given in each of these states to the records, acts and judicial proceedings of the courts and magistrates of every other state.

Article V. For the more convenient management of the general interests of the united states, delegates shall be annually appointed in such manner as the legislature of each state shall direct, to meet in Congress on the first Monday in November, in every year, with a power reserved to each state, to recall its delegates, or any of them, at any time within the year, and to send others in their stead, for the remainder of the Year.

No state shall be represented in Congress by less than two, nor by more than seven Members; and no person shall be capable of being a delegate for more than three years in any term of six years; nor shall any person, being a delegate, be capable of holding any office under the united states, for which he, or another for his benefit receives any salary, fees or emolument of any kind.

Each state shall maintain its own delegates in a meeting of the states, and while they act as members of the committee of the states.

In determining questions in the united states in Congress assembled, each state shall have one vote.

Freedom of speech and debate in Congress shall not be impeached or questioned in any Court, or place out of Congress, and the members of congress shall be protected in their persons from arrests and imprisonments, during the time of their going to and from, and attendance on Congress, except for treason, felony, or breach of the peace.

Article VI. No state without the Consent of the united states in congress assembled, shall send any embassy to, or receive any embassy from, or enter into any conference, agreement, alliance or treaty with any King, prince or state; nor shall any person holding any office of profit or trust under the united states, or any of them, accept of any present, emolument, office or title of any kind whatever from any king, prince or foreign state; nor shall the united states in congress assembled, or any of them, grant any title of nobility.

No two or more states shall enter into any treaty, confederation or alliance whatever between them, without the consent of the united states in congress assembled, specifying accurately the purposes for which the same is to be entered into, and how long it shall continue.

No state shall lay any imposts or duties, which may interfere with any stipulations in treaties, entered into by the united states in congress assembled, with any king, prince or state, in pursuance of any treaties already proposed by congress, to the courts of France and Spain.

No vessels of war shall be kept up in time of peace by any state, except such number only, as shall be deemed necessary by the united states in congress assembled, for the defence of such state, or its trade; nor shall any body of forces be kept up by any state, in time of peace, except such number only, as in the judgment of the united states, in congress assembled, shall be deemed requisite to garrison the forts necessary for the defence of such state; but every state shall always keep up a well regulated and disciplined militia, sufficiently armed and accoutred, and shall provide and constantly have ready for use, in public stores, a due number of field pieces and tents, and a proper quantity of arms, ammunition and camp equipage.

No state shall engage in any war without the consent of the united states in congress assembled, unless such state be actually invaded by enemies, or shall have received certain advice of a resolution being formed by some nation of Indians to invade such state, and the danger is so imminent as not to admit of a delay, till the united states in congress assembled can be consulted: nor shall any state grant commissions to any ships or vessels of war, nor letters of marque or reprisal, except it be after a declaration of war by the united states in congress assembled, and then only against the kingdom or state and the subjects thereof, against which war has been so declared, and under such regulations as shall be established by the united states in congress assembled, unless such state be infested by pirates, in which case vessels of war may be fitted out for that occasion, and kept so long as the danger shall continue, or until the united states in congress assembled shall determine otherwise.

Article VII. When land-forces are raised by any state for the common defence, all officers of or under the rank of colonel, shall be appointed by the legislature of each state respectively, by whom such forces shall be raised, or in such manner as such state shall direct, and all vacancies shall be filled up by the state which first made the appointment.

Article VIII. All charges of war, and all other expences that shall be incurred for the common defence or general welfare, and allowed by the united states in congress assembled, shall be defrayed out of a common treasury, which shall be supplied by the several states, in proportion to the value of all land within each state, granted to or surveyed for any Person, as such land and the buildings and improvements thereon shall be estimated according to such mode as the united states in congress assembled, shall from time to time direct and appoint.

The taxes for paying that proportion shall be laid and levied by the authority and direction of the legislatures of the several states within the time agreed upon by the united states in congress assembled.

Article IX. The united states in congress assembled, shall have the sole and exclusive right and power of determining on peace and war, except in the cases mentioned in the sixth article—of sending and receiving ambassadors—entering into treaties and alliances, provided that no treaty of commerce shall be made whereby the legislative power of the respective states shall be restrained from imposing such imposts and duties on foreigners as their own people are subjected to, or from prohibiting the exploration or importation of any species of goods or commodities, whatsoever—of establishing rules for deciding in all cases, what captures on land or water shall be legal, and in what manner prizes taken by land or naval forces in the service of the united states shall be divided or appropriated—of granting letters of marque and reprisal in times of peace—appointing courts for the trial of piracies and felonies committed on the high seas and establishing courts for receiving and determining finally appeals in all cases of captures, provided that no member of congress shall be appointed a judge of any of the said courts.

The united states in congress assembled shall also be the last resort on appeal in all disputes and differences now subsisting or that hereafter may arise between two or more states concerning boundary, jurisdiction or any other cause whatever; which authority shall always be exercised in the manner following. Whenever the legislative or executive authority or lawful agent of any state in controversy with another shall present a petition to congress stating the matter in question and praying for a hearing, notice thereof shall be given by order of congress to the legislative or executive authority of the other state in controversy, and a day assigned for the appearance of the parties by their lawful agents, who shall then be directed to appoint, by joint consent, commissioners or judges to constitute a court for hearing and determining the matter in question: but if they cannot agree, congress shall name three persons out of each of the united states, and from the list of such persons each party shall alternately strike out one, the petitioners beginning, until the number shall be reduced to thirteen; and from that number not less than seven, nor more than nine names as congress shall direct, shall in the presence of congress be drawn out by lot, and the persons whose names shall be so drawn or any five of them, shall be commissioners or judges, to hear and finally determine the controversy, so always as a major part of the judges who shall hear the cause shall agree in the determination: and if either party shall neglect to attend at the day appointed, without showing reasons, which congress shall judge sufficient, or being present shall refuse to strike, the congress shall proceed to nominate three persons out of each state, and the secretary of congress shall strike in behalf of such party absent or refusing; and the judgment and sentence of the court to be appointed, in the manner before prescribed, shall be final and conclusive; and if any of the parties shall refuse to submit to the authority of such court, or to appear or defend their claim or cause, the court shall nevertheless proceed to pronounce sentence, or judgment, which shall in like manner be final and decisive, the judgment or sentence and other proceedings being in either case transmitted to congress, and lodged among the acts of congress for the security of the parties concerned: provided that every commissioner, before he sits in judgment, shall take an oath to be administered by one of the judges of the supreme or superior court of the state where the cause shall be tried, "well and truly to hear and determine the matter in question, according to the best of his judgment, without favour, affection or hope of reward:" provided also, that no state shall be deprived of territory for the benefit of the united states.

All controversies concerning the private right of soil claimed under different grants of two or more states, whose jurisdictions as they may respect such lands, and the states which passed such grants are adjusted, the said grants or either of them being at the same time claimed to have originated antecedent to such settlement of jurisdiction, shall on the petition of either party to the congress of the united states, be finally determined as near as may be in the same manner as is before prescribed for deciding disputes respecting territorial jurisdiction between different states.

The united states in congress assembled shall also have the sole and exclusive right and power of regulating the alloy and value of coin struck by their own authority, or by that of the respective states—fixing the standard of weights and measures throughout the united states—regulating the trade and managing all affairs with the Indians, not members of any of the states, provided that the legislative right of any state within its own limits be not infringed or violated—establishing and regulating post-offices from one state to another, throughout all the united states, and exacting such postage on the papers passing thro' the same as may be requisite to defray the expences of the said office—appointing all officers of the land forces, in the service of the united states, excepting regimental officers—appointing all the officers of the naval forces, and commissioning all officers whatever in the service of the united states—making rules for the government and regulation of the said land and naval forces, and directing their operations.

The united states in congress assembled shall have authority to appoint a committee, to sit in the recess of congress, to be denominated "A Committee of the States," and to consist of one delegate from each state; and to appoint such other committees and civil officers as may be necessary for managing the general affairs of the united states under their direction—to appoint one of their number to preside, provided that no person be allowed to serve in the office of president more than one year in any term of three years; to ascertain the necessary sums of money to be raised for the service of the united states, and to appropriate and apply the same for defraying the public expences—to borrow Money, or emit bills on the credit of the united states, transmitting every half year to the respective states on account of the sums of money so borrowed or emitted,—to build and equip a navy—to agree upon the number of land forces, and to make requisitions from each state for its quota, in proportion to the number of white inhabitants in such state; which requisition shall be binding, and thereupon the legislature of each state shall appoint the regimental officers, raise the men and cloath, arm and equip them in a soldier like manner, at the expence of the united states; and the officers and men so cloathed, armed and equipped shall march to the place appointed, and within the time agreed on by the united states in congress assembled: But if the united states in congress assembled shall, on consideration of circumstances judge proper that any state should not raise men, or should raise a smaller number than its quota, and that any other state should raise a greater number of men than the quota thereof, such extra number shall be raised, officered, cloathed, armed and equipped in the same manner as the quota of such state, unless the legislature of such state shall judge that such extra number cannot be safely spared out of the same, in which case they shall raise, officer, cloath, arm and equip as many of such extra number as they judge can be safely spared. And the officers and men so cloathed, armed and equipped, shall march to the place appointed, and within the time agreed on by the united states in congress assembled.

The united states in congress assembled shall never engage in a war, nor grant letters of marque and reprisal in time of peace, nor enter into any treaties or alliances, nor coin money, nor regulate the value thereof, nor ascertain the sums and expences necessary for the defence and welfare of the united states, or any of them, nor emit bills, nor borrow money on the credit of the united states, nor appropriate money, nor agree upon the number of vessels of war, to be built or purchased, or the number of land or sea forces to be raised, nor appoint a commander in chief of the army or navy, unless nine states assent to the same: nor shall a question on any other point, except for adjourning from day to day, be determined, unless by the votes of a majority of the united states in congress assembled.

The congress of the united states shall have power to adjourn to any time within the year, and to any place within the united states, so that no period of adjournment be for a longer duration than the space of six Months, and shall publish the Journal of their proceedings monthly, except such parts thereof relating to treaties, alliances or military operations, as in their judgment require secrecy; and the yeas and nays of the delegates of each state on any question shall be entered on the Journal, when it is desired by any delegate; and the delegates of a state, or any of them, at his or their request shall be furnished with a transcript of the said Journal, except such parts as are above excepted, to lay before the legislatures of the several states.

Article X. The committee of the states, or any nine of them, shall be authorized to execute, in the recess of congress, such of the powers of congress as the united states in congress assembled, by the consent of nine states, shall from time to time think expedient to vest them with; provided that no power be delegated to the said committee, for the exercise of which, by the articles of confederation, the voice of nine states in the congress of the united states assembled is requisite.

Article XI. Canada acceding to this confederation, and joining in the measures of the united states, shall be admitted into, and entitled to all the advantages of this union: but no other colony shall be admitted into the same, unless such admission be agreed to by nine states.

Article XII. All bills of credit emitted, monies borrowed and debts contracted by, or under the authority of congress, before the assembling of the united states, in pursuance of the present confederation, shall be deemed and considered as a charge against the united states, for payment and satisfaction whereof the said united states, and the public faith are hereby solemnly pledged.

Article XIII. Every state shall abide by the determinations of the united states in congress assembled, on all questions which by this confederation are submitted to them. And the Articles of this confederation shall be inviolably observed by every state, and the union shall be perpetual; nor shall any alteration at any time hereafter be made in any of them; unless such alteration be agreed to in a congress of the united states, and be afterwards confirmed by the legislatures of every state.

And Whereas it has pleased the Great Governor of the World to incline the hearts of the legislatures we respectively represent in congress, to approve of, and to authorize us to ratify the said articles of confederation and perpetual union. Know Ye that we the undersigned delegates, by virtue of the power and authority to us given for that purpose, do by these presents, in the name and in behalf of our respective constituents, fully and entirely ratify and confirm each and every of the said articles of confederation and perpetual union, and all and singular the matters and things therein contained: And we do further solemnly plight and engage the faith of our respective constituents, that they shall abide by the determinations of the united states in congress assembled, on all questions, which by the said confederation are submitted to them. And that the articles thereof shall be inviolably observed by the states we respectively represent, and that the union shall be perpetual. In Witness whereof we have hereunto set our hands in Congress. Done at Philadelphia in the state of Pennsylvania the ninth day of July, in the year of our Lord one Thousand seven Hundred and Seventy-eight, and in the third year of the independence of America.

[Names omitted]

Appendix C

THE CONSTITUTION OF THE UNITED STATES OF AMERICA

Proposed by Convention September 17, 1787
(effective March 4, 1789)

We the People of the United States, in Order to form a more perfect Union, establish Justice, insure domestic Tranquility, provide for the common defence, promote the general Welfare, and secure the Blessings of Liberty to ourselves and our Posterity, do ordain and establish this CONSTITUTION for the United States of America.

Article I

Section 1. All legislative Powers herein granted shall be vested in a Congress of the United States, which shall consist of a Senate and House of Representatives.

Section 2. The House of Representatives shall be composed of Members chosen every second Year by the People of the several States, and the Electors in each State shall have the Qualifications requisite for Electors of the most numerous Branch of the State Legislature.

No Person shall be a Representative who shall not have attained to the Age of twenty-five Years, and been seven Years a Citizen of the United States, and who shall not, when elected, be an Inhabitant of that state in which he shall be chosen.

Representatives and direct Taxes shall be apportioned among the several States which may be included within this Union, according to their respective Numbers, which shall be determined by adding to the whole Number of free Persons, including those bound to Service for a Term of Years, and excluding Indians not taxed, three fifths of all other Persons. The actual Enumeration shall be made within three Years after the first Meeting of the Congress of the United States, and within every subsequent Term of ten Years, in such Manner as they shall by Law direct. The Number of Representatives shall not exceed one for every thirty Thousand, but each State shall have at Least one Representative; and until such enumeration shall be made, the State of New Hampshire shall be entitled to chuse three, Massachusetts eight, Rhode-Island and Providence Plantations one, Connecticut five, New York six, New Jersey four, Pennsylvania eight, Delaware one, Maryland six, Virginia ten, North Carolina five, South Carolina five, and Georgia three.

When vacancies happen in the Representation from any State, the Executive Authority thereof shall issue Writs of Election to fill such Vacancies.

The House of Representatives shall chuse their Speaker and other Officers; and shall have the sole Power of Impeachment.

Section 3. The Senate of the United States shall be composed of two Senators from each State, chosen by the Legislature thereof, for six Years; and each Senator shall have one Vote.

Immediately after they shall be assembled in Consequence of the first Election, they shall be divided as equally as may be into three Classes. The Seats of the Senators of the first Class shall be vacated at the Expiration of the second Year, of the second Class at the Expiration of the fourth Year, and of the third Class at the Expiration of the sixth Year, so that one-third may be chosen every second Year; and if Vacancies happen by Resignation, or otherwise, during the Recess of the Legislature of any State, the Executive thereof may make temporary Appointments until the next Meeting of the Legislature, which shall then fill such Vacancies.

No Person shall be a Senator who shall not have attained to the Age of thirty Years, and been nine Years a Citizen of the United States, and who shall not, when elected, be an Inhabitant of that State for which he shall be chosen.

The Vice President of the United States shall be President of the Senate, but shall have no vote, unless they be equally divided.

The Senate shall chuse their other Officers, and also a President pro tempore, in the absence of the Vice President, or when he shall exercise the Office of the President of the United States.

The Senate shall have the sole Power to try all Impeachments. When sitting for that purpose they shall be on Oath or Affirmation. When the President of the United States is tried, the Chief Justice shall preside: And no person shall be convicted without the Concurrence of two thirds of the Members present.

Judgment in Cases of Impeachment shall not extend further than to removal from Office, and disqualification to hold and enjoy any Office of honor, Trust, or Profit under the United States: but the Party convicted shall nevertheless be liable and subject to Indictment, Trial, Judgment, and Punishment, according to Law.

Section 4. The Times, Places and Manner of holding Elections for Senators and Representatives, shall be prescribed in each State by the Legislature thereof; but the Congress may at any time by Law make or alter such Regulations, except as to the Places of Chusing Senators.

The Congress shall assemble at least once in every Year, and such Meeting shall be on the first Monday in December, unless they shall by Law appoint a different Day.

Section 5. Each House shall be the Judge of the Elections, Returns and Qualifications of its own Members, and a Majority of each shall constitute a Quorum to do Business; but a smaller number may adjourn from day to day, and may be authorized to compel the Attendance of absent Members, in such Manner, and under such Penalties, as each House may provide.

Each House may determine the Rules of its Proceedings, punish its Members for disorderly Behaviour, and, with the Concurrence of two thirds, expel a Member.

Each House shall keep a Journal of its Proceedings, and from time to time publish the same, excepting such Parts as may in their Judgment require Secrecy; and the Yeas and Nays of the Members of either House on any question shall, at the Desire of one fifth of those Present, be entered on the Journal.

Neither House, during the Session of Congress, shall, without the Consent of the other, adjourn for more than three days, nor to any other Place than that in which the two Houses shall be sitting.

Section 6. The Senators and Representatives shall receive a Compensation for their Services, to be ascertained by Law, and paid out of the Treasury of the United States. They shall in all Cases, except Treason, Felony, and Breach of the Peace, be privileged from Arrest during their Attendance at the Session of their respective Houses, and in going to and returning from the same; and for any Speech or Debate in either House, they shall not be questioned in any other Place.

No Senator or Representative shall, during the Time for which he was elected, be appointed to any civil Office under the Authority of the United States, which shall have been created, or the Emoluments whereof shall have been increased, during such time; and no Person holding any Office under the United States shall be a Member of either House during his continuance in Office.

Section 7. All Bills for raising Revenue shall originate in the House of Representatives; but the Senate may propose or concur with Amendments as on other bills.

Every Bill which shall have passed the House of Representatives and the Senate, shall, before it become a Law, be presented to the President of the

United States; If he approve he shall sign it, but if not he shall return it, with his Objections, to that House in which it shall have originated, who shall enter the objections at large on their Journal, and proceed to reconsider it. If after such Reconsideration two thirds of that House shall agree to pass the bill, it shall be sent, together with the Objections, to the other House, by which it shall likewise be reconsidered, and if approved by two thirds of that House, it shall become a Law. But in all such Cases the Votes of both Houses shall be determined by Yeas and Nays, and the Names of the Persons voting for and against the Bill shall be entered on the Journal of each House respectively. If any Bill shall not be returned by the President within ten Days (Sundays excepted) after it shall have been presented to him, the Same shall be a Law, in like Manner as if he had signed it, unless the Congress by their Adjournment prevent its Return, in which Case it shall not be a Law.

Every Order, Resolution, or Vote to which the Concurrence of the Senate and House of Representatives may be necessary (except on a question of Adjournment) shall be presented to the President of the United States; and before the Same shall take Effect, shall be approved by him, or being disapproved by him, shall be repassed by two thirds of the Senate and House of Representatives, according to the Rules and Limitations prescribed in the Case of a Bill.

Section 8. The Congress shall have Power To lay and collect Taxes, Duties, Imposts and Excises, to pay the Debts and provide for the common Defence and general Welfare of the United States; but all Duties, and Excises shall be uniform throughout the United States;

To borrow money on the credit of the United States;

To regulate Commerce with foreign Nations, and among the several States, and with the Indian Tribes;

To establish an uniform rule of Naturalization, and uniform Laws on the subject of Bankruptcies throughout the United States;

To coin Money, regulate the Value thereof, and of foreign Coin, and fix the Standard of Weights and measures;

To provide for the Punishment of counterfeiting the Securities and current Coin of the United States;

To establish Post Offices and post Roads;

To promote the Progress of Science and useful Arts, by securing for limited Times to Authors and Inventors the exclusive Right to their respective Writings and Discoveries;

To constitute Tribunals inferior to the Supreme Court;

To define and punish Piracies and Felonies committed on the high Seas, and Offenses against the Law of Nations;

To declare War, grant Letters of Marque and Reprisal, and make Rules concerning Captures on Land and Water;

To raise and support Armies, but no Appropriation of Money to that Use shall be for a longer Term than two Years;

To provide and maintain a Navy;

To make Rules for the Government and Regulation of the land and naval forces;

To provide for calling forth the Militia to execute the Laws of the Union, suppress Insurrections and repel Invasions;

To provide for organizing, arming, and disciplining the Militia, and for governing such Part of them as may be employed in Service of the United States, reserving to the States respectively, the Appointment of the Officers, and the Authority of training the Militia according to the discipline prescribed by Congress;

To exercise exclusive Legislation in all Cases whatsoever, over such District (not exceeding ten Miles square) as may, by Cession of particular States, and the acceptance of Congress, become the Seat of the Government of the United States, and to exercise like Authority over all Places purchased by the Consent of the Legislature of the State in which the Same shall be, for the Erection of Forts, Magazines, Arsenals, Dock-yards, and other needful Building;—And

To make all Laws which shall be necessary and proper for carrying into Execution the foregoing Powers, and all other Powers vested by this Constitution in the Government of the United States, or in any Department or Officer thereof.

Section 9. The Migration or Importation of such Persons as any of the States now existing shall think proper to admit, shall not be prohibited by the Congress prior to the Year one thousand eight hundred and eight, but a tax or duty may be imposed on such Importation, not exceeding ten dollars for each Person.

The privilege of the Writ of Habeas Corpus shall not be suspended, unless when in Cases of Rebellion or Invasion the public Safety may require it.

No bill of Attainder or ex post facto Law shall be passed.

No capitation, or other direct, Tax shall be laid unless in Proportion to the Census or Enumeration herein before directed to be taken.

No Tax or Duty shall be laid on Articles exported from any State.

No Preference shall be given by any Regulation of Commerce or Revenue to the Ports of one State over those of another: nor shall Vessels bound to, or from, one State, be obliged to enter, clear, or pay Duties in another.

No Money shall be drawn from the Treasury, but in Consequence of Appropriations made by Law; and a regular Statement and Account of the Receipts and Expenditures of all public Money shall be published from time to time.

No Title of Nobility shall be granted by the United States: And no Person holding any Office of Profit or Trust under them, shall, without the Consent of the Congress, accept of any present, Emolument, Office, or Title, of any kind whatever, from any King, Prince, or foreign State.

Section 10. No State shall enter into any Treaty, Alliance, or Confederation; grant Letters of Marque and Reprisal; coin Money; emit Bills of Credit; make any Thing but gold and silver Coin a Tender in Payment of Debts; pass any Bill Attainder, ex post facto Law, or Law impairing the Obligation of Contracts, or grant any title of Nobility.

No State shall, without the Consent of the Congress, lay any Imposts or Duties on Imports or Exports, except what may be absolutely necessary for executing its inspection Laws; and the net Produce of all Duties and Imposts, laid by any State on Imports or Exports, shall be for the use of the Treasury of the United States; and all such Laws shall be subject to the Revision and Control of the Congress.

No state shall, without the Consent of Congress, lay any duty of Tonnage, keep Troops, or Ships of War in time of Peace, enter into any Agreement or Compact with another State, or with a foreign Power, or engage in War, unless actually invaded, or in such imminent Danger as will not admit of delay.

Article II

Section 1. The executive Power shall be vested in a President of the United States of America. He shall hold his Office during the Term of four years, and, together with the Vice president, chosen for the same Term, be elected, as follows:

Each State shall appoint, in such Manner as the legislature thereof may direct, a Number of Electors, equal to the whole Number of Senators and Representatives to which the State may be entitled in the Congress: but no Senator or Representative, or Person holding an Office of Trust or Profit under the United States, shall be appointed an Elector.

The Electors shall meet in their respective States, and vote by Ballot for two persons, of whom one at least shall not be an Inhabitant of the same State with themselves. And they shall make a List of all the Persons voted for, and of the Number of Votes for each; which List they shall sign and certify, and transmit sealed to the Seat of the Government of the United States, directed to the President of the Senate. The President of the Senate shall, in the Presence of the Senate and House of Representatives, open all the Certificates, and the Votes shall then be counted. The Person having the greatest Number of Votes shall be the President, if such Number be a Majority of the whole Number of Electors appointed; and if there be more than one who have such Majority, and have an equal Number of Votes, then the House of Representatives shall immediately chuse by Ballot one of them for President; and if no Person have a majority, then from the five highest on the List the said House shall in like Manner chuse the President. But in chusing the President, the Votes shall be taken by States, the Representation from each State having one Vote; a quorum for this Purpose shall consist of a Member or Members from two-thirds of the States, and a Majority of all the states shall be necessary to a Choice. In every Case, after the Choice of the President, the Person having the greatest Number of Votes of the Electors shall be the Vice President. But if there should remain two or more who have equal votes, the Senate shall chuse from them by Ballot the Vice President.

The Congress may determine the Time of chusing the Electors, and the Day on which they shall give their Votes; which Day shall be the same throughout the United States.

No person except a natural-born Citizen, or a Citizen of the United States, at the time of the Adoption of this Constitution, shall be eligible to the Office of President; neither shall any Person be eligible to that Office who shall not have attained to the Age of thirty-five Years, and been fourteen Years a Resident within the United States.

In Case of the Removal of the President from Office, or of his Death, Resignation, or Inability to discharge the Powers and Duties of the said Office, the same shall devolve on the Vice President, and the Congress may by Law provide for the Case of Removal, Death, Resignation, or Inability, both of the President and Vice President, declaring what Officer shall then act as President, and such Officer shall act accordingly, until the disability be removed or a President shall be elected.

The President shall, at stated Times, receive for his Services a Compensation, which shall neither be increased nor diminished during the Period for which he shall have been elected, and he shall not receive within that Period any other Emolument from the United States, or any of them.

Before he enter on the execution of his Office, he shall take the following Oath or Affirmation:—"I do solemnly swear (or affirm) that I will faithfully execute the Office of President of the United States, and will, to the best of my Ability, preserve, protect, and defend the Constitution of the United States."

Section 2. The President shall be Commander in Chief of the Army and Navy of the United States, and of the Militia of the several States, when called into the actual Service of the United States; he may require the Opinion, in writing, of the principal Officer in each of the executive Departments, upon any subject relating to the Duties of their respective Offices, and he shall have power to Grant Reprieves and Pardons for Offenses against the United States, except in Cases of Impeachment.

He shall have Power, by and with Advice and Consent of the Senate, to make Treaties, provided two thirds of the Senators present concur; and he shall nominate, and by and with the Advice and Consent of the Senate, shall appoint Ambassadors, other public Ministers and Consuls, Judges of the supreme Court, and all other Officers of the United States, whose Appointments are not herein otherwise provided for, and which shall be established by Law: but the Congress may by Law vest the Appointment of such inferior Officers, as they think proper, in the President alone, in the Courts of Law, or in the Heads of Departments.

The President shall have Power to fill up all Vacancies that may happen during the Recess of the Senate, by granting Commissions which shall expire at the End of their next Session.

Section 3. He shall from time to time give to the Congress Information of the State of the Union, and recommend to their Consideration such Measures as he shall judge necessary and expedient; he may, on extraordinary occasions, convene both Houses, or either of them, and in Case of Disagreement between them, with respect to the Time of Adjournment, he may adjourn them to such Time as he shall think proper; he shall receive Ambassadors and other public Ministers; he shall take care that the Laws be faithfully executed, and shall Commission all the Officers of the United States.

Section 4. The President, Vice President and all civil Officers of the United States, shall be removed from Office on Impeachment for, and Conviction of, Treason, Bribery, or other high Crimes and Misdemeanors.

Article III

Section 1. The judicial Power of the United States, shall be vested in one supreme Court, and in such inferior Courts as the Congress may from time to time ordain and establish. The Judges, both of the supreme and inferior Courts, shall hold their Offices during good Behaviour, and shall, at stated Times, receive for their Services, a Compensation, which shall not be diminished during their Continuance in Office.

Section 2. The judicial Power shall extend to all Cases, in Law and Equity, arising under this Constitution, the Laws of the United States, and Treaties made, or which shall be made, under their Authority; — to all Cases affecting Ambassadors, other public Ministers and Consuls;—to all cases of admiralty and maritime Jurisdiction;—to Controversies to which the United States shall be a Party; — to Controversies between two or more States;— between a State and Citizens of another State;—between Citizens of different States:—between Citizens of the same State claiming Lands under Grants of different States, and between a State, or the Citizens thereof, and foreign States, Citizens or Subjects.

In all Cases affecting Ambassadors, other public Ministers and Consuls, and those in which a State shall be Party, the supreme Court shall have original Jurisdiction. In all the other Cases before mentioned, the supreme Court shall have appellate Jurisdiction, both as to Law and Fact, with such Exceptions, and under such Regulations as the Congress shall make.

The trial of all Crimes, except in Cases of Impeachment, shall be by Jury; and such Trial shall be held in the State where the said Crimes shall have been committed; but when not committed within any State, the Trial shall be at such Place or Places as the Congress may by Law have directed.

Section 3. Treason against the United States, shall consist only in levying War against them, or in adhering to their Enemies, giving them Aid and Comfort. No Person shall be convicted of Treason unless on the Testimony of two Witnesses to the same overt Act, or on Confession in open Court.

The Congress shall have Power to declare the Punishment of Treason, but no Attainder of Treason shall work Corruption of Blood, or Forfeiture except during the Life of the Person attained.

Article IV

Section 1. Full Faith and Credit shall be given in each State to the public Acts, Records, and judicial Proceedings of every other State. And the Congress may by general Laws prescribe the Manner in which such Acts, Records and Proceedings shall be proved, and the Effect thereof.

Section 2. The Citizens of each State shall be entitled to all Privileges and Immunities of Citizens in the several States.

A Person charged in any State with Treason, Felony, or other Crime, who shall flee from Justice, and be found in another State, shall on demand of the executive Authority of the State from which he fled, be delivered up, to be removed to the State having Jurisdiction of the Crime.

No Person held to Service or Labour in one State, under the Laws thereof, escaping into another, shall, in Consequence of any Law or Regulation therein, be discharged from such Service or Labour, but shall be delivered up on Claim of the Party to whom such Service or Labour may be due.

Section 3. New States may be admitted by the Congress into this Union; but no new State shall be formed or erected within the Jurisdiction of any other State; nor any State be formed by the Junction of two or more States, or parts of States, without the Consent of the Legislatures of the States concerned as well as of the Congress.

The Congress shall have Power to dispose of and make all needful Rules and Regulations respecting the Territory or other Property belonging to the United States; and nothing in this Constitution shall be so construed as to Prejudice any Claims of the United States or of any particular State.

Section 4. The United States shall guarantee to every State in this union a Republican Form of Government, and shall protect each of them against Invasion; and on Application of the Legislature, or of the Executive (when the Legislature cannot be convened) against domestic Violence.

Article V

The Congress, whenever two-thirds of both Houses shall deem it necessary, shall propose Amendments to this Constitution, or, on the Application of the Legislatures of two-thirds of the several States, shall call a Convention for proposing Amendments, which, in either Case, shall be valid to all Intents and Purposes, as part of this Constitution, when ratified by the Legislatures of three-fourths of the several States, or by Conventions in three-fourths thereof, as the one or the other Mode of Ratification may be proposed by the Congress; Provided that no Amendment which may be made prior to the Year One thousand eight hundred and eight shall in any Manner affect the first and fourth Clauses in the Ninth Section of the first Article; and that no State, without its Consent, shall be deprived of its equal Suffrage in the Senate.

Article VI

All Debts contracted and Engagements entered into, before the Adoption of this Constitution, shall be as valid against the United States under this Constitution, as under the Confederation.

This Constitution, and the Laws of the United States which shall be made in Pursuance thereof; and all Treaties made, or which shall be made, under the Authority of the United States, shall be the supreme Law of the Land; and the Judges in every State shall be bound thereby, any Thing in the Constitution or Laws of any State to the Contrary notwithstanding.

The Senators and Representatives before mentioned, and the Members of the several State Legislatures, and all executive and judicial Officers, both of the United States and of the several States, shall be bound by Oath or Affirmation to support this Constitution; but no religious Test shall ever be required as a qualification to any Office or public Trust under the United States.

Article VII

The Ratification of the Conventions of nine States shall be sufficient for the Establishment of this Constitution between the States so ratifying the same.

Done in Convention by the Unanimous Consent of the States present the Seventeenth Day of September in the Year of our Lord one thousand seven hundred and Eighty seven, and of the Independence of the United States of America the Twelfth. In Witness whereof We have hereunto subscribed our Names.

[Names omitted]

Articles in Addition to, and Amendment of, the Constitution of the United States of America, Proposed by Congress, and Ratified by the Legislatures of the Several States, Pursuant to the Fifth Article of the Original Constitution.

[The first ten amendments went into effect in 1791.]

Amendment I

Congress shall make no law respecting an establishment of religion, or prohibiting the free exercise thereof; or abridging the freedom of speech, or of the press; or the right of the people peaceably to assemble, and to petition the Government for a redress of grievances.

Amendment II

A well regulated Militia, being necessary to the security of a free State, the right of the people to keep and bear Arms shall not be infringed.

Amendment III

No Soldier shall, in time of peace, be quartered in any house, without the consent of the Owner, nor in time of War, but in a manner to be prescribed by law.

Amendment IV

The right of the people to be secure in their persons, houses, papers, and effects, against unreasonable searches and seizures, shall not be violated, and no Warrants shall issue, but upon probable cause, supported by Oath or affirmation, and particularly describing the place to be searched, and the persons or things to be seized.

Amendment V

No person shall be held to answer for a capital or otherwise infamous crime, unless on a presentment or indictment of a Grand Jury, except in cases arising in the land or naval forces, or in the Militia, when in actual service in time of War or public danger; nor shall any person be subject for the same offence to be twice put in jeopardy of life or limb; nor shall be compelled in any criminal case to be a witness against himself, nor be deprived of life, liberty, or property, without due process of law; nor shall private property be taken for public use, without just compensation.

Amendment VI

In all criminal prosecutions, the accused shall enjoy the right to a speedy and public trial, by an impartial jury of the State and district wherein the crime shall have been committed, which district shall have been previously ascertained by law, and to be informed of the nature and cause of the accusation; to be confronted with the witnesses against him; to have compulsory process for obtaining witnesses in his favour, and to have the Assistance of Counsel for defence.

Amendment VII

In suits at common law where the value in controversy shall exceed twenty dollars, the right of trial by jury, shall be preserved, and no fact tried by a jury shall be otherwise reexamined in any Court of the United States, than according to the rules of the common law.

Amendment VIII

Excessive bail shall not be required, nor excessive fines imposed, nor cruel and unusual punishments inflicted.

Amendment IX

The enumeration in the Constitution, of certain rights, shall not be construed to deny or disparage others retained by the people.

Amendment X

The powers not delegated to the United States by the Constitution, nor prohibited by it to the States, are reserved to the States respectively, or to the people.

Amendment XI (1798)

The Judicial power of the United States shall not be construed to extend to any suit in law or equity, commenced or prosecuted against one of the United States by Citizens of another State, or by Citizens or Subjects of any Foreign State.

Amendment XII (1804)

The Electors shall meet in their respective States and vote by ballot for President and Vice-President, one of whom, at least, shall not be an inhabitant of the same State with themselves; they shall name in their ballots the person voted for as President, and in distinct ballots the person voted for as Vice-President, and they shall make distinct lists of all persons voted for as President, and of all persons voted for as Vice-President, and of the number of votes for each, which lists they shall sign and certify, and transmit sealed to the seat of the government of the United States, directed to the President of the Senate;—The President of the Senate shall, in the presence of the Senate and House of Representatives, open all the certificates and the votes shall then be counted; — The person having the greatest number of votes for President, shall be the President, if such number be a majority of the whole number of Electors appointed; and if no person have such majority, then from the persons having the highest numbers not exceeding three on the list of those voted for as President, the House of Representatives shall choose immediately, by ballot, the President. But in choosing the President, the votes shall be taken by states, the representation from each state having one vote; a quorum for this purpose shall consist of a member or members from two-thirds of the states, and a majority of all the states shall be necessary to a choice. And if the House of Representatives shall not choose a President whenever the right of choice shall devolve upon them, before the fourth day of March next following, then the Vice-President shall act as President, as in the case of the death or other constitutional disability of the President.— The person having the greatest number of votes as Vice-President, shall be the Vice-President, if such number be a majority of the whole number of Electors appointed, and if no person have a majority, then from the two highest numbers on the list, the Senate shall choose the Vice-President; a quorum for the purpose shall consist of two-thirds of the whole number of Senators, and a majority of the whole number shall be necessary to a choice. But no person constitutionally ineligible to the office of President shall be eligible to that of Vice-President of the United States.

Amendment XIII (1865)

Section 1. Neither slavery nor involuntary servitude, except as a punishment for crime whereof the party shall have been duly convicted, shall exist within the United States, or any place subject to their jurisdiction.

Section 2. Congress shall have power to enforce this article by appropriate legislation.

Amendment XIV (1868)

Section 1. All persons born or naturalized in the United States, and subject to the jurisdiction thereof, are citizens of the United States and of the State wherein they reside. No State shall make or enforce any law which shall abridge the privileges or immunities of citizens of the United States; nor shall any State deprive any person of life, liberty, or property, without due process of law; nor deny to any person within its jurisdiction the equal protection of the laws.

Section 2. Representatives shall be apportioned among the several States according to their respective numbers, counting the whole number of persons in each State, excluding Indians not taxed. But when the right to vote at any election for the choice of electors for President and Vice-President of the United States, Representatives in Congress, the Executive and Judicial officers of a State, or the members of the Legislature thereof, is denied to any of the male inhabitants of such State, being twenty-one years of age, and citizens of the United States, or in any way abridged, except for participation in rebellion, or other crime, the basis of representation therein shall be reduced in the proportion which the number of such male citizens shall bear to the whole number of male citizens twenty-one years of age in such State.

Section 3. No person shall be a Senator or Representative in Congress, or elector of President and Vice-President, or hold any office, civil or military, under the United States, or under any State, who, having previously taken an oath, as a member of Congress, or as an officer of the United States, or as member of any State legislature, or as an executive or judicial officer of any State, to support the Constitution of the United States, shall have engaged in insurrection or rebellion against the same, or given aid or comfort to the enemies thereof. But Congress may by a vote of two-thirds of each House, remove such disability.

Section 4. The validity of the public debt of the United States, authorized by law, including debts incurred for payment of pensions and bounties for services in suppressing insurrection or rebellion, shall not be questioned. But neither the United States nor any State shall assume or pay any debt or obligation incurred in aid of insurrection or rebellion against the United States, or any claim for the loss or emancipation of any slave; but all such debts, obligations, and claims shall be held illegal and void.

Section 5. The Congress shall have the power to enforce, by appropriate legislation, the provisions of this article.

Amendment XV (1870)

Section 1. The right of citizens of the United States to vote shall not be denied or abridged by the United States or by any State on account of race, color, or previous condition of servitude—

Section 2. The Congress shall have power to enforce this article by appropriate legislation.

Amendment XVI (1913)

The Congress shall have power to lay and collect taxes on incomes, from whatever source derived, without apportionment among the several States, and without regard to any census or enumeration.

Amendment XVII (1913)

The Senate of the United States shall be composed of two Senators from each State, elected by the people thereof, for six years; and each Senator shall have one vote. The electors in each State shall have the qualifications requisite for electors of the most numerous branch of the State legislatures.

When vacancies happen in the representation of any State in the Senate, the executive authority of such State shall issue writs of election to fill such vacancies: *Provided,* That legislature of any State may empower the executive thereof to make temporary appointments until the people fill the vacancies by election as the legislature may direct.

This amendment shall not be so construed as to affect the election or term of any Senator chosen before it becomes valid as part of the Constitution.

Amendment XVIII (1919)

Section 1. After one year from the ratification of this article the manufacture, sale, or transportation of intoxicating liquors within, the importation thereof into, or the exportation thereof from the United States and all territory subject to the jurisdiction thereof for beverage purposes is hereby prohibited.

Section 2. The Congress and the several States shall have concurrent power to enforce this article by appropriate legislation.

Section 3. This article shall be inoperative unless it shall have been ratified as an amendment to the Constitution by the legislatures of the several States, as provided in the Constitution, within seven years from the date of the submission hereof to the States by the Congress.

Amendment XIX (1920)

The right of citizens of the United States to vote shall not be denied or abridged by the United States or by any State on account of sex.

Congress shall have power to enforce this article by appropriate legislation.

Amendment XX (1933)

Section 1. The terms of the President and Vice-President shall end at noon on the 20th day of January, and the terms of Senators and Representatives at noon on the 3d day of January, of the years in which such terms would have ended if this article had not been ratified; and the terms of their successors shall then begin.

Section 2. The Congress shall assemble at least once in every year, and such meeting shall begin at noon on the 3d day of January, unless they shall by law appoint a different day.

Section 3. If, at the time fixed for the beginning of the term of the President, the President elect shall have died, the Vice-President elect shall become President. If a President shall not have been chosen before the time fixed for the beginning of his term, or if the President elect shall have failed to qualify, then the Vice-President elect shall act as President until a President shall have qualified; and the Congress may by law provide for the case wherein neither a President elect nor a Vice-President elect shall have qualified, declaring who shall then act as President, or the manner in which one who is to act shall be selected, and such person shall act accordingly until a President or Vice-President shall have qualified.

Section 4. The Congress may by law provide for the case of the death of any of the persons from whom the House of Representatives may choose a President whenever the right of choice shall have devolved upon them, and for the case of the death of any of the persons from whom the Senate may choose a Vice-President whenever the right of choice shall have devolved upon them.

Section 5. Sections 1 and 2 shall take effect on the 15th day of October following the ratification of this article.

Section 6. This article shall be inoperative unless it shall have been ratified as an amendment to the Constitution by the legislatures of three-fourths of the several States within seven years from the date of its submission.

Amendment XXI (1933)

Section 1. The eighteenth article of amendment to the Constitution of the United States is hereby repealed.

Section 2. The transportation or importation into any State, Territory, or possession of the United States for delivery or use therein of intoxicating liquors, in violation of the laws thereof, is hereby prohibited.

Section 3. This article shall be inoperative unless it shall have been ratified as an amendment to the Constitution by conventions in the several States, as provided in the Constitution within seven years from the date of the submission hereof to the States by the Congress.

Amendment XXII (1951)

Section 1. No person shall be elected to the office of the President more than twice, and no person who has held the office of President, or acted as President, for more than two years of a term to which some other person was elected President shall be elected to the office of the President more than once.

But this Article shall not apply to any person holding the office of President when this Article was proposed by the Congress, and shall not prevent any person who may be holding the office of President, or acting as President, during the term within which this article becomes operative from holding the office of President or acting as President during the remainder of such term.

Section 2. This article shall be inoperative unless it shall have been ratified as an amendment to the Constitution by the legislatures of three-fourths of the several states within seven years from the date of its submission to the states by the Congress.

Amendment XXIII (1961)

Section 1. The District constituting the seat of Government of the United States shall appoint in such manner as the Congress may direct:

A number of electors of President and Vice-President equal to the whole number of Senators and Representatives in Congress to which the District would be entitled if it were a State, but in no event more than the least populous State; they shall be in addition to those appointed by the States, but they shall be considered, for the purposes of the election of President and Vice-President, to be electors appointed by a State; and they shall meet in the District and perform such duties as provided by the twelfth article of amendment.

Section 2. The Congress shall have power to enforce this article by appropriate legislation.

Amendment XXIV (1964)

Section 1. The right of citizens of the United States to vote in any primary or other election for President or Vice President, for electors for President or Vice President, or for Senator or Representative in Congress, shall not be denied or abridged by the United States or any other State by reason of failure to pay any poll tax or other tax.

Section 2. The Congress shall have the power to enforce this article by appropriate legislation.

Amendment XXV (1967)

Section 1. In case of the removal of the President from office or of his death or resignation, the Vice President shall become President.

Section 2. Whenever there is a vacancy in the office of the Vice President, the President shall nominate a Vice President who shall take office upon confirmation by a majority vote of both Houses of Congress.

Section 3. Whenever the President transmits to the President pro tempore of the Senate and the Speaker of the House of Representatives his written declaration that he is unable to discharge the powers and duties of his office, and until he transmits to them a written declaration to the contrary, such powers and duties shall be discharged by the Vice President as Acting President.

Section 4. Whenever the Vice President and a majority of either the principal officers of the executive departments or of such other body as Congress may by law provide, transmit to the President pro tempore of the Senate and the Speaker of the House of Representatives their written declaration that the President is unable to discharge the powers and duties of his office, the Vice President shall immediately assume the powers and duties of the office as Acting President.

Thereafter, when the President transmits to the President pro tempore of the Senate and the Speaker of the House of Representatives his written declaration that no inability exists, he shall resume the powers and duties of his office unless the Vice President and a majority of either the principal officers of the executive departments or of such other body as Congress may by law provide, transmit within four days to the President pro tempore of the Senate and the Speaker of the House of Representatives their written declaration that the President is unable to discharge the powers and duties of his office. Thereupon Congress shall decide the issue, assembling within forty-eight hours for that purpose if not in session. If the Congress, within twenty-one days after receipt of the latter written declaration, or, if Congress is not in session, within twenty-one days after Congress is required to assemble, determines by two-thirds vote of both Houses that the President is unable to discharge the powers and duties of his office, the Vice President shall continue to discharge the same as Acting President; otherwise, the President shall resume the powers and duties of his office.

Amendment XXVI (1971)

Section 1. The right of citizens of the United States, who are eighteen years of age or older, to vote shall not be denied or abridged by the United States or by any State on account of age.

Section 2. The Congress shall have the power to enforce this article by appropriate legislation.

Appendix D

INDEX GUIDE TO THE CONSTITUTION

Control of territories by Congress.

Guarantees to the States.

ARTICLE V. Method of amendment.

ARTICLE VI. Supremacy of the Constitution, laws, and treaties of the United States.

Oath of office—prohibition of a religious test.

ARTICLE VII. Method of ratification of the Constitution.

AMENDMENTS

I.	Freedom of religion, speech, press and assembly; right of petition.
II.	Right to keep and bear arms.
III.	Limitations in quartering soldiers.
IV.	Protection from unreasonable searches and seizures.
V.	Due process in criminal cases. Limitation on right of eminent domain.
VI.	Right to speedy trial by jury, and other guarantees.
VII.	Trial by jury in suits at law.
VIII.	Excessive bail or unusual punishments forbidden.
IX.	Retention of certain rights by the people.
X.	Undelegated powers belong to the States or to the people.
XI.	Exemption of States from suit by individuals.
XII.	New method of electing President.
XIII.	Abolition of slavery.
XIV.	Definition of citizenship. Guarantees of due process and equal protection against State action. Apportionment of Representatives in Congress. Validity of public debt.
XV.	Voting rights guaranteed to freedmen.
XVI.	Tax on incomes "from whatever source derived."
XVII.	Popular election of Senators.
XVIII.	Prohibition of intoxicating liquors.
XIX.	Extension of suffrage to women.
XX.	Abolition of "lame duck" session of Congress. Change in presidential and congressional terms.
XXI.	Repeal of 18th Amendment.
XXII.	Limitation of President's terms in office.
XXIII.	Extension of suffrage to District of Columbia in presidential elections.

XXIV.   Abolition of poll tax requirement in national elections.
XXV.   Presidential succession and disability provisions.
XXVI.   Extension of suffrage to eighteen-year olds.

Appendix E

THE FEDERALIST NO. 10

(First published November 22, 1787)

TO THE PEOPLE OF THE STATE OF NEW YORK:
Among the numerous advantages promised by a well-constructed Union, none deserves to be more accurately developed than its tendency to break and control the violence of faction. The friend of popular governments never finds himself so much alarmed for their charter and fate, as when he contemplates their propensity to this dangerous vice. The instability, injustice, and confusion introduced into the public councils, have, in truth, been the mortal diseases under which popular governments have everywhere perished; as they continue to be the favorite and fruitful topics from which the adversaries to liberty derive their most specious declamations. The valuable improvements made by the American constitutions on the popular models, both ancient and modern, cannot certainly be too much admired; but it would be an unwarrantable partiality to contend that they have as effectively obviate the danger on this side as was wished and expected. Complaints are everywhere heard from our most considerate and virtuous citizens, equally the friends of public and private faith, and of public and personal liberty, that our governments are too unstable, that the public good is disregarded in the conflicts of rival parties, and that measures are too often decided, not according to the rules of justice and the rights of the minor party, but by the superior force of an interested and overbearing majority. However anxiously we may wish that these complaints had no foundation, the evidence of known facts will not permit us to deny that they are in some degree true. . . . [The] distresses under which we labor [must] be chiefly, if not wholly, effects of the unsteadiness and injustice with which a factious spirit has tainted our public administrations.

By a faction, I understand a number of citizens, whether amounting to a majority or minority of the whole, who are united and actuated by some common impulse of passion, or of interest, adverse to the rights of other citizens, or to the permanent and aggregate interests of the community.

There are two methods of curing the mischiefs of faction: the one, by removing its causes; the other, by controlling its effects.

There are again two methods of removing the causes of faction: the one by destroying the liberty which is essential to its existence; the other, by giving to every citizen the same opinions, the same passions, and the same interests.

It could never be more truly said than of the first remedy, that it was worse than the disease. Liberty is to faction what air is to fire, an aliment without which it instantly expires. But it could not be less folly to abolish liberty, which is essential to political life, because it nourishes faction, than it would be to wish the annihilation of air, which is essential to animal life, because it imparts to fire its destructive agency.

The second expedient is as impracticable as the first would be unwise. As long as the reason of man continues fallible, and he is at liberty to exercise it, different opinions will be formed. As long as the connection subsists between his reason and his self-love, his opinions and his passions will have a reciprocal influence on each other; and the former will be objects to which the latter will attach themselves. The diversity in the faculties of men, from which the rights of property originate, is not less an insuperable obstacle to a uniformity of interests. The protection of these faculties is the first object of government. From the protection of different and unequal faculties of acquiring property, the possession of different degrees and kinds of property immediately results; and from the influence of these on the sentiments and views of the respective proprietors, ensues a division of the society into different interests and parties.

The latent causes of faction are thus sown in the nature of man; and we see them everywhere brought into different degrees of activity, according to the different circumstances of civil society. A zeal for different opinions, concerning religion, concerning government, and many other points, as well as speculation as of practice; an attachment to different leaders ambitiously contending for preeminence and power; or to persons of other descriptions whose fortunes have been interesting to the human passions, have, in turn, divided mankind into parties, inflamed them with mutual animosity, and rendered them much more disposed to vex and oppress each other than to co-operate for their common good. So strong is this propensity of mankind to fall into mutual animosities, that where no substantial occasion presents itself, the most frivolous and fanciful distinctions have been sufficient to kindle their unfriendly passions and excite their most violent conflicts. But the most common and durable source of factions has been the various and unequal distribution of property. Those who hold and those who are without property have ever formed distinct interests in society. Those who are creditors, and those who are debtors, fall under a like discrimination. A landed interest, a manufacturing interest, a mercantile interest, a moneyed interest, with many lesser interests, grow up of necessity in civilized nations, and divide them into different classes, actuated by different sentiments and views. The regulation of these various and interfering interests forms the principal task of modern legislation, and involves the spirit of party and faction in the necessary and ordinary operations of the government.

No man is allowed to be a judge in his own cause, because his interest would certainly bias his judgment, and, not improbably, corrupt his integrity. With equal, nay with greater reason, a body of men are unfit to be both judges and parties at the same time; yet what are many of the most important acts of legislation, but so many judicial determinations, not indeed concerning the rights of single persons, but concerning the rights of large bodies of citizens? And what are the different classes of legislators but advocates and parties to the cause which they determine? Is a law proposed concerning private debts? It is a question to which the creditors are parties on one side and the debtors on the other. Justice ought to hold the balance between them. Yet the parties are, and must be, themselves the judges; and the most numerous party, or, in other words, the most powerful faction must be expected to prevail. Shall domestic manufacturers be encouraged, and in what degree, by restrictions on foreign manufactures? are questions which would be differently decided by the landed and the manufacturing classes and probably by neither with a sole regard to justice and the public good. . . .

It is in vain to say that enlightened statesmen will be able to adjust these clashing interests, and render them all subservient to the public good. Enlightened statesmen will not always be at the helm. . . .

The inference to which we are brought is, that the *causes* of faction cannot be removed, and that relief is only to be sought in the means of controlling its *effects*.

If a faction consists of less than a majority, relief is supplied by the republican principle, which enables the majority to defeat its sinister views by regular vote. It may clog the administration, it may convulse the society; but it will be unable to execute and mask its violence under the forms of the Constitution. When a majority is included in a faction, the form of popular government, on the other hand, enables it to sacrifice to its ruling passion or interest both the public good and the rights of other citizens. To secure the public good and private rights against the danger of such a faction, and at the same time to preserve the spirit and the form of popular government, is then the great object to which our inquiries are directed. Let me add that it is the great desideratum by which this form of government can be rescued from the opprobrium under which it has so long labored, and be recommended to the esteem and adoption of mankind.

By what means is this object attainable? Evidently by one of two only: Either by the existence of the same passion or interest in a majority at the same time must be prevented, or the majority, having such coexistent passion or interest, must be rendered, by their number and local situation, unable to concert and carry into effect schemes of oppression. If the impulse and the opportunity be suffered to coincide, we well know that neither moral nor religious motives can be relied on as an adequate control. They are not found to be such on the injustice and violence of individuals, and lose their efficacy in proportion to the number combined together, that is, in proportion as their efficacy becomes needful.

From this view of the subject it may be concluded that a pure democracy, by which I mean a society consisting of a small number of citizens, who assemble and administer the government in person, can admit of no cure for the mischiefs of faction. A common passion or interest will, in almost every case, be felt by a majority of the whole; a communication and concert result from the form of government itself; and there is nothing to check the inducements to sacrifice the weaker party or an obnoxious individual. Hence it is that such democracies have ever been spectacles of turbulence and contention; have ever been found incompatible with personal security or the rights of property; and have in general been as short in their lives as they have been violent in their deaths. Theoretic politicians, who have patronized this species of government, have erroneously supposed that by reducing mankind to a perfect equality in their political rights, they would, at the same time, be perfectly equalized and assimilated in their possessions, their opinions, and their passions.

A republic, by which I mean a government in which the scheme of representation takes place, opens a different prospect, and promises the cure for which we are seeking . . . .

The two great points of difference between a democracy and a republic are: first, the delegation of the government, in the latter, to a small number of citizens elected by the rest; secondly, the greater number of citizens, and greater sphere of country, over which the latter may be extended.

The effect of the first difference is, on the one hand, to refine and enlarge the public views, by passing them through the medium of a chosen body of citizens, whose wisdom may best discern the true interest of their country, and whose patriotism and love of justice will be least likely to sacrifice it to temporary or partial considerations. Under such a regulation, it may well happen that the public voice, pronounced by the representatives of the people, will be more consonant to the public good than if pronounced by the people themselves, convened for the purpose. On the other hand, the effect may be inverted. Men of factious tempers, of local prejudices, or of sinister designs, may, by intrigue, by corruption, or by other means, first obtain the suffrages, and then betray the interests of the people. The question resulting is whether small or extensive republics are more favorable to the election of proper guardians of the public weal; and it is clearly decided in favor of the latter by two obvious considerations:

In the first place, it is to be remarked that, however small the republic may be, the representatives must be raised to a certain number, in order to guard against the cabals of a few; and that, however large it may be, they must be limited to a certain number, in order to guard against the confusion of a multitude. Hence the number of representatives in the two cases not being in proportion to that of the two constituents, and being proportionally greater in the small republic, it follows that, if the proportion of fit characters be not less in the large than in the small republic, the former will present a greater option, and consequently a greater probability of a fit choice.

In the next place, as each representative will be chosen by a greater number of citizens in the large than in the small republic, it will be more difficult for unworthy candidates to practice with success the vicious arts by which elections are too often carried; and the suffrages of the people being more free, will be more likely to centre in men who possess the most attractive merit and the most diffusive and established characters.

It must be confessed that in this, as in most other cases, there is a mean, on both sides of which inconveniences will be found to lie. By enlarging too much the numbers of electors, you render the representative too little acquainted with all their local circumstances and lesser interests as by reducing it too much, you render him unduly attached to these, and too little fit to comprehend and pursue great and national objects. The federal Constitution forms a happy combination in this respect; the great and aggregate interests being referred to the national, the local and particular to the State legislatures.

The other point of difference is, the greater number of citizens and extent of territory which may be brought within the compass of republican than of democratic government; and it is this circumstance principally which renders factious combinations less to be dreaded in the former than in the latter. The smaller the society, the fewer probably will be the distinct parties and interests composing it; the fewer the distinct parties and interests, the more frequently will a majority be found of the same party; and the smaller the number of individuals composing a majority, and the smaller the compass within which they are placed, the more easily will they concert and execute their plans of oppression. Extend the sphere, and you take in a greater variety of parties and interests; you make it less probable that a majority of the whole will have a common motive to invade the rights of other citizens; or if such a common motive exists, it will be more difficult for all who feel it to discover their own strength, and to act in unison with each other. Besides other impediments, it may be remarked that where there is a consciousness of unjust or dishonorable purposes, communication is always checked by distrust in proportion to the number whose concurrence is necessary.

Hence, it clearly appears, that the same advantage which a republic has over a democracy, in controlling the effects of faction, is enjoyed by a large over a small republic,—is enjoyed by the Union over the States composing it. Does the advantage consist in the substitution of representatives whose enlightened views and virtuous sentiments render them superior to local prejudices and to schemes of injustice? It will not be denied that the representation of the Union will be most likely to possess these requisite endowments. Does it consist in the greater security afforded by a greater variety of parties, against the event of any one party being able to outnumber and oppress the rest? In an equal degree does the increased variety of parties comprised within the Union, increase this security? Does it, in fine, consist in the greater obstacles opposed to the concert and accomplishment of the secret wishes of an unjust and interested majority? Here, again, the extent of the Union gives it the most palpable advantage.

The influence of factious leaders may kindle a flame within their particular States, but will be unable to spread a general conflagration through the other States. A religious sect may degenerate into a political faction in a part of the Confederacy; but the variety of sects dispersed over the entire face of it must secure the national councils against any danger from that source. A rage for paper money, for an abolition of debts, for an equal division of property, or for any other improper or wicked project, will be less apt to pervade the whole body of the Union than a particular member of it; in the same proportion as such a malady is more likely to taint a particular county or district than an entire State.

In the extent and proper structure of the Union, therefore, we behold a republican remedy for the diseases most incident to republican government. And according to the degree of pleasure and pride we feel in being republicans, ought to be our zeal in cherishing the spirit and supporting the character of Federalists.

Publius [*James Madison*]

Appendix F

THE MONROE DOCTRINE

Message to Congress from President James Monroe (December 2, 1823)

. . . At the proposal of the Russian Imperial Government, made through the minister of the Emperor [the Russian Tsar] residing here, a full power and instructions have been transmitted to the minister of the United States at St. Petersburg to arrange by amicable negotiations the respective rights and interests of the two nations on the northwest coast of this continent. A similar proposal had been made by His Imperial Majesty to the Government of Great Britain, which has likewise been acceded to. The Government of the United States has been desirous by this friendly proceeding of manifesting the great value which they have invariably attached to the friendship of the Emperor and their solicitude to cultivate the best understanding with his Government. In the discussions to which this interest has given rise and in the arrangements by which they may terminate, the occasion has been judged proper for asserting, as a principle in which the rights and interests of the United States are involved, that the American continents, by the free and independent condition which they have assumed and maintain, are henceforth not to be considered as subjects for future colonization by any European powers. . . .

It was stated at the commencement of the last session that a great effort was then making in Spain and Portugal to improve the condition of the people of those countries, and that it appeared to be conducted with extraordinary moderation. It need scarcely be remarked that the result has been so far very different from what was then anticipated. Of events in that quarter of the globe, with which we have so much intercourse and from which we derive our origin, we have always been anxious and interested spectators. The citizens of the United States cherish sentiments the most friendly in favor of the liberty and happiness of their fellow-men on that side of the Atlantic. In the wars of the European powers in matters relating to themselves we have never taken any part, nor does it comport with our policy so to do. It is only when our rights are invaded or seriously menaced that we resent injuries or make preparation for our defense. With the movements in this hemisphere we are of necessity more immediately connected, and by causes which must be obvious to all enlightened and impartial observers. The political system of the allied powers is essentially different in this respect from that of America. This difference proceeds from that which exists in their respective Governments; and to the defense of our own, which has been achieved by the loss of so much blood and treasure, and matured by the wisdom of their most enlightened citizens, and under which we have enjoyed unexampled felicity. . . . We owe it, therefore, to candor and to the amicable relations existing between the United States and those [allied] powers to declare that we should consider any attempt on their part to extend their system to any portion of this hemisphere as dangerous to our peace and safety. With the existing colonies or dependencies of any European power we have not interfered and shall not interfere. But with the [Latin American] Governments who have declared their independence and maintained it, and whose independence we have, on great consideration and on just principles, acknowledged, we could not view any interposition for the purpose of oppressing them, or controlling in any other manner their destiny, by any European power in any other light than as the manifestation of any unfriendly disposition toward the United States. In the war between those new Governments and Spain we declared our neutrality at the time of their recognition, and to this we have adhered, and shall continue to adhere, provided no change shall occur which, in the judgment of the competent authorities of this Government, shall make a corresponding change on the part of the United States indispensable to their security.

The late events in Spain and Portugal show that Europe is still unsettled. Of this important fact no stronger proof can be adduced than that the allied powers should have thought it proper, on any principle satisfactory to themselves, to have interposed by force in the internal concerns of Spain. To what extent such interposition may be carried, on the same principle, is a question in which all independent powers whose governments differ from theirs are interested, even those most remote, and surely none more so than the United States. Our policy in regard to Europe, which was adopted at an early stage of the wars which have so long agitated that quarter of the globe, nevertheless remains the same, which is, not to interfere in the internal concerns of any of its powers; to consider the government *de facto* as the legitimate government for us; to cultivate friendly relations with it, and to preserve those relations by a frank, firm, and manly policy, meeting in all instances the just claims of every power, submitting to injuries from none.

But in regard to those continents circumstances are eminently and conspicuously different. It is impossible that the allied powers should extend their political system to any portion of either continent without endangering our peace and happiness; nor can anyone believe that our southern brethren, if left to themselves, would adopt it of their own accord. It is equally impossible,therefore, that we should behold such interposition in any form with indifference. If we look to the comparative strength and resources of Spain and those new [Latin American] Governments, and their distance from each other, it must be obvious that she can never subdue them. It is still the true policy of the United States to leave the parties to themselves, in the hope that other powers will pursue the same course. . . .

Appendix G

WOMEN'S RIGHTS

Declaration of Sentiments and Resolutions
Woman's Rights Convention
(Seneca Falls, N.Y., July 19, 1848)

I. Declaration of Sentiments

When, in the course of human events, it becomes necessary for one portion of the family of man to assume among the people of the earth a position different from that which they have hitherto occupied, but one to which the laws of nature and of nature's God entitle them, a decent respect to the opinions of mankind requires that they should declare the causes that impel them to such a course.

We hold these truths to be self-evident: that all men and women are created equal; that they are endowed by their Creator with certain inalienable rights; that among these are life, liberty, and the pursuit of happiness; that to secure these rights governments are instituted, deriving their just powers from the consent of the governed. Whenever any form of government becomes destructive of these ends, it is the right of those who suffer from it to refuse allegiance to it, and to insist upon the institution of a new government, laying its foundation on such principles, and organizing its powers in such form, as to them shall seem most likely to effect their safety and happiness. Prudence, indeed, will dictate that governments long established should not be changed for light and transient causes; and accordingly all experience hath shown that mankind are more disposed to suffer while evils are sufferable, than to right themselves by abolishing the forms to which they are accustomed. But when a long train of abuses and usurpations, pursuing invariably the same object, evinces a design to reduce them under absolute despotism, it is their duty to throw off such government, and to provide new guards for their future security. Such has been the patient sufferance of the women under this government, and such is now the necessity which constrains them to demand the equal station to which they are entitled.

The history of mankind is a history of repeated injuries and usurpations on the part of man toward woman, having in direct object the establishment of an absolute tyranny over her. To prove this, let facts be submitted to a candid world.

He has never permitted her to exercise her inalienable right to the elective franchise.

He has compelled her to submit to laws, in the formation of which she has no voice.

He has withheld from her rights which are given to the most ignorant and degraded men—both natives and foreigners.

Having deprived her of this first right of a citizen, the elective franchise, thereby leaving her without representation in the halls of legislation, he has oppressed her on all sides.

He has made her, if married, in the eye of the law, civilly dead.

He has taken from her all right in property, even to the wages she earns.

He has made her, morally, an irresponsible being, as she can commit many crimes with impunity, provided they be done in the presence of her husband. In the covenant of marriage, she is compelled to promise obedience to her husband, he becoming, to all intents and purposes, her master—the law giving him power to deprive her of her liberty, and to administer chastisement.

He has so framed the laws of divorce, as to what shall be the proper causes, and in case of separation, to whom the guardianship of the children shall be given, as to be wholly regardless of the happiness of women— the law, in all cases, going upon a false supposition of the supremacy of man, and giving all power into his hands.

After depriving her of all rights as a married woman, if single, and the owner of property, he has taxed her to support a government which recognizes her only when her property can be made profitable to it.

He has monopolized nearly all the profitable employments, and from those she is permitted to follow, she receives but a scanty remuneration. He closes against her all the avenues to wealth and distinction which he considers most honorable to himself. As a teacher of theology, medicine, or law, she is not known.

He has denied her the facilities for obtaining a thorough education, all colleges being closed against her.

He allows her in Church, as well as State, but a subordinate position, claiming Apostolic authority for her exclusion from the ministry, and, with some exceptions, from any public participation in the affairs of the Church.

He has created a false public sentiment by giving to the world a different code of morals for men and women, by which moral delinquencies which exclude women from society, are not only tolerated, but deemed of little account in man.

He has usurped the prerogative of Jehovah himself, claiming it as his right to assign for her a sphere of action, when that belongs to her conscience and to her God.

He has endeavored, in every way that he could, to destroy her confidence in her own powers, to lessen her self-respect and to make her willing to lead a dependent and abject life.

Now, in view of this entire disfranchisement of one-half the people of this country, their social and religious degradation—in view of the unjust laws above mentioned, and because women do feel themselves aggrieved, oppressed, and fraudulently deprived of their most sacred rights, we insist that they have immediate admission to all the rights and privileges which belong to them as citizens of the United States.

In entering upon the great work before us, we anticipate no small amount of misconception, misrepresentation, and ridicule; but we shall use every instrumentality within our power to effect our object. We shall employ agents, circulate tracts, petition the State and National legislatures, and endeavor to enlist the pulpit and the press in our behalf. We hope this Convention will be followed by a series of Conventions embracing every part of the country.

II. Resolutions

WHEREAS, The great precept of nature is conceded to be, that "man shall pursue his own true and substantial happiness." [William] Blackstone in his *Commentaries* [on the Laws of England 3(1765-69)] remarks, that this law of Nature being coeval with mankind, and dictated by God himself, is of course superior in obligation to any other. It is binding over all the globe, in all countries and at all times; no human laws are of any validity if contrary to this, and such of them as are valid, derive all their force, and all their validity, and all their authority, mediately and immediately, from this original; therefore,

Resolved, That all laws which prevent woman from occupying such a station in society as her conscience shall dictate, or which place her in a position inferior to that of man, are contrary to the great precept of nature, and therefore of no force or authority.

Resolved, That woman is man's equal—was intended to be so by the Creator, and the highest good of the race demands that she should be recognized as such.

Resolved, That the women of this country ought to be enlightened in regard to the laws under which they live, that they may no longer publish their degradation by declaring themselves satisfied with their present position, nor their ignorance, by asserting that they have all the rights they want.

Resolved, That inasmuch as man, while claiming for himself intellectual superiority, does accord to woman moral superiority, it is pre-eminently his duty to encourage her to speak and teach, as she has an opportunity, in all religious assemblies.

Resolved, That the same amount of virtue, delicacy, and refinement of behavior that is required of woman in the social state, should also be required of man, and the same transgressions should be visited with equal severity on both man and woman.

Resolved, That the objection of indelicacy and impropriety, which is so often brought against woman when she addresses a public audience, comes with a very ill-grace from those who encourage, by their attendance, her appearance on the stage, in the concert, or in feats of the circus.

Resolved, That woman has too long rested satisfied in the circumscribed limits which corrupt customs and a perverted application of the Scriptures have marked out for her, and that it is time she should move in the enlarged sphere which her great Creator has assigned her.

Resolved, That it is the duty of the women of this country to secure to themselves their sacred right to the elective franchise.

Resolved, That the equality of human rights results necessarily from the fact of the identity of the race in capabilities and responsibilities.

Resolved, That the speedy success of our cause depends upon the zealous and untiring efforts of both men and women, for the overthrow of the monopoly of the pulpit, and for the securing to women an equal participation with men in the various trades, professions, and commerce.

Resolved, therefore That, being invested by the Creator with the same capabilities, and the same consciousness of responsibility for their exercise, it is demonstrably the right and duty of woman, equally with man, to promote every righteous cause by every righteous means; and especially in regard to the great subjects of morals and religion, it is self-evidently her right to participate with her brother in teaching them, both in private and in public, by writing and by speaking, by any instrumentalities proper to be used, and in any assemblies proper to be held; and this being a self-evident truth growing out of the divinely implanted principles of human nature, any custom or authority adverse to it, whether modern or wearing the hoary sanction of antiquity, is to be regarded as a self-evident falsehood, and at war with mankind.

Appendix H

THE EMANCIPATION PROCLAMATION

Proclamation by President Abraham Lincoln
(January 1, 1863)

Whereas, on the twenty-second day of September, in the year of our Lord one thousand eight hundred and sixty-two, a proclamation was issued by the President of the United States, containing, among other things, the following, to wit:

"That on the first day of January, A.D. 1863, all persons held as slaves within any State or designated part of a State, the people whereof shall then be in rebellion against the United States, shall be then, thence forward, and forever free; and the executive government of the United States, including the military and naval authority thereof, will recognize and maintain the freedom of such persons, and will do no act or acts to repress such persons, or any of them, in any efforts they may make for their actual freedom.

"That the executive will on the first day of January aforesaid, by proclamation, designate the states and parts of states, if any, in which the people thereof, respectively, shall then be in rebellion against the United States; and the fact that any state, or the people thereof, shall on that day be in good faith represented in the Congress of the United States, by members chosen thereto at elections wherein a majority of the qualified voters of such states shall have participated, shall, in the absence of strong countervailing testimony, be deemed conclusive evidence that such state, and the people thereof are not then in rebellion against the United States."

Now, therefore, I, Abraham Lincoln, President of the United States, by virtue of the power in me vested as Commander-in-Chief of the Army and Navy of the United States, in time of actual armed rebellion against the authority and government of the United States, and as a fit and necessary war measure for suppressing said rebellion, do, on this first day of January, in the year of our Lord one thousand eight hundred and sixty-three, and in accordance with my purpose so to do, publicly proclaimed for the full period of one hundred days from the day first above mentioned, order and designate as the States and parts of States wherein the people thereof, respectively, are this day in rebellion against the United States, the following, to wit:

Arkansas, Texas, Louisiana (except the parishes of St. Bernard, Plaquemines, Jefferson, St. John, St. Charles, St. James, Ascension, Assumption, Terre Bonne, Lafourche, St. Mary, St. Martin, and Orleans, including the city of New Orleans), Mississippi, Alabama, Florida, Georgia, South Carolina, North Carolina, and Virginia (except the forty-eight counties designated as West Virginia, and also the counties of Berkeley, Accomac, Northampton, Elizabeth City, York, Princess Anne, and Norfolk, including the cities of Norfolk and Portsmouth), and which excepted parts are for the present left precisely as if this proclamation were not issued.

And by virtue of the power and for the purpose aforesaid, I do order and declare that all persons held as slaves within said designated States and parts of States are, and henceforward shall be, free; and that the Executive Government of the United States, including the military and naval authorities thereof, will recognize and maintain the freedom of said persons.

And I hereby enjoin upon the people so declared to be free to abstain from all violence, unless in necessary self-defense; and I recommend to them that, in all cases when allowed, they labor faithfully for reasonable wages.

And I further declare and make known that such persons of suitable condition will be received into the armed service of the United States to garrison forts, positions, stations, and other places, and to man vessels of all sorts in said service.

And upon this act, sincerely believed to be an act of justice, warranted by the Constitution upon military necessity, I invoke the considerate judgment of mankind and the gracious favor of Almighty God.

In witness whereof, I have hereunto set my hand and caused the seal of the United States to be affixed. . . .

Index

G